Tarell Alvin McCraney

Tarell Alvin McCraney

Theater, Performance, and Collaboration

✦

Edited by
Sharrell D. Luckett, David Román,
and Isaiah Matthew Wooden

NORTHWESTERN UNIVERSITY PRESS
EVANSTON, ILLINOIS

Northwestern University Press
www.nupress.northwestern.edu

Printed in the United States of America

10 9 8 7 6 5 4 3 2 1

Library of Congress Cataloging-in-Publication Data

Names: Luckett, Sharrell D., editor. | Román, David, editor. |
    Wooden, Isaiah Matthew, editor.
Title: Tarell Alvin McCraney : theater, performance, and collaboration /
    edited by Sharrell D. Luckett, David Román, and Isaiah Matthew Wooden.
Description: Evanston, Illinois : Northwestern University Press, 2020.
Identifiers: LCCN 2019027256 | ISBN 9780810141940 (paperback) |
    ISBN 9780810141957 (cloth) | ISBN 9780810141964 (ebook)
Subjects: LCSH: McCraney, Tarell Alvin—Criticism and interpretation. |
    McCraney, Tarell Alvin—Dramatic production. | American drama—
    21st century—History and criticism. | African American dramatists.
Classification: LCC PS3613.C38625 Z88 2020 | DDC 812.6—dc23
LC record available at https://lccn.loc.gov/2019027256

CONTENTS

ILLUSTRATIONS

ACKNOWLEDGMENTS

This book is a reflection of and testament to the power of collaboration. We would like to express our sincerest thanks and appreciation to the many people who helped make it possible. Gianna Francesca Mosser, former editor in chief at Northwestern University Press, supported the project from the very beginning and ensured that it had a smooth journey through the various stages of review. Trevor Perri and Patrick Samuel at Northwestern University Press have been instrumental in ushering the book to publication. We thank them and the entire NUP team for being wonderful colleagues. The feedback provided by the anonymous reviewers enhanced every page of the book. We have benefited tremendously from their diligence.

The book's contributors answered our call enthusiastically and without hesitation. Our gratitude to them is incalculable. We are especially grateful for the rigor, vigor, and thoughtfulness they brought to every aspect of this process.

While this book has multiple origin stories, a panel on McCraney's work that the three of us participated in at the 2015 Association for Theatre in Higher Education (ATHE) conference in Montreal is perhaps the most significant. We are grateful to the Black Theater Association (BTA) and the LGBTQ Focus Group for sponsoring the session. We owe thanks to BTA for sponsoring a second roundtable on McCraney's work that we organized at the 2018 ATHE conference in Boston. We are grateful for the support of the Charles Phelps Taft Research Center, the Helen Weinberger Center for Drama and Playwriting at the University of Cincinnati, and Dorothy L. Hodgson, dean of the School of Arts and Sciences at Brandeis University. An auspicious encounter with Harvey Young set our work with NUP into motion. We thank him for his encouragement and goodwill. We also want to acknowledge Stephanie Batiste, Cheryl Black, Harry J. Elam, Artisia Green, Kathy Perkins, Nicole Hodges Persley, Jordan Schildcrout, Marianna Vertullo, and Helen Wheeler for their support.

Tarell Alvin McCraney is as kind as he is brilliant. We thank him for his incredible body of work *and* for moving through the world with grace, compassion, and a spirit of generosity. We are grateful to Corinne Hayoun and to Tarell's assistants, Christopher Betts and Boafoa Darko, for their timely responses to our many inquiries.

There are several people and institutions that we would like to acknowledge individually:

Sharrell would like to thank Isaiah and David for being such thoughtful and generous coeditors; it has been great to work with them on this volume. She would also like to thank her colleagues and students in the Departments of English and Comparative Literature, Africana Studies, Women's, Gender, and Sexuality Studies, and the College-Conservatory of Music (CCM) at the University of Cincinnati. Special thanks to Dr. Jonathan Lassiter, Rahbi Hines, Juel Lane, Frederick Marte, her family, and her ancestors for their contributions to this work.

David would like to thank Isaiah and Sharrell for everything they've done to bring this volume to life. He is especially grateful for the extended community of artists he has befriended over the years through Tarell Alvin McCraney's work. He would also like to thank the press departments at Steppenwolf Theatre and Manhattan Theatre Club; Joan Marcus and Michael Brosilow for permission to use their photographs; and Karen Tongson, the former events editor at *American Quarterly*, who encouraged his essay.

Isaiah would like to thank Sharrell and David for being exemplary collaborators. He would also like to thank his colleagues at Brandeis University and the many students who have joined him in engaging McCraney's work critically and creatively over the years. He is lucky to count La Marr Jurelle Bruce, Jakeya Caruthers, Tabitha Chester, Soyica Diggs Colbert, Julius B. Fleming, Jr., Eric M. Glover, Kamilah Holder, Khalid Y. Long, Maya Roth, Lisa B. Thompson, and DeRon Williams as interlocutors. He dedicates his work in this volume to Harry J. Elam, Jr., who first introduced him to McCraney's plays, and to his family, whose love continues to prove sustaining.

Tarell Alvin McCraney

✦

A Career Chronology

Sharrell D. Luckett

October 17, 1980 Tarell Alvin McCraney is born to Stephen McCraney and Marian Alvin in Miami, Florida. The family resides in the Liberty City community.

1995 McCraney auditions for and becomes a member of Village Improv. Founded by Teo Castellanos, Village Improv is a nonprofessional youth theater company that devises work focusing on HIV/AIDS and substance abuse awareness and prevention. One year later, McCraney's hard work earns him the position of assistant director. The company is active from 1995 to 2000.

1999 McCraney graduates from New World School of the Arts in Miami, Florida.

HONORS AND AWARDS: YoungArts Winner in Theater from the National YoungArts Foundation; Exemplary Artist Award and the Dean's Award in Theater at New World School of the Arts.

2003 McCraney earns his B.F.A. in acting from the Theatre School at DePaul University in Chicago, Illinois. His father, grandmother, and brother attend his graduation, but his mother is too ill to make the trip. She succumbs to an AIDS-related illness five weeks after his graduation. McCraney becomes a founding member of Teo Castellanos's D-Projects, a Miami-based dance and theater company.

HONORS AND AWARDS: Sarah Siddons Award from The Theatre School at DePaul University.

2006   *In the Red and Brown Water* is produced in the Yale
          School of Drama's Carlotta Festival of New Plays. The
          production is directed by Anna Jones, a Yale M.F.A. stu-
          dent in directing. *The Brothers Size* is developed at the Yale
          School of Drama. The production is directed by Tea Alagić,
          a Yale M.F.A. student in directing. *The Breach* (cowritten
          with Catherine Filloux and Joe Sutton) is commissioned by
          Southern Rep Theatre in New Orleans, Louisiana.

2007   McCraney receives his M.F.A. in playwriting from the
          Yale School of Drama. While at Yale, he assists August
          Wilson on the final play in his *Century Cycle*, *Radio Golf*
          (2005). *Marcus; Or the Secret of Sweet* is produced in the
          Yale School of Drama's Carlotta Festival of New Plays.
          Jessi D. Hill, a Yale M.F.A. directing student, stages the
          production. *The Brothers Size* makes its Off-Broadway
          debut at the Public Theater as part of the Under the
          Radar Festival. The play is produced by the Foundry
          Theatre, and directed by Tea Alagić. *The Brothers Size*
          premieres at London's Young Vic, coproduced with the
          Actors Touring Company (ATC) and directed by Bijan
          Sheibani. *Wig Out!* is developed at the Sundance Institute
          Theatre Lab, directed by Kent Gash. *The Breach* (cow-
          ritten with Catherine Filloux and Joe Sutton) premieres
          at Southern Rep Theatre in New Orleans, Louisiana,
          directed by Ryan Rilette. The production marks the two-
          year anniversary of Hurricane Katrina in New Orleans.
          The Breach is also staged at Seattle Rep in early 2008.

          HONORS AND AWARDS: Cole Porter Playwriting Award
          from the Yale School of Drama; *The Brothers Size* at the
          Young Vic is nominated for a Laurence Olivier Award for
          Outstanding Achievement in an Affiliate Theatre; Whiting
          Award from the Whiting Foundation.

2008   *In the Red and Brown Water* premieres at the Alliance
          Theatre in Atlanta, Georgia. Tina Landau directs the pro-
          duction. The Alliance Kendeda Playwriting award, which
          McCraney received in 2007, guaranteed the play a pro-
          duction at the Alliance. While at the Vineyard Theatre in
          New York City, McCraney works on *Wig Out!* and *The
          Brother/Sister Plays*. *Wig Out!* premieres at the Vineyard
          Theatre. Tina Landau directs the production. The Young
          Vic produces *In the Red and Brown Water* in October,
          with Walter Meierjohann as the director.

HONORS AND AWARDS: Paula Vogel Playwriting Award from the Vineyard Theatre in New York City; RSC/ Warwick International Playwright in Residence from the Royal Shakespeare Company (2008–2010); London's *Evening Standard* Award for Most Promising Playwright; Outstanding New American Play Award from the National Endowment for the Arts for *The Brother/Sister Plays* (administered by Arena Stage in Washington, D.C.).

2009   *The Brother/Sister Plays* premieres at the McCarter Theatre Center in Princeton, New Jersey in the spring and is later staged Off-Broadway at the Public Theater. Tina Landau directs *In the Red and Brown Water* and Robert O'Hara directs *The Brothers Size* and *Marcus; Or the Secret of Sweet* for both runs.

HONORS AND AWARDS: Hodder Fellow at the Lewis Center for the Arts at Princeton University; Inaugural *New York Times* Outstanding Playwright Award for *The Brothers Size*; the GLAAD (Gay and Lesbian Alliance Against Defamation) Award for Outstanding New York Theatre for the Vineyard's 2008 production of *Wig Out!*; Steinberg Playwright Award.

2010   McCraney becomes the forty-third member of Steppenwolf Theatre Company. He directs the Young Person's *Hamlet* for the Royal Shakespeare Company, which opens in the Courtyard Theatre at Stratford-upon-Avon in May and eventually tours ten schools in London. Steppenwolf Theatre Company produces *The Brother/Sister Plays*. Tina Landau directs the productions.

2011   *American Trade* premieres in London. The production is coproduced by the Royal Shakespeare Company and Hampstead Theatre, and directed by Jamie Lloyd.

2012   *Choir Boy* premieres in London at the Royal Court, directed by Dominic Cooke. McCraney serves as a panelist in the Theater Category for the YoungArts Awards.

2013   *Choir Boy* is produced at Manhattan Theatre Club's Studio at Stage II, directed by Trip Cullman. *Head of Passes* premieres at Steppenwolf Theatre Company in Chicago, with Tina Landau as the director. McCraney adapts and directs Shakespeare's *Antony and Cleopatra* for the Royal Shakespeare Company, coproduced with GableStage in

Miami and the Public Theater in New York City. He sets the play in the Caribbean.

HONORS AND AWARDS: John D. and Catherine T. MacArthur Foundation Fellowship; Windham-Campbell Prize in Drama; PlayTime Developmental Studio Award from New Dramatists for *Wig Out!*

2014   McCraney's adaptation and direction of *Antony and Cleopatra* makes its U.S. premiere with a production at GableStage in Miami from January 10 to February 9, followed by a production at the Public Theater from February 18 to March 23 (officially opening March 5).

HONORS AND AWARDS: Doris Duke Artist Award; Honorary Doctorate from the University of Warwick; 2013–2014 Outer Critics Circle Award for Outstanding New Off-Broadway Play for *Choir Boy*.

2015   McCraney joins the University of Miami's faculty as professor of theater and civic engagement in the Department of Theatre Arts. He teaches an "Introduction to Acting" class and leads a program that supports performing arts training for female high school students. The Marin Theatre Company produces the Bay Area premiere of *Choir Boy*, directed by Kent Gash. *Head of Passes*, directed by Tina Landau, makes its West Coast premiere at Berkeley Rep.

2016   *Moonlight* premieres in movie theatres. The film is directed by Barry Jenkins and is adapted by McCraney and Jenkins from an unpublished work written by McCraney years earlier titled "In Moonlight Black Boys Look Blue."

2017   Yale School of Drama appoints McCraney as Chair of the Playwriting Program, Eugene O'Neill Professor in the Practice of Playwriting, and Yale Repertory Theatre Playwright-in-Residence. *Head of Passes* opens at the Public Theater. Tina Landau directs the production.

HONORS AND AWARDS: McCraney and Jenkins win an Oscar for Best Adapted Screenplay at the 89th Academy Awards. The film also wins Oscars for Best Supporting Actor (Mahershala Ali) and Best Picture. Select additional *Moonlight* awards include: Golden Globe for Best Drama; Gotham Award for Best Feature; NAACP Image Award for Best Independent Film; WGA Award for Best Original Screenplay; the Visionary Arts Award from the Human

Rights Campaign; Best Original Screenplay from the
Writers Guild of America; Three Gold Derby Awards; Six
Independent Spirit Awards, including Best Picture and Best
Screenplay; Six Seattle Film Critics Awards; and Best Origi-
nal Screenplay Award from the Writers Guild of America.
McCraney wins a PEN/Laura Pels Theater Award from
PEN America.

2018   Manhattan Theatre Club remounts *Choir Boy* for its
                Broadway performance. Previews begin on December 12.

                HONORS AND AWARDS: McCraney is named one of the
                United Artists 2018 Fellows for Theatre and Performance.

2019   *Choir Boy* opens on January 8 at the Samuel J. Friedman
                Theatre in New York City with Trip Cullman as the
                director, marking McCraney's Broadway debut. The pro-
                duction garners four Tony nominations, including a nod
                for Best New Play. *High Flying Bird*, a movie written by
                McCraney and directed by Steven Soderbergh, appears
                on Netflix. McCraney cowrites *Ms. Blakk for President*
                with Tina Landau, and he performs the role of Joan Jett
                Blakk. The show is produced at Steppenwolf Theatre
                Company and is conceived and directed by Tina Landau.
                David Makes Man, an hour-long drama series conceived by
                McCraney and produced by several key players, including
                Oprah Winfrey and Michael B. Jordan, premieres August
                14 on the Oprah Winfrey Network (OWN).

The author has consulted the following sources for the chronology.

Broadway World. "McCraney Wins 1st NY Times Outstanding Playwright Award
    for *The Brothers Size*." May 12, 2009. https://www.broadwayworld.com
    /article/McCraney-Wins-1st-NY-Times-Outstanding-Playwright-Award-For
    -The-Brothers-Size-20090512.
Broadway World. "'The Brother/Sister Plays' *In the Red and Brown Water* Pre-
    views Tonight, 10/30." October 30, 2009. https://www.broadwayworld.com/off
    -broadway/article/THE-BROTHERSISTER-PLAYS-IN-THE-RED-BROWN
    -WATER-Previews-Tonight-1030-.
Castellanos, Teo. "Question about D-Projects and Tarell." Email message to
    Luckett, 2019.
Dolen, Christine. "Tarell Alvin McCraney is teaching at UM and launching a high
    school program." *Miami Herald*, October 9, 2015. https://www.miamiherald
    .com/entertainment/performing-arts/article38395932.html.
GableStage. "Antony and Cleopatra by William Shakespeare: Adapted by Tarell
    Alvin McCraney." Accessed March 30, 2019. http://www.gablestage.org
    /past-seasonsold/antony-cleopatra/.

Hirschman, Bill. "Tarell Alvin McCraney's American Premiere of His New Antony and Cleopatra at GableStage in 2014." Florida Theater On Stage. November 12, 2012. http://www.floridatheateronstage.com/news/tarell-alvin-mccraneys -american-premiere-of-his-new-antony-and-cleopatra-at-gablestage-in-2014/.

IMDB. "Tarell Alvin McCraney." Accessed March 20, 2019. http://www.imdb .com/name/nm4144120/otherworks?ref_=nm_pdt_wrk_sm.

MacArthur Foundation. "Tarell McCraney." Accessed February 16, 2019. https:// www.macfound.org/fellows/897/.

Macnaughton Lord Representation. "Tarell Alvin McCraney." Accessed March 15, 2019. http://www.mlrep.com/client.php?id=86.

Magic Theatre. "The Brothers Size." Accessed March 20, 2019. http://magicthe atre.org/past-productions/the-brothers-size-by-tarell-alvin-mccraney.

Marin Theatre Company. "Marin Theatre Company produces the Bay area premiere of *Choir Boy* by Tarell Alvin McCraney." Accessed March 25, 2019. http:// www.marintheatre.org/press/press-releases/choir-boy-bay-area-premiere.

Moniuszko, Sara M. "'Moonlight,' 'Arrival' take top WGA honors." *USA Today*, February 20, 2017. https://www.usatoday.com/story/life/movies/2017/02/20 /writers-guild-of-america-awards-moonlight-arrival/98148510/.

Montgomery, Daniel. "Gold Derby Film Awards 2017: 'La La Land' sweeps with 9 wins including Best Picture." Gold Derby, February 21, 2017. https://www .goldderby.com/article/2017/2017-gold-derby-film-award-winners-la-la-land -moonlight/.

National Endowment for the Arts. "NEA New Play Development Program Selections." *NEA Arts Magazine* 1 (2009): 15. Accessed March 30, 2019. https:// www.arts.gov/NEARTS/2009v1-reaching-millions-art/nea-new-play -development-program-selections.

National YoungArts Foundation. "Tarell Alvin McCraney to be honored at National YoungArts Foundation Backyard Ball." Accessed March 25, 2019. https://beta.youngarts.org/storage/app/uploads/public/5a1/483/a56/5a1483 a56f9e4439006492.pdf.

New Dramatists. "PlayTime Developmental Studio: Tarell Alvin McCraney." Accessed March 14, 2019. https://newdramatists.org/topics/48.

New World School of the Arts. "'Moonlight,' based on the play by NWSA alumnus Tarell Alvin McCraney wins Three Academy Awards: Best Picture, Best Adapted Screenplay, Best Supporting Actor." February 27, 2017. https://nwsa. mdc.edu/nwsa-college-about/latest-nwsa-college-news/882-"moonlight", -based-on-the-play-by-nwsa-alumnus-tarell-alvin-mccraney-wins-three-acad emy-awards-best-picture,-best-adapted-screenplay,-best-supporting-actor .html.

New York Theatre Guide. "Steinberg Playwright Awards go to Bruce Norris, Tarell Alvin McCraney and David Adjmi." September 17, 2010. https://www .newyorktheatreguide.com/news-features/steinberg-playwright-awards-go-to -bruce-norris-tarell-alvin-mccraney-and-david-adjmi.

Padla, Steven. "Noted playwright Tarrell [*sic*] Alvin McCraney appointed chair of the playwriting department." YaleNews, December 6, 2016. https://news .yale.edu/2016/12/06/noted-playwright-tarrell-alvin-mccraney-appointed-chair -playwriting-department.

PEN America. "Pen American Literary Awards." Accessed March 25, 2019. https://pen.org/pels-theater-awards/.

Public Theater. "The Brothers Size." Accessed March 17, 2019. https://www.publictheater.org/Tickets/Calendar/PlayDetailsCollection/UTR/2007/The-Brothers-Size/.

Ramanathan, Lavanya. "Studio stages Tarell Alvin McCraney's 'Marcus; Or the Secret of Sweet.'" *Washington Post*, January 6, 2011. http://www.washingtonpost.com/wp-dyn/content/article/2011/01/05/AR2011010505743.html.

Royal Shakespeare Company. "Tarell Alvin McCraney 2013 Production." Accessed February 27, 2019. https://www.rsc.org.uk/antony-and-cleopatra/past-productions/tarell-alvin-mccraney-2013-production.

Shufro, Cathy. "'That beautiful music of a new voice.'" *Yale Alumni Magazine*, September/October 2014. https://yalealumnimagazine.com/articles/3944-tarell-alvin-mccraney.

———. "Three Young Playwrights. Three New Plays. Now Comes the Hard Part." *Yale Alumni Magazine*, July/August 2006. http://archives.yalealumnimagazine.com/issues/2006_07/playwrights.html.

Steppenwolf. "Member Profiles: Tarell Alvin McCraney." Accessed March 2, 2019. https://www.steppenwolf.org/ensemble/member-pages/tarell-alvin-mccraney/.

Sundance Institute. "Sundance Institute Announces Acting Ensemble for this summer's Theatre lab." Accessed March 13, 2009. http://www.sundance.org/pdf/press-releases/Sundance%20Institute%20PR_2007%20Theatre%20Lab%20Acting%20Company.pdf.

Theatre Communications Group. "Marcus or the Secret of Sweet." Accessed March 25, 2019. http://www.tcg.org/Default.aspx?TabID=3052.

Theatre School at DePaul University. "Tarell Alvin McCraney receives United States Artists Fellowship." January 17, 2018. https://blogs.depaul.edu/theatre-school-news/2018/01/17/tarell-alvin-mccraney-receives-united-states-artists-fellowship/.

Ubuntu Biography Project. "tarell alvin mccraney." October 17, 2017. https://ubuntubiographyproject.com/2017/10/17/terell-alvin-mccraney/.

Vineyard Theatre. "Paula Vogel Playwriting Award." Accessed March 25, 2019. https://www.vineyardtheatre.org/paula-vogel-playwriting-award/.

Warwick: The Capital Centre. "Tarell Alvin McCraney." Accessed March 18, 2019. https://warwick.ac.uk/fac/cross_fac/capital/about/people/playwright/mccraney/.

Yale Bulletin and Calendar. "Talents of drama students showcased in Carlotta Festival." May 11, 2007. Vol. 35 No. 28. http://archives.news.yale.edu/v35.n28/story12.html.

Tarell Alvin McCraney

Ogun Size Enters; or, An Introduction

✦

Isaiah Matthew Wooden

This book dedicates rigorous critical attention to the work of Tarell Alvin McCraney, one of the most significant writers and theater-makers of the twenty-first century. Featuring essays, interviews, and commentaries by scholars and artists who span generations, geographies, and areas of interests—and, importantly, who bring fresh and diverse perspectives to their observations and analyses—the volume reflects a particular commitment to engaging and interrogating the vastness of McCraney's theatrical imagination, the singularity of his writerly voice, the incisiveness of his cultural insights and critiques, the creativity he displays through stylistic and formal qualities, and the unorthodoxies of his personal and professional trajectories. Contributors consider McCraney's ingenuities as a playwright, adapter, director, performer, teacher, and collaborator. In so doing, they expand and enrich the conversations on his much-celebrated and deeply resonant oeuvre. They also provide springboards for further examinations of the performance texts they investigate, thereby enhancing and encouraging the growth of the emerging field of "McCraney studies." As a way to introduce the volume and, indeed, McCraney's broader artistic project, I will briefly trace some of the topics and themes that are already beginning to preoccupy and shape the field and, correspondingly, the substance of this book. In addition to supplying greater context for the work under consideration, I also contemplate its aesthetic, cultural, and pedagogical significance.

McCraney, in a wide-ranging conversation with fellow playwright-director-actor Kwame Kwei-Armah in 2014, offered the following response when asked about how he has negotiated some of the challenges artists perennially face: "I always look for the weird model . . . I always find the weird model . . . the outlier in the system that's, you know, going to change and revolutionize things."[1] It had been a desire to find and pursue "the weird model" that led the theater-maker and his classmates at the Yale School of Drama to present his play *The Brothers Size* as a part of the Public Theater's Under the Radar

Festival some seven years earlier. Directed by Tea Alagić and featuring three budding actors who have since gone on to enjoy impressive performance careers—Gilbert Owuor (Ogun Size), Brian Tyree Henry (Oshoosi Size), and Elliot Villar (Elegba)—the stark, arresting production announced McCraney as one of the most daring and innovative artists creating new work for the stage. *New York Times* critic Jason Zinoman helped stir up excitement about the emerging writer when he declared, "Tarell Alvin McCraney, a third-year student at the Yale School of Drama, is one of the few playwrights in the Under the Radar Festival who is actually under the radar—but not for long."[2] Zinoman's unequivocal proclamation would prove prescient. Indeed, in the months following *The Brothers Size*'s triumphant New York premiere, McCraney would distinguish himself as a formidable "outlier in the system," one distinctly committed to and capable of revolutionizing the theatrical and cultural landscapes.

It is not hyperbolic to say that McCraney has experienced unprecedented success since making his professional debut as a playwright in 2007. The various accolades that he's earned—among them, the Steinberg Playwright Award, the Windham-Campbell Prize for Drama, the MacArthur Fellowship, the Academy Award for Best Adapted Screenplay, as well as residencies at the Royal Shakespeare Company and New Dramatists—certainly attest to this and, moreover, to his ever-growing prominence and influence. McCraney's greatest achievements, however, are the performance texts that he has written for both stage and screen, which evidence his investments in dramatizing the richness and complexities of black life, culture, and experience. To date, they include the plays *American Trade*, *Choir Boy*, *Head of Passes*, *Ms. Blakk for President* (with Tina Landau), *The Breach* (with Catherine Filloux and Joe Sutton), *Wig Out!*, and the critically acclaimed trilogy *The Brother/Sister Plays*: *In the Red and Brown Water*, *The Brothers Size*, and *Marcus; Or the Secret of Sweet*; the Oscar Award–winning film *Moonlight*, which was based on his unpublished story "In Moonlight Black Boys Look Blue"; the Steven Soderbergh–directed movie *High Flying Bird*; the television series *David Makes Man*; and adaptations of William Shakespeare's *Hamlet* and *Antony and Cleopatra*; as well as several other ongoing film, television, and theater projects.

McCraney's dramatic texts have appeared on stages throughout the United States and internationally, garnering productions at an array of notable theaters. The success of *Moonlight* and *David Makes Man* has served to further expand the artist's reach, acquainting new audiences across the globe with the suppleness of his storytelling. Powerfully, no matter when or where they have been presented, McCraney's works have afforded an intergenerational mix of black performers vital opportunities to embody characters abounding in emotional, cultural, and symbolic meaning. They have also marked a disruption to the status quo, beckoning collaborators, spectators, and critics to imagine and pursue new possibilities—for the performing and media arts, as well as for the world more broadly.

An Outlier in the *Other* America

While it has become somewhat unfashionable for artists to openly discuss how much they draw on personal experiences for creative inspiration, McCraney has been rather vocal about his penchant for integrating biographical details into his work. Accordingly, it is useful to begin any examination of his artistic achievements and aesthetic sensibilities by exploring and understanding the ways particular life events and circumstances have informed their development. Born on October 17, 1980, and raised in Miami's Liberty City community, McCraney confronted myriad obstacles while traveling the path that would ultimately lead him to pursue writing and theatermaking professionally. Routinely shuttling between the homes of his father and grandparents, devoted Baptists, and the unit that his mother rented in one of the most impoverished housing project communities in the nation during his youth, he found particular solace in telling dramatic stories. These early made-up tales drew inspiration from his grandfather's dynamic Sunday sermons, the colorful figures he encountered while maneuvering the Liberty City streets, and his own pressing needs to better understand the world and the space he, his family, and his community inhabited within it. Importantly, they provided the aspiring artist a means to reckon with some of the questions and uncertainties that regularly seized his attention. As he explained in a 2009 interview with writer Patrick Healy, "Ever since I was young, I was writing plays, sometimes little ones, that were basically about how you fit with people, how they fit with you and how you fit in the world . . . These were questions that I always thought about growing up. And I'm still having a conversation with myself about them."[3] A flair for the dramatic cast McCraney as an outlier in his childhood communities, where people were more apt to privilege those activities and qualities—athletics and hustling, for example—that might help them escape or survive some of the perils that often plague inner city life. Of course, what he at times experienced as estrangement and alienation only further intensified his motivations to create and tell stories that spotlighted the lifeworlds of the overlooked, marginalized, disenfranchised, and the queer among them.

It was his collaborations with Teo Castellanos, the founder and artistic director of the Miami-based dance and theater company D-Projects, during his teen years that exposed McCraney to some of the transformative possibilities of creating socially conscious and politically engaged performance works. The projects that he and his peers produced under Castellanos's direction mostly served a pedagogical purpose. They would tour the devised pieces, which covered topics such as HIV prevention and the hazards of drug use, to local youth rehabilitation and correctional facilities. In the "Backstage Pass" chapter of this volume, Castellanos recalls that, even in his adolescence, McCraney was a compelling performer: "Once we performed in a detention center . . . I asked him to walk up a stairwell, on some 'site specific' improvised direction. He went up there, and when he began to deliver his monologue, the inmates and the staff became so captivated you could hear a pin drop in that jail."[4] As was the case with many of his cocreators, the stories that the ensemble developed and performed often resonated with McCraney personally. His mother's battles with addiction and her struggles to manage HIV had supplied him with an intimate knowledge of some of the challenges facing many of the people he regularly encountered.

Coming of age in "the other America" amid the various epidemics that would wreak havoc on poor, black communities in the 1980s and '90s endowed McCraney with greater empathy for those left out of the nation's dominant narratives. He speaks to this point in the artist statement that he crafted for the McCarter Theater Company's 2009 productions of *The Brother/Sister Plays*:

> There were days I thought I was born into a third world country. Partly from overzealous imagination, but also from the scarce ability to keep running water in our home coupled with the battle to keep the rampant rodents that plagued our project from chomping into my baby sister . . . I was brought up near the tropic of Capricorn, hurricanes common as mosquito bites. Sea breezes strong enough to send you sailing and starry nights that made the voyages of Columbus seem distant and not yet present. Yet there in the midst of that beauty were drug lords who ran the street corner like Wall Street and Beirut combined. I lived in the other America; the America that doesn't always get depicted in the cinema. The America that we are told to pretend isn't there.[5]

It was a desire to, as he puts it, "create theater that told untold stories, that gave voice to another half of America" that compelled McCraney to direct his attention more fully to writing.[6]

Before entering the M.F.A. program in playwriting at the Yale School of Drama in 2004, McCraney, it is worth noting, mostly pursued opportunities to enhance his skills as a performer. He studied acting and dance in the high school theater program at Miami's New World School of the Arts and, upon graduating in 1999, moved to Chicago to enroll in the Theatre School at DePaul University to receive his B.F.A. in acting. While at DePaul, he would meet several people who would become longtime mentors and collaborators, including the director Tina Landau, the playwright Carlos Murillo, and the actor Cheryl Lynn Bruce. Although he displayed considerable talent as an actor, even catching the eye of influential director Peter Brook, who tapped him to do workshops of Can Themba's *Le Costume/The Suit* and Marie-Hélène Estienne's adaptation of *Tierno Bokar* soon after earning his undergraduate degree, he quickly discovered that he no longer had a passion for pursuing the profession. "I felt like I was going to end up in therapy, or in Lake Michigan when it's 32 degrees out. I had to stop [acting]. There are braver people than me. There are people who are hungrier for it than I am," he explained in an interview with Dan Rubin.[7] He transitioned to playwriting, in part, because he wanted to conjure up the kinds of worlds and roles for other performers that he himself had once desired to inhabit and portray. He would notably make a triumphant return to the stage in 2019, performing the role of Ms. Joan Jett Blakk, the drag persona of activist and 1992 presidential candidate Terence Smith, in the premiere production of *Ms. Blakk for President* at Steppenwolf Theatre Company.

McCraney began crafting several new pieces the summer after graduating from DePaul—most notably, "In Moonlight Black Boys Look Blue." The story featured many of the questions and themes that reverberated throughout the artist's early life and have since become hallmarks of his dramaturgy: namely, race, class, gender, sexuality, spirituality, geography, and family. Written in the wake of his mother's premature death, it also grappled with questions of loss, grief, and mourning. Its protagonist was, like McCraney, an outlier who lived in the *other* America. Its pages reflected the artist's deep commitments to exploring and interrogating both formally and narratively some of the existential and socio-cultural concerns and circumstances that those who identify with its central character negotiate in their everyday lives. It was an early entry into what has become a larger project aimed at "giving voice to the voiceless" and allowing "the light from the moon to shine on the privileged and the marginalized alike," as McCraney put it in the acceptance speech he delivered for the Human Rights Campaign (HRC) 2017 Visionary Award.[8] Though McCraney would table the project once he arrived at the Yale School of Drama, he would remain unwavering in his conviction to use his writing to bring nuance and texture to lives and stories often made invisible by dominant narratives, particularly the lives and stories of the black and queer.

Ogun Size Enters in the Distant Present

Among the many remarkable things about McCraney's writing are the ways in which it often shrewdly repeats and revises what Harry J. Elam and Douglas A. Jones call "normative dramaturgical formations" to spin fresh stories about the here and now that consciously and provocatively blend the old with the new.[9] His engagement with what I have referred to elsewhere as an "aesthetics of recycling" dramatically opens space for him to wrestle with the pleasures and perils of contemporary black life.[10] Undoubtedly, in reading or seeing any of McCraney's plays, it becomes immediately apparent that his influences are many—from Yoruba cosmology, black music, and Miami and bayou cultures, to the work of William Shakespeare, Alvin Ailey, Federico García Lorca, Reinaldo Arenas, Essex Hemphill, Suzan-Lori Parks, and Lynn Nottage, among numerous others. The writer that McCraney is perhaps most frequently likened to is playwright August Wilson, who had a tremendous impact on McCraney's artistic development early on in his career. McCraney notably served as Wilson's assistant on the 2005 production of *Radio Golf* at Yale Repertory Theatre, an experience, he told *Los Angeles Times* critic Charles McNulty, that gifted him with a profound understanding of "what it means to be a generous theater artist."[11] From Wilson, who succumbed to liver cancer a few months after their time working together, he learned "the importance of collaboration, of talking it out, of fighting it out in the room . . . [that] it's important to trust the people you've gathered."[12] He also got to see and experience up close the benefits of drawing on and synthesizing various expressive and artistic forms—among them, poetry, song, dance, storytelling, and ritual—in his dramaturgy. Of course, while many critics were rushing to hail McCraney as Wilson's heir apparent, audiences were recognizing and celebrating the distinctiveness and dynamism of his writing and artistic vision.

Central to that vision are the various dramaturgical strategies and theatrical devices that McCraney deploys to fashion his complex narratives. Beginning with *In the Red and Brown Water* and *The Brothers Size*, he has, for example, set many of his plays in what he calls "the distant present," a queer temporal configuration that forges myriad possibilities to imagine, explore, and render lives, experiences, and stories that impede or refuse the logic and imposition of normative time. By situating his work in "time frames at once familiar yet somewhat removed," McCraney "forces us to consider when the contemporary moves from now to then," David Román argues.[13] Simultaneously, he uses distance to compel audiences to contend with the ways that, for far too many, the present is merely not enough—and, indeed, it does not necessarily get better, despite the progressive narratives that we are bombarded with purporting otherwise. Significantly, for McCraney, distancing the present serves as an important means to blur the boundaries between past, present, and future. It also creates space to worry the lines between the real, the fictive, and the mythic while, in many instances, throwing into sharp relief parallels between the worlds of his plays and the lifeworlds of their spectators.

McCraney's incorporation of a distinct form of dialogue that requires characters to announce their stage directions ("Ogun Size enters") and, at times, communicate their intentions and emotions ("Oya sad, smiles") in many of his scripts similarly serves to collapse divisions between performers and spectators. While this technique has been effectively employed by various cultural practitioners over the years—including the sixteenth- and seventeenth-century English dramatists that McCraney often cites as influences, avant-gardists such as Samuel Beckett and Suzan-Lori Parks, and the playwright's own grandfather, whose spirited preaching proved formative for the artist—it performs an especially vital and singular function in McCraney's dramaturgy. Most notably, it aids in reemphasizing and reinvigorating the artist's investment in an idea of "theater as community."[14] As Jill Dolan highlights in *Utopia in Performance*, a distinguishing characteristic of live performance—theater, in particular—is its potential and capacity to "provide a place where people [can] come together, embodied and passionate, to share experiences of meaning making and imagination" and to "feel themselves allied with each other, and with a broader more capacious sense of a public, in which social discourse articulates the possible, rather than insurmountable obstacles to human potential."[15] McCraney suggests that theater is at its best (and, indeed, its most "holy") when "for the hour or so onstage the audience and actor are one, and all those people, though each seeing it slightly differently, are believing—following the same course or going on a journey."[16] In his dramaturgy, the spoken stage directions, then, serve to inspire what we might call, following Dolan (and anthropologists like Victor Turner), *communitas*: experiences in which audiences and/or participants "feel themselves become part of the whole in an organic, nearly spiritual way" and, correspondingly, share a deep if fleeting sense of belonging.[17] According to McCraney, they also aim to engender call-and-response: "The actors speak stage directions that invite the audience to remember that they are in a theater and that the story that is being told is for them and to feel free to call and respond back."[18]

As the chapters in this volume powerfully illuminate, there is tremendous synergy between form and content in McCraney's work and, as such, the substance of his dramaturgy also tends to provoke a sense of *communitas* and call-and-response. His particular facility for finding and exposing the universal in the specific and, indeed, blending the epic with the intimate affords his audiences a number of entry points for engaging, understanding, and perhaps even empathizing with the characters and tales he plots. Whether he's sharpening focus on an older African American woman forced to confront difficult questions about righteousness, suffering, and faith while living amid the sinking lands of the Mississippi River Delta, as he does in *Head of Passes*, or dramatizing the struggles of a black youth coming of age and coming to terms with his sexual identity in a world that is persistently hostile to difference, as he does in *Marcus; Or the Secret of Sweet*, McCraney fills his work with bold, honest, and sometimes painful reflections and representations of the human condition. It is perhaps because of the adversities he's witnessed and negotiated in his own life that McCraney does not shy away from exploring provocative or controversial topics and themes, always approaching them with acuity, curiosity, and generosity.

While there is rich evidence to substantiate the profound care with which McCraney contends with complex subjects throughout his oeuvre, I want to draw attention briefly to a subtle though especially illustrative example from

The Brothers Size that speaks to the thoughtful and sophisticated ways his dramaturgy takes on urgent issues and calls us to interrogate our assumptions about what we think we already know. Since its earliest performances, many have responded positively to the stirring portrait of black brotherhood and manhood that McCraney depicts in the play. Sandra L. Richards, for example, praises the drama for providing a "sensitive exploration of black men's interiority in the context of a United States that imagines them primarily as strong, hypersexual bodies without minds or regard for social propriety," while Jeffrey McCune commends the ways McCraney "makes black men speak as poets, masters of linguistic twists and turns—which allows the spectator/reader to not only understand these men as creators of new language, but also the architects of a new world."[19] What, however, frequently goes unremarked in analyses of the play are the nuanced ways that McCraney recuperates and refigures the prison cell as a fecund site of queer possibility and as a space for rehearsing otherwise illegible forms of black masculinity.

Through a recurring dream marked by questions, hums, moans, unease, and ellipses, the play beckons spectators to ponder whether the bond between Oshoosi and Elegba might go beyond friendship and, indeed, whether the pair perhaps might feel greater freedom to express same-sex desire in a place—prison—that often circulates discursively as antonymic to any meaningful sociality. In so doing, it prompts considerations of the suppressions and repressions of difference, deviance, and delinquency necessary for the maintenance of hegemonic and heteronormative discourses—suppressions and repressions that the very existence of prison helps make possible. Simultaneously, the play presses audiences to contend with the conditions and realities of a racist prison system that not only incarcerates black people at astronomical rates in the United States but also labors to cast those who find themselves in its grip as unworthy of love and devoid of humanity. Ogun Size exposes the fraudulence of these latter suppositions when he declares to his younger sibling, who once again finds himself a fugitive of the law, in the play's final scene: "You still my brother . . . I swear."[20] It is a beautiful reminder that, despite any insistence otherwise, this brother, this black man, remains significant to somebody.

A Beam through Darkness, Pure in Its Source

McCraney's work abounds with explorations of the potential in forging and embracing different kinds of connections, networks, affiliations, and other forms of collectivity. Having been rejected by their relatives, many of the characters in *Wig Out!*, for example, construct alternative kinships and families through their participation in the houses, rituals, events, and cultural practices that animate the drag and ballroom communities that have provided refuge for many poor and working-class black and Latinx gay and transgender people throughout the United States since the nineteenth century. The prep school protagonists in *Choir Boy* similarly build deep bonds by joining their voices together to sing in harmony. It should come as little surprise, then, that in addition to remarking on the form, style, and substance of his work, many of the artists whose voices we include in this volume echo Michael Boyd, former artistic director of the Royal Shakespeare Company, in describing McCraney as a "consummate collaborator."[21]

While writing is generally thought of as a solitary pursuit, creating new work for the theater is unique in that, at a certain point, it requires engaging a broader collaborative community. In her book *Playwrights in Rehearsal: The Seduction of Company*, Susan Letzler Cole describes a scene in which Suzan-Lori Parks, for example, gathers a group of actors in a room at the Public Theater to read her play, *In the Blood*. "During the reading of scene 2, the author picks up her pen, crosses out lines on a page of the script, makes a note on her pad, crosses out more lines, and makes another note."[22] For Parks, assembling a group of people and absorbing how they give voice and definition to the characters, rhythms, moods, and events she has sketched on the page became crucial to the process of playmaking. For McCraney, that process sometimes also includes preparing a delicious meal for his colleagues, as Tea Alagić recounts in "Backstage Pass."

I had a chance to experience McCraney's graciousness as a collaborator firsthand when, while directing *In the Red and Brown Water* at Georgetown University in 2014, he visited the campus and spent two days in rehearsal with my students. In addition to the wise counsel and gentle mentoring he provided the aspiring performers, what stood out during the residency were the ways that, while hearing the play read aloud by the group, he felt inspired to make slight adjustments to the text. It became clear in those moments that McCraney understood his script as a living document, one with the potential to invite new worlds and an array of interpretations.

There is a line in *Head of Passes* that perhaps speaks best to how McCraney's colleagues generally view him as a collaborator. After her family has met with unspeakable tragedy, Shelah takes to praying, asking God to plant grace and salvation in all who deserve divine pity. God's grace and salvation, she remarks, "shines like a beam through the darkness, pure in its source."[23] Surely, a similar thing might be said of McCraney's writing, which, as the chapters, interviews, and commentaries in this volume illuminate, has fundamentally altered our dramatic and dramaturgical tastes and expectations. Most of the volume's contributors have notably opted to approach their analyses with "critical generosity," even while recognizing that there are aspects of McCraney's writing, dramaturgy, and theatermaking processes that demand additional consideration or critique.[24] Our collective hope is that the readings, interpretations, reflections, and appraisals in the pages that follow will engender even more readings, interpretations, reflections, and appraisals—as well as critiques—of McCraney's body of work, thereby opening up further lines of inquiry for considering the significance of the artist's contributions to dramatic literature and theater history, as well as to the study of race, gender, sexuality, culture, and performance more broadly.

The Dramatic Imagination of Tarell Alvin McCraney

We have organized *Tarell Alvin McCraney* into three parts to draw attention to some of the repetitions, revisions, resonances, and reverberations reflected in and across McCraney's oeuvre. The chapters in part 1, "Space, Faith, and Touch," explore how McCraney at once queries and queers spatial, spiritual, and haptic matters in his work, bringing particular critical attention to the ways these topics emerge in *Head of Passes*, *Wig Out!*, *Choir Boy*, *The Breach*, and *Moonlight*. The chapters in part 2, "Brothers, Sisters, and the Gods among Us," examine signal themes and dramaturgical strategies in *The Brother/ Sister Plays*, probing the acclaimed triptych for fresh meanings and interpretations. Part 3, "Art, Creation, and Collaboration," centers the voices of some of McCraney's most important coconspirators, thereby creating space to contemplate the critical and/in the creative. The volume concludes with a short interview that the editors conducted with McCraney in which he further demonstrates the distinctiveness of his artistic voice and imagination. Evidenced throughout the volume's multiple parts is the rigor with which contributors, who deploy a range of methodologies to carry out their examinations and analyses, have approached their engagements with McCraney's work. I provide a précis of each chapter here to help orient readers to the volume's ample offerings.

In "Juxtaposing Creoles: Miami in the Plays of Tarell Alvin McCraney," Donette Francis explores the ways McCraney's work is informed by and infused with a distinctly "Miami sensibility." Turning attention to what she calls McCraney's "black southern hemispheric epics"—notably, *The Brother/ Sister Plays*, *Head of Passes*, and *Moonlight*—Francis proposes that, even when they are not explicitly set in Miami, McCraney's works often draw from and comment on the city's unique geopolitical past and present. The foundational role that water plays in McCraney's "black southern hemispheric epics," she intimates, stems from the natural substance's importance to the social and physical ecology of Miami. Francis interrogates the ways that McCraney evinces a "consciousness of place" in his writing that is deeply rooted in his relationship to his hometown.

Patrick Maley meditates on McCraney's explorations of faith, spirituality, and religiosity in "Theodicy and Hope: Tarell Alvin McCraney's Scrutiny of Religiosity." Presenting *Head of Passes* and *Wig Out!* as signal examples, Maley directs us to think of the ways that McCraney's dramaturgy at once reveals a deep skepticism of religiosity's efficacy while, at the same time, exampling a "theodicy of hope." Even as McCraney's plays "interrogate divine care for humanity (theodicy) without any conviction of affirmation (skeptical)," they remain "open to affirmation and productive aesthetic humanism (hope)," Maley argues. In this way, they allow for less conclusive, more ambivalent engagements with divine and spiritual matters.

In "The Distant Present of Tarell Alvin McCraney," a revisiting of his 2014 *American Quarterly* essay, David Román suggests that McCraney's work is emblematic of a new millennial "renaissance moment in African American theatre." He proposes that what distinguishes McCraney from some of his peers in this "renaissance moment" is his persistent focus on the contemporary. Primarily analyzing the premiere productions of *Head of Passes* at Steppenwolf Theatre Company and *Choir Boy* at Manhattan Theatre Club, Román examines how, in rendering the present distant, McCraney creates opportunities for both his characters and audiences to grapple with some of the knottiness that often attends conversations on faith, education, spirituality, and sexuality. He demonstrates how both plays powerfully affirm McCraney's commitments to experimenting with dramatic form while offering up fresh cultural insights.

Bryant Keith Alexander examines *Wig Out!*'s representations of "gendered becoming" in "'My Grandmother Wore a Wig': On Tarell Alvin McCraney's Mapping of Queer Origins in *Wig Out!*" Sharpening focus on the "My grandmother wore a wig" soliloquies featured in the play, Alexander considers the space these "cameo" moments afford characters to reckon with past traumas and personal histories and, correspondingly, to negotiate their complex feelings about their own gender and sexual identities. A central effect of these soliloquies, Alexander asserts, is to prompt audiences to contend with the complexities of identity formation. Alexander reveals some of the personal insights that attending to these complexities can yield by engaging the principles of performative writing in the chapter.

Katherine Nigh maintains in "*The Breach*: A Rupture in the National Narrative of Katrina" that McCraney and his collaborators on the lesser known play *The Breach* (Catherine Filloux and Joe Sutton) render post-Katrina New Orleans in a more intimate, more empathetic key. Tracing the history of the play's development and its earliest stagings in New Orleans, Seattle, and New York City, Nigh argues that the drama provides an important counter to the dominant narratives proliferated by the media in the aftermath of the devastating weather event, especially those that constructed New Orleans's black and poor residents in pathological and criminal terms. The chapter draws particular attention to the ways that, through the plotline McCraney crafts, the play recuperates those queer people and communities erased from the official record on Hurricane Katrina.

While I. Augustus Durham gestures toward the ways matters of space and spirituality manifest in the Oscar Award–winning film *Moonlight* in "'Certainly No Clamor for a Kiss': When Black Men Touch," his primary focus is "the work that the haptic does in the film." The chapter explores what the film conveys about black men and touch in particular. Through touch,

Durham asserts, black men not only experience particular awakenings in *Moonlight* but also "the breaking of a world broken." The concluding entry in part 1 of the volume, Durham's highly intertextual and theoretically rich chapter opens up new lines of inquiry for studying Jenkins and McCraney's much-celebrated film.

In "Scenes of Vulnerability: Desire, Historical Secrecy, and Black Queer Experience in *Marcus; Or the Secret of Sweet*," which shifts the volume's focus in part 2 to *The Brother/Sister Plays*, GerShun Avilez situates *Marcus; Or the Secret of Sweet* in a genealogy of works by black queer writers invested in conveying the nuances of black queer experience. Avilez demonstrates how, even as it renders black queer life as a "constant negotiation of serial loss," *Marcus; Or the Secret of Sweet* brings to the surface the power of intimacy to assuage loneliness and vulnerability, although not always enduringly. The chapter analyzes the experiences of connection—same-sex intimacy and linkages to a queer past—that McCraney affords the play's protagonist throughout the drama. *Marcus; Or the Secret of Sweet*, Avilez argues, reveals the ways that queer desire "can undo alienation, work against feelings of powerlessness, and bridge the past and present."

Like Avilez, Freda Scott Giles also situates *The Brother/Sister Plays* in a genealogy of black writing in "Hip-Hop Nommo: Orishas for the Millennium Generation," albeit one with more Afrocentric roots. Charting the ways that Pepe Carril's *Shango de Ima*, August Wilson's *Joe Turner's Come and Gone*, and McCraney's *In the Red and Brown Water* incorporate elements of Yoruba cosmology, Giles suggests that there is a continuum of "paradigms for representing and re-presenting the New World African in the postcolonial era." McCraney, she offers, is an exemplar of a more recent iteration of this paradigm wherein connections to Africa are assumed and do not necessarily require explanation.

Soyica Diggs Colbert closely reads *In the Red and Brown Water* in "Black Movements and Tarell Alvin McCraney's *In the Red and Brown Water*" to explore "how black performance moves through bodies, places, and time and, in that motion, extends black political movements." One of the earliest scholars to critically examine McCraney's work, Colbert returns to the epilogue of her first book, *The African American Theatrical Body: Reception, Performance, and the Stage*, to explicate further her assertions about the relationship between embodied and political movements.[25] The chapter investigates what insights *In the Red and Brown Water* exposes about what Colbert calls "black movements"—that is, "embodied actions . . . that further political movements . . . that in turn rearrange time and space."

Omi Osun Joni L. Jones poetically contemplates the ways *The Brother/Sister Plays* elucidate what she theorizes as "The Black Real" in "*The Brother/Sister Plays* and The Black Real." Jones outlines how the Black Real is manifested through three mutually supporting and influencing characteristics in the trilogy: notably, its engagements with self-naming/self-narrating, indeterminacy, and interaminating diaspora. For Jones, "self-narrating/self-naming is understood as agency and community building; indeterminacy as 'the break' (space of creativity and spirituality), transtemporality, erotic autonomy, and choice; and an interanimating diaspora as a spiritually and politically driven experience."

Jeffrey Q. McCune Jr. attends to the ways that *The Brothers Size* stages the everyday lives of black men in "One *Size* Does Not Fit All: Voicing Black Masculinities in a Pursuit of 'Freedoms.'" McCune argues that McCraney carves out "rich, complex black masculinities through the deployment of new dramatic language, an emphasis on 'brother-ness,' and the use of a small-scale set that allows for spectators to activate their own imaginings" in the play. In so doing, he asserts, *The Brothers Size* elicits "reading practices for its audience wherein black men's personal stories escape the metonymic trap and act as filters to the intersections of black men's lives and their unique departures."

The centerpiece of part 3, "Backstage Pass: An Artist Roundtable on the Work of Tarell Alvin McCraney," features prominent artists and theater practitioners—Tea Alagić, Jabari Ali, Alana Arenas, Michael Boyd, Cheryl Lynn Bruce, Teo Castellanos, Trip Cullman, Oskar Eustis, Shirley Jo Finney, Tina Landau, Carlos Murillo, and Robert O'Hara—discussing their engagements with both McCraney and his work. Curated and introduced by volume coeditor Sharrell D. Luckett, the roundtable is thick with information about the theatermaking process and the transformational power of creating work in community. It is an invaluable resource for those interested in teaching and staging McCraney's plays.

McCraney himself reflects on his personal and artistic journey in a brief interview with the volume's coeditors in the book's final chapter.

Significant throughout *Tarell Alvin McCraney* are the distinctive critical frameworks and analytical tools that contributors supply readers to approach, unpack, and analyze McCraney's ever-evolving body of work. To be sure, the volume's chapters not only augment conversations on the writer's artistic contributions but also make a case for why his work will continue to remain relevant, resonant, and worthy of study for decades to come.

Part 1

✦

Space, Faith, and Touch

Juxtaposing Creoles

Miami in the Plays of Tarell Alvin McCraney

Donette Francis

People from Miami get the mix, we understand how even our accents are a mix of different accents, *overlaid* on top of each other . . . We lived in a neighborhood where there was a voo-doo lady, and the Santería people are not far away, if you want to find them; they are down the street in the other direction. People think I am making things up, but in a place where drugs and guns exist also exist these other, mythical things, and many people do believe there is a good and evil spiritual fight in the world . . . Some critics can't stand my work say it's folksy . . . But . . . I would . . . *invite them to live in my neighbourhood and see that is actually what happens.*

—Tarell Alvin McCraney

In Miami, we love a blend. We tout our diversity. Even though we have miles to go in true equality, *still* in art, colors and genres begin to mix and blend.

—Tarell Alvin McCraney

Tarell Alvin McCraney is a third-generation Black Miamian.[1] While many of his early plays are set in the bayous of Louisiana (*The Brother/Sister Plays* and *Head of Passes*, for example),[2] at an April 2017 lecture at the University of Miami, the playwright decisively claimed, "All of my plays are about Miami; the bayous are the Everglades."[3] McCraney's mapping of Miami's topography onto rural Louisiana draws attention to these subtropical wetlands as fragile habitats vulnerable to climate change and man-made manipulations of ecosystems. Coastal erosion, compounded by oil production and oil spills in the Gulf of Mexico, has had adverse environmental impact on Louisiana's bayous and the entire Gulf coast. Consequently, cities like New Orleans experience storm surges from hurricanes that now reach farther inland. Juxtaposing these landscapes serves as a particularly apt reminder for what the vagaries of climate change portend for Miami's future, especially amid the city's aggressive real estate development schemes. But the juxtaposition of these two cities, New Orleans, founded in 1718, and Miami, incorporated more than a century later in 1896, also signals more.[4] Indeed, given the playwright's Miami-framed creole orientation, which includes the city's racial, cultural, and ecological landscapes, it is neither accidental nor incidental that his early works draw upon Louisiana's established creole vernacular. Creolization generally seeks to make sense of people and traditions born and remade in the new world, the creation of hybrid languages in such contact zones, and the power plays that establish hierarchies of value among people and their cultures in terms of race, space, architecture, and cosmologies.[5] In this regard, creolization is universal across all societies and changes over time. However, within the United States, Louisiana's long history of creolization more readily recognizes the Louisiana-born people, cultures, and conditions that resulted from the conflicts and contradictions of French, Spanish, and, later, U.S. imperial rule of that territory.[6] More recently, in the aftermath of Hurricane Katrina in 2005, New Orleans immediately signals in the national imaginary the effects of structural and environmental racism on Afro-creole bodies.

In what I term McCraney's "Black southern hemispheric epics," which mix literary and biblical classics, cities and cosmologies, as well as race and architecture, the playwright uses waterscapes to build a palimpsest of geographies and identities overlaid with the traces of earlier histories that are the sediment of the present.[7] Water actually materializes the hemispheric as the substance which literally touches Louisiana, Miami, and the Caribbean simultaneously. Here I am trying to capture what we might think of as water's DNA that actually retains the histories of even those marginalized bodies in the contemporary cityscape. Sedimentation itself is a process that comprises mixing and layering with a keen awareness of the mixing between the layers themselves. Sediment as a metaphor for Black life in Miami, therefore, recognizes these stratified layers of sediment, where the top layers have access to more oxygen and settled matter can be catalyzed by elements such as the strong winds and waves of hurricanes. Thinking about the plurality of Blackness through the metaphor of sediment draws attention to both the mixed and layered traces of Black ethnicity, which are always on, or just below, the surface and never wholly subsumed by an undifferentiated, settled, or uncontaminated idea of Blackness as the sole identity marker. Furthermore, the playwright's declarative statement about the similitude of the bayous and the Everglades turns to biospheres where water, mud, and land are indistinguishable and the possibility of one's very movement is encumbered by sedimentation, which includes the material refuse that floats on top. In pointing to such wetlands characterized by their density, McCraney reaches for a murky hemispheric imaginary—a geopolitical structuring that, though governed by the national, orients to the hemisphere. As he asserts in the first of the opening epigraphs, denizens of this U.S. southern metropolis are keenly attuned to living inside of and hearing the layered and varied diasporic histories of migration, settlement, and sedimentation.

Pursuing the playwright's invitation to read the instructive similarities of southern Louisiana and South Florida that inform his aesthetic practice, I utilize the phrase "Black southern hemispheric epics" in this essay to bring together the necessary triangulation of the Black, southern, and hemispheric in order to grasp all the relevant geopolitical and cultural frames necessary to read place in McCraney's oeuvre. In particular, I analyze how a "Miami sensibility" affects the dramaturgy of *Head of Passes*, which unfolds near the mouth of the Mississippi River, and I examine *The Brother/Sister Plays*, set in Louisiana's public housing, alongside *Moonlight*'s setting in Miami's Liberty Square projects and its sur- rounding environs.[8] Incorporated in 1896 as a sinking city built on swampland for agricultural and tourist economies, Miami's fragile habitat is compounded by the precariousness of Black life in the city, where racial segregation has his- torically meant the inland isolation of Blacks in inner-city neighborhoods, while the more desirable properties were reserved for whites on, or in close proximity to, the beaches.[9] With recent attention to rising sea levels, these once-isolated Black neighborhoods—ten feet above the current sea level—are now highly sought after by developers, with the ensuing mass displacement of low-income Black and brown peoples.[10] In addition to the city's relative youth, its geopoliti- cal multi-directionality simultaneously references urban cities in the northern United States, the politics of Jim Crow segregation in the southern United States, and the multiple and shifting imperial histories of the broader global "Souths," which include the Caribbean and Central and South America. McCraney brings such a consciousness of place to his plays set in Louisiana, where he interrogates the ways the elements, ecological vulnerability, Black precarity, *and* plurality are a part of everyday sensibilities.

While critics have previously addressed select themes in McCraney's work, less attention has been given to how these themes intersect with the particulars of Miami as a place.[11] Understanding the multiple features of the playwright's dramaturgy, including the ethos of synthesizing the mythic with the quotidian, necessitates an appreciation of the lifeworld of his upbringing in Liberty City. With phrases like "the poorest and most dangerous neighborhood in Miami- Dade County," a discourse surrounds Liberty City that renders it analogous to representations of Haiti in the global imagination as the "poorest nation in the Western hemisphere." In this regard, Miami is drawn into hemispheric as well as national racializations of power. McCraney's Black southern hemi- spheric epics counter such reductive geopolitical frames by rendering the more multifaceted lifeworlds of Liberty City, which, at its core, has been and remains a cosmopolitan Black space: first, in the late nineteenth century, Bahamian and African American laborers (primarily from North Florida, Georgia, and Alabama) were foundational to incorporating and building the city; second, national observers reported the city's Black cosmopolitan character in the 1942

Miami special issue of *The Crisis Magazine*, stating, "Here are found peoples from South Africa, Central and East Africa, India, South America, Central America, Canada, Bermuda and all the islands of the West Indies, composing a city of about 40,000 colored inhabitants"; and finally, in the post-1970s Miami of McCraney's plays, the presence of Haitians, Afro-Latinos, Bahamians, and other immigrants from the Anglophone Caribbean demonstrate the plurality with which African American identity is lived.[12] Likewise, the languages publicly spoken accentuate the linguistic and cultural multiplicities of the Americas, which adds another layer of cosmopolitanism since, in addition to the various dialects of English—including African American and Caribbean Creoles—the Black population speaks Spanish, French, and Kreyol. However, where Spanish has become a dominant language of commerce and prestige in the city's public cultures, Haitian Kreyol, by comparison, is devalued. In attending to such layered complexities, McCraney centralizes the nuances of everyday Black life, where one lives in and among Black difference and its attending hierarchies.

A central ethos of McCraney's dramaturgy is to perform the mythical on stage while violence is implicitly narrated, remaining off the page and off the stage to avoid repeating visual iconographies of inner-city Black violence. Thus, rather than the singular focus on drugs and gun violence, McCraney details their coexistence with various spiritual cosmologies, ranging from Christianity in *Choir Boy* to Vodou in *Antony and Cleopatra*. As such, dreamscapes are staged to render the lack of distinction between the otherworldly and the quotidian. In his repurposed Greek, Shakespearean, or biblical epics, original source texts do not disappear but are *overlaid* with the mundane particulars of ordinary Black life to illustrate Black universality. By deploying grand literary forms to stage Black local specificities, McCraney underscores that these Black stories not only transcend the temporality of their present, but that attention given to structural differences in the human condition does not equate to abject exceptionality. For McCraney, the sources that matter most and inspire his work are the family, the community, and the city that inspire the work.[13] Nonetheless, the playwright's subtle spatial and gendered demarcation in the opening epigraph that locates ungendered Santería (Hispanic) and female Vodou (Haitian) practitioners on opposite ends of the neighborhood gestures toward ethnic and gender antagonisms within Blackness in terms of who can practice these African-derived cosmologies and where. While being careful not to romanticize an unproblematic Black mosaic, I argue that McCraney's Miami-inflected creole aesthetic lays out the city's complicated hemispheric and southern U.S. urban history of race, space, and Black worldmaking.

Creole Miami: Crossroads and Crossings

Miami is often positioned as outside the United States, with its own peculiar hemispheric sovereignty, rather than as a quintessentially southern U.S. city.[14]

Much of this contemporary popular understanding is marked by the decisive set of events that unfolded in the 1980s, with new waves of Cuban and Haitian refugees arriving in the city, as well as the Miami race riots in Liberty City following the death of Arthur McDuffie. These events and the ensuing cultural wars catalyzed Miami's acculturation into a Spanish-dominant, bicultural city in which the upper- and middle-class white Hispanic population normalized the idea and practice of a *cosmopolitan hemispheric creole whiteness* rather than assimilating successive generations of immigrants into a U.S.-national-Anglo model of "becoming American." Fissured by inequalities based on race, immigration, class, and language, by the end of the 1980s the city would at once become functionally Hispanicized *and* despondently Black.[15] As citizens of the hemisphere met up in this relatively young city without a longstanding Anglo-Saxon hegemony, a white "Latinness" (both largely and initially Cuban) eclipsed and then toppled an Anglo-American identity by making claims to the city's political and cultural institutions.[16] Subsequent generations of Haitian and English-speaking Caribbean immigrants have attempted to deploy this acculturation model, but have been confronted with how Blackness limits incorporation. These fault lines between white Latinness and Blackness, which includes the uncertain and often invisible position of Afro-Latinos, illustrate how multiculturalism manifests differently in Miami than in other U.S. cities. It also makes visible identities and contradictions not readily apparent through the conventional Black/white binary lens of U.S. racial formation.[17] In other words, *cosmopolitan hemispheric creole whiteness* is the operative logic of white supremacy in Miami, which understands itself as less provincial than Anglo-American whiteness.

Locating Miami at the crossroads between the Black United States South, the Circum-Caribbean, and Latin America, McCraney reaches for affective and physical resemblances across these landscapes.[18] While I am not the first to point to Miami's post-1980s racial and ethnic mélange, the primary focus is often on the Latinx presence with Blackness as an addendum; or, with those studies that do focus on Blackness, Latinx is rendered the antagonistic supplement.[19] Seldom do we get a sustained intersectional analysis about how all these features come together and make meaning. More pointedly, rarely do we critically dwell on what it means to think the hemisphere from a Black point of view that holds in tension the region's layered racial, ethnic, and linguistic plurality.[20] To acknowledge Miami's specific U.S. history of creolization calls attention to a place where different hemispheric understandings and valuation of racial and ethnic mixture meet and a white hegemony of a different, Spanish-inflected kind emerges. Louisiana's longer francophone history of creolization is well documented, therefore, I will not rehearse it here.[21] Alternatively, I explore the ways understanding Miami through a discourse of creolization reveals a Black freedom struggle that utilized accommodationist strategies to resolve racial tensions in order to preserve the viability of its tourist and agricultural industries, as well as the different hemispheric powerbrokers that accede to power in the city.[22] Situating the national with the hemispheric offers a *Black hemispheric imaginary* to our ongoing national conversations about race, the meanings of Blackness, and its aesthetic practices. Such a hemispheric imaginary complicates contemporary discourses that focus on the impending browning of America, but fail to grapple with the fact that brown bodies may in fact be white-identified, allied, and aligned. It insists that it is not enough to point to shifting demographic statistics; instead, one needs also to capture the nuances of racial, ethnic, *and* linguistic identifications or disidentifications.[23] As scholars often turn to this city to forecast the future of the United States, a careful reading of Miami and its discriminatory practices of *cosmopolitan hemispheric creole whiteness* can serve to illustrate what that future potentially holds.

McCraney characterizes Miami and its arts practices through the multivalent meanings of creole, and, for him, three features distinguish the city's art practice: one, it is staged and performed outside; two, it embodies the call-and-response of religious practices and the carnivalesque; and three, it incorporates the figure of Papa Legba as "the gateway god . . . or party starter . . . These traditions . . . are homegrown mixtures of the worlds left behind to create a new one."[24] The playwright calls on Afro-Atlantic rituals of spiritual and carnivalesque play—features that readily apply to Louisiana's Afro-creole cultures, as well as Afro-Caribbean and Afro-Latinx art practices. New Orleans, for example, is understood as a theatrical city with very public expressive cultures such as the ubiquitous second line. McCraney draws attention to how Miami's creole aesthetic is also very conscious of the publicness of its performativity. The momentum of his epics moves between such expressiveness and the contrasting quiet.[25] Yet, precisely because the greater metropolitan area still encompasses the persistent remains of residential segregation, his creole vision of Miami claims the right of Black bodies to occupy outdoor public spaces for artistic expression and recreation.[26] The monthly Friday night playing of Rara, Haitian religious processional festival music in the streets of Little Haiti, is but one example.[27] While McCraney positions Miami itself as the crossroads of the Americas, he also addresses the embodied quotidian crossings that characters navigate to both inhabit themselves and their physical environments. His epics bring to center stage characters who are precarious, peripheral, and imperfect. He also dramatizes the perilous stakes involved in traversing such crossings, which as Darnell L. Moore reminds us, "can be precarious spaces to occupy for those who must dodge multiple arrows of racism, homophobia, sexism and so much else daily."[28] How does one live as a poor Black gay male from Liberty City plotting a course through the city's elite arts high school institutions? How does one survive the crack epidemic as a single Black female in 1980s Miami and, relatedly, how does one survive as the son of such a mother? How does a young Black woman survive the loss of a reproductive future in a Black community that valorizes motherhood as a rite of passage and a larger national culture saturated in discourses of pathological Black female hyper-reproduction? Such explorations reveal the layered ways crossroads and crossings converge in the playwright's oeuvre with the recurring spatial imagery of waterways and porches as liminal spaces for imagining, negotiating, and rescripting Black freedom dreams—not as completed action, but as transformative, and in some cases ephemeral, yet transcendent, moments of encounter.[29]

Bayous, Beaches, and Bathtubs

Water is foundational to the social and physical ecology of Miami. The southern metropolis sits on the tip of the Florida peninsula, which itself is situated between the Gulf of Mexico, the Atlantic Ocean, and the Florida Straits. Downtown Miami has the Atlantic Ocean to its east and the Everglades to its west. Encircled by the sea, the city literally sits on a porous bedrock of limestone, and its foundation is comprised of swampland. Following Vanessa Agard-Jones's provocation to attend to "what the sand remembers" as a way of reading the local materiality of Caribbean histories, I suggest that these waterscapes—where water, sand, and land merge—are particularly useful to think about sediments and the incessant impurity, indeterminancy, and intermingling of such waterscapes, and, by analogy, these hemispheric identities and histories.[30] Unlike what has become the necessary focus on the Black Atlantic as a site of tragic Middle Passage crossings and the afterlives of slavery or as romantic waterways travelled by sailors who gathered and relayed information for political mobilization across the Atlantic,[31] my focus on Black sediments holds onto these entangled Middle Passage histories even while turning to a place persistently attuned to the wrath of seasonal hurricanes as well as the contemporary layers of the embodied histories of the city's inhabitants that are traceable in the biosphere of water, sand, and land.

McCraney's Liberty City is located in the northwest corridor of mainland Miami. Drive south one hour—or thirty-seven miles from Liberty City—and you are at the Homestead entrance of the Everglades National Park, a diverse biosphere where water, mud, and land become undifferentiated, and where the Everglades's very composition is in a state of constant flux. Equally important is that such a drive takes one through the Miccosukee Indian reservation. While this encounter should provide a forceful indictment of indigenous jurisdiction and U.S.-settler colonialism, at the very least, it reminds travelers of the indigenous histories sedimented in the present as living and dynamic rather than an extinct part of the city's cartography. Drive fifteen minutes east from Liberty City and you are on Miami Beach, where residential racial restrictions once limited Black access. Jim Crow Miami meant that renowned Black artists performed on stage at various venues on Miami Beach but had to seek hotel accommodations inland in the city's Black neighborhoods of Overtown and Brownsville. Animated by the ecosystems

Landscape sediments in Miami. Photograph copyright © Michael Elliott.

of both place and family, McCraney's epics demonstrate how water, this pervasive but limited natural element, shapes possibilities or impossibilities. And for the playwright, the very texture of water accrues distinct meanings in different geographical contexts. For example, in *The Brother/Sister Plays*, the waterways of the moonlit bayous unveil repressed desires and reveal the possibilities for new forms of sociality. In *Head of Passes*, torrential rains bring generational destruction and yet potential renewal. In *Moonlight*, the ocean engenders moments of quiet, transcendent, but ultimately temporary freedom.[32]

Whether bayous, beaches, or bathtubs, waterways are structuring spaces of catalytic movement and reflection that propel both grand and quiet dramatic action. McCraney's epics often span three generations and follow a plot structure highlighting the importance of lessons learned and improved upon by the next generation. In his family ecosystems, generations are compressed, comprised of teenaged parents and young adults living short lives. In *In the Red and Brown Water*, two generations die relatively young respectively by the drama's end. Many of these generational lessons, nevertheless, are learned through dream sequences, which again serve to highlight the imbrications of the otherworldly and the everyday. Elsewhere I have identified this generation-based, yet anti-heterosexual normative teleology as the plot structure of the Caribbean anti-romance to account for the post-1990s critical intervention of Caribbean women's writings into grand masculinist narratives of either triumph or tragedy.[33] Jafari Allen more overtly queers my formulation to argue for a Black radical anti-romance that returns "to the not-too-distant past" of the 1980s as a spatiotemporal moment where "the idea of Black/queer/diaspora solidarity emerges" and gives visibility to "the everyday actions of Black LGBTQ and same gender loving people on the ground—mixing, moving, and engaging the world virtually or in the flesh."[34] Allen's Black queer temporality lines up with the biographical context that inspires McCraney's oeuvre. Born in 1980, McCraney enters the world on the cusp of the decade Allen asserts is central to the emergence of "Black/queer/diaspora solidarity"; yet, McCraney's epic stories about the quotidian lifeworld of Liberty City (where the community writ large is decimated by the crack epidemic and HIV/AIDS) underscore that Black temporalities are often already queered since they are structured by the impossibilities of heterosexual romances and straight time—as both heterosexual reproductive unions and linear teleogy.

In *The Brother/Sister Plays*, one encounters what the subtitle for *In the Red and Brown Water* describes as "a fast and loose play on Spanish Yerma and African Oya/Oba." Indicating the significance of Yoruban deities, McCraney is nonetheless more interested in pointing to syncretic Miami, where these West African rituals have already been mediated through the Caribbean and the Black South, and where he encountered this repertoire in urban archipelagos rather than in continental Africa or in textbooks, thereby accentuating that these practices change in and across time and space.[35] As such, this essay will not take as its principal concern the West African cosmologies in the plays, but rather their expression of a Miami sensibility. Casting directions in the production notes call for "creole" cast members for the trilogy (the character Elegba is creole), which is specific to the embodied politics of racial formation in Louisiana. Yet, in the world of McCraney's Black southern hemispheric epics, creole characters also serve to draw attention to how color distinctions play out within Black communities, particularly their treatment of the ways dark-skinned girls see themselves and are seen within the community's own hierarchal standards of desire. The trilogy's creole sensibility is also evinced in its exploration of racialized identities that live in proximate relations. Certainly, these epics focus on the internal world of the Black community; yet they also mark out contact with the white population and the sociocultural boundaries that cannot be crossed. Deeply local and integrated forms of whiteness appear as service providers—such as the local shopkeeper of *In the Red and Brown Water* and the community's family doctor in *Head of Passes*—which opens space to explore what it means to provide the essential food supply or healthcare in a Jim Crow South. These whites understand themselves as members of the shared community. O Li Roon, the shopkeeper in *In the Red and Brown Water*, articulates such a sentiment as he reprimands Elegba about stealing candy: "I was raised here too. Right on the Bayou. Yo mama's beat my ass with you when you got in trouble" (59). Notably, these examples do not mean equality but rather intimate touches as members of proximate communities in solidarity, and as a way of distinguishing the various forms of whiteness.[36]

Unfolding first in the chronology of the three plays, *In the Red and Brown Water* dramatizes the story of Oya, a promising young Black female track athlete who foregoes an athletic scholarship to the state university in order to stay home and care for her ailing mother, Mama Moja. The majority of the staged action occurs on Oya's front porch, especially after her mother's death in what would have been Oya's first year in college, thereby showing the compression of these generations. By setting most of the action on the porch, McCraney draws attention to the architectural feature of the "project porches" of southern public housing in Miami and Louisiana. Prominently showcased in McCraney's epics, these pivotal interstitial spaces between public and private underscore the ways in which low-income Black people live their private lives outdoors—a publicness that invites intrusion. With no physical divide between neighbors, project porches are sites to surveil and be surveilled. In the close living quarters of *The Brother/Sister Plays*, porches are suited both to external sociality as well as to overhearing conversations intended for some degree of privacy.[37]

After her mother's death, Oya lives alone, without kin, but with the support of her godmother, Aunt Elegua. Oya spends a lot of time on the porch and, as such, negates the need for visitors to seek an invitation. Consequently, there is nothing private about Oya's life. It is the public scene of her courtships with two suitors, Shango and Ogun Size. A fixture in the rocking chair on her porch, Oya watches, and is excluded from, neighborhood rituals, including baby showers and parties. It is here where even a young toddler taunts her with "you ain't my mama," indicating that already in this young toddler's cognition is an awareness that Oya cannot fulfill the community's version of the reproductive heterosexual romance, which might resemble single Black motherhood or children produced in nonmarital partnerships (87). Unbeknownst to this toddler, she taps into Oya's longing for a child that manifests in her sitting on the porch waiting, which elicits the following response from her lover:

OGUN:
You stay outside too much Oya.
You need stay in sometimes.
It ain't right for you to be out here all the time.
One day you'll have something to stay in for. (93)

In this scenario, inside is associated with domesticity and childrearing. While Oya will unsuccessfully consult "A woman of magic, a bruja,/ A hoodoo-voodoo lady . . ." in an attempt to remedy her infertility, by the drama's end she loses out on love as well as a reproductive future (104). It is important to

Project porches in Miami. Photograph copyright © Michael Elliott.

underscore that once again McCraney flags both the Latinx and Haitianness of the African-derived cosmology of Oya's neighborhood, demonstrating how the Black plurality of his Miami neighborhood transfers to his plays. Oya's loss of a reproductive future leads to her self-inflicted death, resulting in the end of this second generation and the family line.

Yet, Oya's death is foreshadowed in Elegba's opening dream where he yells his salutations to announce himself well before arriving on Oya and Mama Moja's front porch. To stave him off, Mama Moja emerges onto the porch and listens as he relays his dream:

ELEGBA:
It's always about the water, my dreams.
Near it or around it. Sometimes I stand
In the *high tide* and I can't breathe but I
Can breathe. And I walk on the bottom on
The floor of the waters and they's these people
Walk alongside me but they all bones and they
Click the bone people, they talk in the click.
I say, "Where yall going?" And they say, "Just
Walking for a while." I say, "Don't you want
To go home . . ." They say, "When we walk there, it
Wasn't there no more." I feel bad for them. . . .

> Then they click and I come up on the mud part,
> Like they send me to the land part, And I'm
> Sitting there waiting 'cause I know they want
> Me to wait I wait there looking and on
> Top of the waters is Oya. . . .
> Oya girl floating on top of the water. . . .
> Brown skin in the red water. (22–23, emphasis mine)

If we center the opening lines where Elegba "stand[s] in the *high tide* and [he] can't breathe," we reorient away from more conventional Middle Passage readings to foreground the presentness of hurricane seasons and rising sea levels as a Miami sensibility that understands its and other coastal geographies as fragile habitats. In this way, the entire trilogy should be read as a meditation on climate change and hurricane time—that is, how the annual recurrence of tropical storms and hurricanes affects the pace and sensibility of both the people and the city.[38] In this dream sequence, dead ancestors present as bone people who live underneath the ocean floor and whose homes, once there, "wasn't there no more." To live with a high tide sensibility means an awareness of both the erosion and disappearance of landscape, built environment, and people washed away by water, a repeating threat each hurricane season. But the red and brown water of the play's title at once symbolizes the red blood of Oya's death and the disruption that brings sedimented elements on the ocean floor to mix with its top layers, thus changing the very color and texture of the water's composition.

McCraney plots a seasonal—yet less visible—story about the material effects of weather-based displacements on contemporary Black bodies lost to the sea, especially during hurricane season. These bone people are not boat people in the sense of migratory bodies risking it all in search of refuge; they are national citizens left unprotected at home from various degrees of precarity and, indeed, from the weather's collateral damage. Thus, interwoven into the very narrative arc of this story about ancestors is the contemporary reality of rising sea levels and recurring weather-based traumas that Carole Boyce Davies would describe as "micro Middle Passages."[39] As with the effects of Hurricane Katrina a decade before, in the aftermath of the 2017 hurricane season with Irma's and Maria's devastating effects across the Circum-Caribbean, the entire region and the U.S. mainland had to make sense of the extent to which the United States exercises a far-reaching imperial presence in the Caribbean Basin, with uneven access to sustainable infrastructure and resources becoming more pronounced. Such structural inequities were especially evident in the lack of aid campaigns and media coverage of Barbuda's near-complete destruction, Dominica's invisibility to U.S. fundraising drives, and the commonwealths of the British and U.S. Virgin Islands as well as Puerto Rico explicitly reckoning with their second-class citizenship status vis-à-vis their respective imperial states. A Black hemispheric imaginary accentuates such colonial legacies, their multiple imperial entanglements, and the material impact on bodies made subaltern.

Bayous feature more principally in the latter two plays of *The Brother/ Sister Plays*, where they are spaces outside social censorship that operate as sites of clearing and sites where repressed desires surface. Many of the trips to the bayou in *The Brothers Size* and *Marcus; Or the Secret of Sweet* happen when there is moonlight, a time in the evening when a different, more twilight sensibility comes into being. Theorizing such twilight times and spaces as "Caribbean spaces," Boyce Davies describes the "unreality between night and day, where spirits begin to roam and objects that seem perfectly normal in the daylight assume strange patterns and shapes, that gap between different realities, that zone of instability between darkness and light, that time when transformation happens."[40] These twilight times and spaces are central to *The Brother/Sister Plays* where the plays's culminating actions occur in the twilight of day. In *The Brothers Size*, the once incarcerated brother, Oshoosi Size, is out on parole and dreams of being able to drive to the bayou in his own car as something akin to the feeling of "the ultimate freedom" (156). Yet, it is the fulfillment of this dream in the twilight of an evening drive that lands him back in the orbit of the carceral state. In sharp contrast, the bayou in *Marcus; Or the Secret of Sweet* serves as a place of clearing and as a space where sexual truth can be revealed. Throughout the trilogy, characters reappear from one story to the next. And, in this final play, Marcus, the son of Elegba from the earlier two plays, struggles to come to terms with his homosexuality, a fact his community already recognizes as a "tacit subject," which Carlos Decena defines as "neither secret nor silent" since "coming out can be a verbal declaration of something that is already understood or assumed—tacit—in an exchange."[41] The bayou here becomes the stage for the public outing of the visiting stranger from the Bronx, Shua, who is romantically involved with both Marcus and his female best friend Osha. Rethinking the geography of liberalism, the play discloses that the Black urban North is not more liberated or progressive than the Black South, especially as it relates to public acknowledgment of Black gay male sexuality.

Following *The Brother/Sister Plays*, *Head of Passes* is set in a deteriorating house located in the marshlands on the mouth of the Mississippi River. The play brings together the ecosystems of water, families, and the architecture of porches. McCraney revisits the biblical story of Job through Shelah Reynolds, the family matriarch. He reworks heroic male narratives to confront the gendered and generational legacies of Black housing for the middle classes, and the sexual secrets held in these houses. Most of this play's dramatic action is staged in the Florida room. In contrast to project porches, Florida rooms are enclosed structures adjoined to an existing house that enable a better flow of sunlight and fresh air. However, they also immediately signal class distinctions in their very construction, as these front rooms allow for a greater amount of privacy from the street while still providing the ability to enjoy the outdoors from a remove.

The play's action begins and ends in the Florida room, which has been inundated with rain and, correspondingly, six inches of rising water. The opening stage directions for act 1 read:

> There is the wind, heard first, like a voice or a cry. Then steady, constant, like yearning, or wood bending, there is the Gulf of Mexico; home to Pirate Ships and lore near forgot. A string of lights, hung across the Florida Room of the former Bed and Breakfast, fizzle on . . . SHELAH steady, *constant like the Gulf*, coming down the stairs . . . She looks towards the Florida Room. (3, emphasis mine)

From the start, the unfolding story is framed by how the environment shapes individuals. The audience first encounters the wind as an embodied yearning and crying sound. Rain and the leak in the living room's roof literally floods the action of the play. The audience learns that one generation prior, the Reynolds left the publicness of the parish and the Black community on the mainland and bought the right to privacy by living in this marshland on the Gulf. But their privacy comes at a cost since they have to monetize their house as a bed-and-breakfast, catering to itinerant Texans drilling on oil barges on the Gulf of Mexico who require short-term accommodations. After her husband's death, Shelah stops operating this business. Aubrey, the eldest son, is eager to sell the house and plot of land to developers, but his mother reminds him of the racial legacy of their land acquisition, as there was "nothing else 'cept catfish and rednecks" in the Passes when they first moved (40). There is both a precariousness and a speculativeness to living in this landscape of the bottom that houses the lowest rung of human and animal species. As bottom-feeders, catfish feed near the bottom of the ocean floor and in parts of the U.S. South are referred to as "mud cats" signaling the very physical granular muddiness of the bottom. Unincorporated in the mainland of American citizenship, the Reynolds family engages in the speculative gesture of living on and developing this inhospitable terrain on the Gulf and are able to create an interracial community of solidarity based on mutual values of fairness and care.

Through such subtle nuances, McCraney's treatment of geography in the play draws attention to sand's heterogeneity. The specificities of the local environment, in this case Louisiana's sand, shape labor power and industries of capital accumulation.

SHELAH:
Listen, I wasn't never for the business, I was raised on a farm,
But you can't really grow nothing to sustain,
Out here too long that sandy salty silt, it'll fool

You cause you can get a seedling but I'm looking at nothing
Growing out the earth and I had to. . . . We had to provide.
But honey, they get that oil running out there (31–32).

Coming from McCraney's Miami topography where the fecundity of a
despoiled Everglades supports the growth of sugarcane, this play highlights
that Louisiana's bayous are brackish salt water where nothing grows. This
land's very ecology, therefore, left the family few options for monetization.
Yet the promise of property ownership is particularly resonant in Black communities, where redlining and other forms of residential restrictions sought to
make this marker of the ultimate fulfillment of the American Dream inaccessible to the descendants of slaves.

Even while addressing the fiscal precarity of Black homeownership, *Head
of Passes* also tackles the intimate underbelly of privatized living. Set on the
evening of Shelah's birthday, the rainstorm that rages during the play serves
as a catalytic element that destroys this family and exposes their secrets. As
the night draws to a close, Shelah's three adult children go out separately into
the storm and before daybreak she loses all three to death: one by stabbing;
another by drug overdose; and the third by vehicular death. In the opening
scene of act 2, Shelah lies on her side on the Florida room's floor lamenting
that her family had long been destroyed by the internal secrets of sexual
abuse that were revealed the preceding night (67). The final act and last scene
of the play opens with the sound of the tide coming back in: "It is steadily,
slowly rising. It's already taken parts of the house; the once open Florida
Room has become/is becoming an island, surrounded by water on at least two
sides. Shelah has not moved. She will not be moved" (85). The first and last
one on stage, Shelah opens and closes the play. Unlike the project porches of
The Brother/Sister Plays where no privacy means less space for secrets, this
play moves from an enclosed Florida room that houses the secrets of sexual
abuse to a room that has become an island where water has washed away its
secrets, making Shelah at once more vulnerable to the elements while also,
perhaps paradoxically, more reliant on and open to the greater community
for her own care. Shelah remains; and though she herself is fatally ill, the play
suggests that with the community's help, she will be the one to provide care
for her daughter's two orphaned sons, the third generation.

Where the waterscape scenes in McCraney's plays set in Louisiana seek to
create possibilities in the midst of tragedy, in *Moonlight* the sea provides the
protagonist space to learn how to trust and manage his surrounding elements as sites of freedom-making. Viewers first enter the film *Moonlight*
through sound as Boris Gardiner's song "Every Nigger Is a Star" plays over
a black screen followed by the sound of ocean waves in what looks like
black, moonlit sky.[42] Thus on a contemporary story of urban Miami are
the sediments of the 1970s Kingston, Jamaica, of the song's origins, which
itself had the overlay of the visual iconography of U.S. Blaxploitation film

vernacular. This particular coming together is itself a creole triangulation—
Liberty City, Kingston, and the Blaxploitation genre—indicative of the Black
hemispheric imaginary. Additionally, that this overlay is also key to fellow
Liberty City filmmaker Barry Jenkins's filmic protocol confirms McCraney's
assertion that people from Miami instinctively "get the mix," which they both
understand and practice aesthetically. Behind the wheels of a blue Chevrolet
Impala, Juan brings the viewer into the world of Liberty City. For the film's
first nine minutes and twenty-two seconds, the protagonist does not speak;
in fact, choosing opacity, he refuses speech. And when he finally does speak,
he states his name: "My name is Chiron; people call me Little." This statement is followed by Chiron locating himself as coming from Liberty City. In
these first nine and a half minutes of quiet, Chiron gives the viewer searing,
contemplative, judgmental, and vulnerable looks. Eight minutes later, or sev-
enteen and a half minutes into the film, Chiron enters the ocean with Juan for
a transformative swimming lesson during which he will also receive tutelage
on race, identity, geography, and where and how to seize temporary moments
of freedom. Viewers watch as Chiron discovers how to maneuver his hands
and body in the ocean, but he also learns how to trust.

Freedom here has a geography and a temporality linked to intergenerational
male bonding communicated through Juan's statement: "I got you and I'm
not gonna let you go. You in the middle of the world." That "in the middle of
the world" is, indeed, in the middle of the ocean gestures toward an endless
horizon, where both Juan and Chiron are liberated from the inland confines
of Liberty City and the strictures of performing Black hypermasculinity. The
racial logic of Jim Crow Miami should not be lost on the viewer since, through
the mid-1960s, Blacks were prohibited from public recreational spaces such
as city beaches and pools. Here, nonetheless, away from the public gaze, they
can hug and be held. If home space represents restrictions as they carry the
burdens and baggage of black masculinity, then, the ocean, in contrast, is
an endless space of levity, plentitude, and possibility. Yet, these moments are
temporary, quiet, and ephemeral.

It is in one such moment that Juan relates to Chiron his own backstory
about the invisible Afro-Cuban presence in Miami: "Let me tell you something man there are Black people everywhere. Remember that, OK? There ain't
no place you can go in the world where ain't no Black people. We were the
first on this planet. I've been here a long time, but I'm from Cuba. *A lot of
Black folks in Cuba, but you wouldn't know that from being here*" (Juan;
emphasis mine). It is important to note the use of the conjunction "but" rather
than "and," announcing the seemingly local disjuncture of Blackness and
Cubanness. In Miami, the Afro-Cuban presence is often registered as following the 1980s Mariel boatlift. Juan's use of "long time" records a longer
history, and his storytelling relates the film's titular logic through the voice of
an older Afro-Cuban woman as Juan recounts her saying to him in her vari-
ation of Spanish-accented English: "Running around catching all the light.

In moonlight, Black boys look blue. That what I'm going to call you, Blue"
(24:24). Vocalizing the title of McCraney's original 2006 script, "In Moonlight Black Boys Look Blue," this revoicing of the older Afro-Cuban woman
is the Miami palimpsest—a city of overlaid accents and sediment histories. It
is here where the two Americas meet (African America and Afro-Cuba), and
ideas are passed on. If the Afro-Cuban is invisible in the white racialized logic
of Cuban Miami, Juan aligns himself with a global Blackness and gestures
toward a hemispheric orientation that insists on the long history of a Black
hemispheric presence and thought. While the ethnicity of Juan's girlfriend
Teresa remains unaddressed in the film, the Ibero-Romantic linguistic spelling of her name, "Teresa," rather than the Anglo "Theresa" gestures, at the
very least, to ethnic ambiguity or the possibility of her Afro-Latinadadness.
Such subtle ambiguities are the hallmark of McCraney's plots.

The afternoon ocean scene is both formative and transformative for Chiron. It is important to connect this occurrence to the one that follows where
Chiron associates for himself water as a site of temporary freedom-making.
This next sequence in the film finds Chiron entering his home after school to
notice the absent TV. Immediately and instinctively, he knows his mother has
pawned it, and his response is to draw himself a bubble bath out of dish deter-
gent and water warmed from the kitchen stove. Home alone and immersed in
the quiet of the bathtub, Chiron re-creates the feeling of temporary freedom
first experienced with Juan in the ocean. Whether in the ocean or the bathtub,
these water scenes are quiet intimate spaces of possibility. As the film progresses in the close living quarters of Liberty City, viewers are placed in the
interior courtyard of the public housing scheme devoid of trees and vegeta-
tion, inviting the question, what does it mean to navigate the hot sun without
shade? This scene stands in contrast to the lush yardscape of the house that
Juan occupies with Teresa, which illustrates that within walking distance
of Chiron's Liberty Square projects exist different kinds of privatized Black
housing. In fact, viewers notice that Teresa relocates after Juan's death since
presumably she cannot financially maintain such housing. Nonetheless, the
various spaces of the film's Black world—the open field by the train tracks,
the high school and Juan and Teresa's homes—try to capture the breadth of
Liberty City so as to not conflate Liberty Square housing projects with the
entire neighborhood.

The inner courtyard of public housing is the site where Chiron is publicly
mocked about his mother's monetized sexual transactions to support her
drug habit. In contrast to this loud courtyard scene of shaming in the confines
of public housing, beach scenes of smoking weed on the sand by the sea create quiet spaces for Black queer male vulnerability. With the reprieve of the
beach, Kevin and Chiron have intimate exchanges, not just sexual encounters. These spaces enable them to articulate their mutual vulnerabilities and
sexual contact happens only after such intimacies are communicated. In the
first of these scenes as teenagers, post–sexual contact, they both leave traces

of their sexual intimacy as sediments in the sand; Kevin rubs the sands' residue off his hand while Chiron grips a handful of sand upon reaching orgasm, which he too releases back to the sand. These traces of Black queer encounters remind us, as Agard-Jones advances, of "what the sand remembers."

Throughout the film's first and second acts, Kevin instructs Chiron on how to perform the masquerade of a "non-soft" heteromasculinity as a defense against navigating the neighborhood homophobia. Yet, they are both caught up in the restrictions of performing hard Black hypermasculinity evinced in the game of "Knock Down, Stay Down" initiated by the school bully Terrel. It is Kevin who delivers the lifelong physical and psychological blows to Chiron. Recalling the Battle Royal scene in Ralph Ellison's *Invisible Man*, where young Black men are coerced to fight viciously for the entertainment of the white onlookers, these two boys do not want to fight, but because Kevin's masculinity is at stake, he fights to perform the bully's standard of Black inner-city heteromasculinity. Chiron notably returns to the solace of water after this violent encounter, soaking his bruised face in his kitchen sink with ice water to soothe the pain and swelling. As the film draws to a close years after this incident, during which time Chiron has become a drug dealer in Altanta, Kevin and Chiron reunite in Miami. Here Kevin invites Chiron to stop wearing the mask represented by his buff body and gold-plated grills: "That ain't you Chiron . . . Why you got them damn fronts man?"[43] For many, these gold-plated grills are a constitutive part of a Black, working-class, Miami, or, more broadly, an urban aesthetic. One could, therefore, read Kevin's reprimand as reproducing a logic that instructs that the only way to become a fully actualized human is to shed the grills that are embraced as a distinctive marker of one's status from below. Kevin and Chiron return to the former's apartment on the beach in the film's final minutes. It is a liminal space of possibility where both men are able once again to reject the masquerade of hypermasculinity and embrace Black queerness. Those that call for a romantic ending with the consummation of the sex act should remember that the last encounter between the two young men was the traumatic, violent fight that literally altered Chiron's course in masculinity.

The film ends where it begins: with the sound of the ocean and the younger Chiron, played by Alex R. Hibbert, looking back from the water's endless horizon to confront the viewer with his piercing Black look. It closes with a quiet look, an invitation to this Black hemispheric point of view that looks to sea/see what is on the immediate horizon—even while negotiating quotidian limits. These are not grand liberation narratives but rather narratives of how ordinary Black people live and make meaning in the everyday. Contextualizing McCraney's oeuvre—his Black southern hemispheric epics—through a Miami sensibility insists on reading the sediments of Black plurality and its consequent Black hemispheric geopolitical horizons, which bring to light Black lifeworlds surviving within the often-precarious rhythms of both the city and the sea.

Theodicy and Hope

✦

Tarell Alvin McCraney's Scrutiny of Religiosity

Patrick Maley

In the closing moments of Tarell Alvin McCraney's *Head of Passes*, Shelah sits and waits. The pious matriarch, who, after losing her children and home in one terrible night, has spent much of the play's second half raging against the God she calls "a thief in the Night!" decides to "sit and see" (82, 77).[1] This action is indeterminate: Shelah waits for God's next move but recognizes no response. The play ends without closure of Shelah's grief. God has little place in *Wig Out!*, McCraney's play exploring the drag community's complex dynamics, which he suggests are generative of identity: "During the day, one might get stared at, called a name on a street corner or, worse, accosted by someone outside the circle, but for that night at the ball one could be literally the *queen of it all*."[2] Although *Wig Out!* may seem to reject frequently normative concepts like religion in favor of a self-sustaining community, the play complicates such a notion by including characters with names like Venus, Loki, and Deity. *Wig Out!* thus intimates the presence of the divine without directly engaging its force.

Although prominent throughout McCraney's work, religiosity—the condition of being religious, often considering human life to be in dialogue with or affected by deific force—is neither ameliorative nor destructive for his characters. Instead, McCraney's plays scrutinize religion, querying the degree to which it contributes productively to human challenges of identity and community. In this way, his work recalls biblical theodicy, a process through which religious humans work to justify divine benevolence among persistent human struggle. Such efforts are prominent throughout the Hebrew Bible, which starkly juxtaposes God's desire to love and protect his chosen people with extensive Hebrew suffering. For biblical authors, suffering must be the fault of humanity for provoking God's anger. But McCraney's theodicy is more skeptical; like a courtroom jury, his dramatic worlds are willing to be convinced of divine power, but will not offer affirmation without adequate evidence. McCraney thus signifies on biblical theodicy by questioning both the possibility of divine grace and the human desire for it.

The fact that religiosity remains prominent in McCraney's plays despite persistent skepticism suggests that wrestling with the possibility of the divine offers something essential to his dramaturgy. Indeed, the definitive absence or presence of deific forces would drastically alter the playwright's world. More important than answering questions of divine attendance, therefore, is the human struggle with the question. Jacob wrestles God in Genesis, and faithful Yoruba work to determine their patron orisha through Ifá divination, but McCraney's characters strive with the very premise that deities exist and are benevolent. The plays seem willing to embrace either affirmation or negation of that premise, but nowhere in the playwright's work is either answer reached.

McCraney's oeuvre therefore constitutes a skeptical theodicy of hope. This means that his plays interrogate divine care for humanity (theodicy) without any conviction of affirmation or even of divine existence (skepticism), but are nonetheless open to both affirmation and productive atheistic humanism (hope). "Hope wrestles with despair, but it doesn't generate optimism," Cornel West observes, "It just generates this energy to be courageous, to bear witness, to see what the end is going to be."[3] McCraney's dramaturgy wrestles with despair by allowing for the possibility of a deleterious absence or oppressive presence of the divine, potential realities that his work is comfortable considering while also being unwilling to forfeit either the struggle for congress with deific forces or the potential of productive atheism. In this way, McCraney restructures the model of biblical theodicies.

In the Pentateuch, God promises the Hebrews prosperity in exchange for faith, but by the sixth century B.C.E., the Hebrew nation had been dispersed and lived under terrible oppression. "Theodicies as theological exercises attempt to deal with dissonance caused by holding three propositions concurrently," argues Craig Prentiss, "that evil exists, that God is omnipotent, and that God is synonymous with goodness. Within a theistic system, approaching a satisfactory response requires that at least one of these propositions be nuanced or eliminated."[4] Thus, sixth-century Hebrews might have pondered God's abandonment, or a lack of God's goodness, but biblical theodicy rejects such notions, attempting to understand instead how humans might conduct themselves more effectively within God's grace. Biblical theodicy articulates solutions rather than hope, suggesting that following its prescriptions will lead believers back into God's grace (or to understanding that grace was never lacking). McCraney's work is more skeptical, wondering first whether or not deific forces, if they exist (as posited by a wide variety of religious traditions), are invested in human struggles, and second whether or not humans should care.

This strategy is prominent in *Head of Passes*, the play McCraney says is "inspired by the Book of Job," and an illuminating juxtaposition emerges by considering *Wig Out!* in light of Ecclesiastes.[5] The Book of Job suggests that humans cannot know the justification for God's actions, and that any investigation into the matter is sinful folly. Pious Job loses everything simply because God wants to prove a point to Satan. After a long, fruitless dialogue between Job and some friends who seek to help him understand his suffering, God appears at the book's close—first admonishing the humans for trying to understand his inconceivable nature, and finally praising Job when he at last shows humility. The book suggests that God's actions are beyond conception of the human mind, and so utter piety is always due. Ecclesiastes makes a similar point about the difficulty of humans understanding God's whims but argues that clues exist in the pleasures of life. "I commend enjoyment, for there is nothing better for people under the sun than to eat, and drink, and enjoy themselves," the book's narrator suggests, arguing that goodness available to humans is God's gift, which is intended to be enjoyed.[6] Job's theodicy argues that God's goodness is inconceivable, while Ecclesiastes insists that evidence lies before any humans pious enough to accept it.

Reading *Head of Passes* and *Wig Out!* as signifying on Job and Ecclesiastes thus shows McCraney traveling a wide spectrum of theodicy while shunning conclusions. Instead, McCraney's work queries the foundation of black religiosity, wondering ultimately not how to justify the interplay of human suffering and joy with God's goodness but rather how to conduct oneself within a human community marked by such conflicting conditions as pain, joy, struggle, celebration, angst, and wonder when divine benevolence remains an open question. McCraney's dramaturgy seeks a functional strategy for operating within theodicy's inconclusiveness. This complex dynamic of religiosity underscores the importance of community within individual and social projects of becoming, one of McCraney's master themes. Neither moralistic nor teleological, his plays make no guarantees that their characters will come to clear understandings of themselves or their places within a web of relationships. He nonetheless supports his characters' search for racial, sexual, gender, and familial identity, a quest he nurtures by broadening their communities to include a potential divine presence. Thus, although he shows deep skepticism of religiosity's efficacy in projects of becoming, by not banishing religion, the playwright reveals an abiding hope that communion with the divine can be a productive component in the project of defining self and community, and that it can offer some form of redress from generational struggle.

McCraney's Skepticism and Shelah's Desperate Religiosity: *Head of Passes*

Head of Passes takes place in a house that had long seemed a warm home. Here Shelah and her husband ran a bed-and-breakfast while also raising three children. But those days are long eclipsed by uncertain present conditions:

adult children have moved on, Shelah's husband has died, and the house is in terrible disrepair. The opening of act 2 will find the house destroyed by a storm, but cracks in Shelah's home appear long before that. Her health is failing; she learns belatedly that her daughter Cookie's drug addiction has roots in childhood sexual abuse by Shelah's husband, who fathered Cookie out of wedlock and brought her home for Shelah to raise (echoing August Wilson's *Fences*); and Shelah ruminates over how to reveal her illness to her children. But throughout the trouble of act 1, Shelah's faith remains strong. She addresses God regularly in moments of struggle, and she insists that the Devil's name not be uttered under her increasingly compromised roof, even in reference to delicious egg hors d'oeuvres. She is not certain that hers or her family's lives are on the right track, but she believes God will show the way.

That unflinching devotion faces challenges in act 2. Her house crumbles, and Shelah gradually learns that each of her three children died during the night. Here the resonances of Job become strongest: like her biblical predecessor, Shelah loses the entirety of her home and her family in shockingly little time (Shelah's plight might in fact be worse than Job's, whose wife survives the divine attack). The bulk of the long Book of Job centers on a repetitive dialogue between Job and three friends who fail to justify God's justice. But McCraney departs from his model and leaves Shelah alone to rage—more like Lear on the heath or a mourning Hecuba than like Job—against absent forces. Over the course of her long, passionate speech, Shelah moves in and out of fury, anguish, bewilderment, penitence, petulance, and self-righteousness before resolving that she has said enough and that she is ready to await God's response. "I'll sit and see," she asserts at the play's closing, waiting for God's comfort before realizing that she is merely at the outset of grieving: "Day 1 and Nothing" (82). The play does not show day two or anything after, leaving audiences unaware of whether Shelah finds peace or even how long she lives before her health fails, but McCraney also does not shut down the possibility of Shelah's solace. The play closes as an open question.

Shelah is convinced that the Judeo-Christian God exerts major influence over her world. McCraney proves to be less certain. The play sets up a stark juxtaposition between Shelah's convictions and the recognizable results of her religiosity. On the one hand, she is certain that God loves and protects her; on the other, she receives no solace from her invocations. But the play does not suggest that solace is unattainable. Perhaps, as Shelah wonders, God is punishing her for "the ways in which [her] blind faith had produced many blind spots," as Isaiah Matthew Wooden puts it; most notably, she wonders if her suffering is penance for failing to act on her suspicion of sexual abuse in her home.[7] "For *Head of Passes*," says McCraney, "I was taken with the idea behind unyielding faith and how we hold onto it"; the play may therefore be showing that utter religious devotion produces lapses in human responsibility.[8] Or perhaps God comes to Shelah as a bird. Shortly before the play's conclusion, Shelah grows annoyed by a chirping robin: "Quit making all that damn . . . don't you see I'm trying to lay a burden down?" (81). Given the play's biblical framework, this robin may be God. Throughout the Bible, God appears in unexpected forms, from a burning bush before Moses to a "sound of sheer silence" before Elijah, so it is feasible that Shelah's anger blinds her to God answering her prayer in the form of a bird.[9] The lack of line breaks and capitalization in the script during the bird's brief appearance indicates that this is the only section of Shelah's monologue spoken in prose, as if she is too enveloped in the high-minded poetry of her performative faith to recognize her prosaic theophany. Or perhaps God is a fiction that distracts Shelah from reality. The religious conditions of *Head of Passes* are capacious enough for all these possibilities and more, but the play shows no interest in settling the question of Shelah's faith. Instead, *Head of Passes* leaves that question open, eager to dwell on its complications but unwilling to offer conclusions.

Certainly the end of *Head of Passes* could intimate religious emptiness, suggesting that Shelah's "Day 1 and Nothing" is indicative of all her days to come. Neither God nor any of his agents appear overtly in the play, so it is reasonable to see Shelah's faith as foolishly misplaced. In fact, McCraney made an atheistic reading more plausible with his revision for the play's 2016 run at the Public Theater in New York City. Both the 2013 world premiere at Steppenwolf Theatre Company in Chicago and the 2015 production at Berkeley Rep contained a laconic angel that only Shelah could see, appearing throughout the play in times of great distress, but the playwright eliminated this indicator of God's presence before opening in New York.[10] As the play evolved, the playwright thus seems to have grown more interested in Shelah's isolation, in examining how she would fare in the face of a radical lack of ratification for her faith. The revisions reveal the play growing starker, and the skepticism of McCraney's theodicy deepening. So perhaps God and his destructive or redemptive forces are totally absent in *Head of Passes*, and Shelah's belief in God's love is as delusional as her hope for the resurrection of her children. This reading is plausible because the play makes no efforts to shut it down. Instead, the playwright allows for uncertainty, for the perfectly reasonable conclusion that *Head of Passes* exists in a godless world.

Importantly, however, the play also insists that audiences consider Shelah's abiding faith seriously. Faith is by necessity operative either without evidence or in the face of contrary evidence, and so blithely rejecting Shelah's devotion as empirically misplaced would be irresponsible. Instead, it is necessary to follow the lead of Shelah and her playwright into an open-ended theological struggle. The absence of God is a valid potential result of this struggle, but it is by no means the condition determined by the play's conclusion. Instead, Shelah is deeply entwined in a wrestling match on at least two levels. Within the framework of the play, Shelah, Jacob-like, grapples with God for spiritual benefits. Jacob wrestles with God's force from nightfall until daybreak before finally pinning his opponent and insisting, "I will not let you go, unless you bless me"; the human overpowers the divine and presses his advantage to secure himself a valuable blessing.[11] This outcome is Shelah's goal: "I'm calling YOU!" she screams upon learning of her children's deaths, and then later she becomes more direct: "I call on you, my God I call your name. Where is the promise? . . . Where are you! / Show yourself!" (71, 78–80). She calls on God with the desperate force of one struggling mightily against a foe: "With your breath you can restore life, that's the promise! / I can blink and again the loves of my life / will have theirs and I swear I . . . Ah! Please! / Please! I just want my babies, Lord. Do it for me, Lord!" (80). Shelah feels as though she has earned advantages through her life of piety, and now she hopes that she is in a position to capitalize like Jacob.

But on another important level—one accessible only to McCraney's audience—Shelah is wrestling with the very idea of divine investment in human suffering. Like Job existing as a Hebrew parable for the wrongheadedness of humans inquiring after God, Shelah stands in for the questions McCraney asks about the efficacy of religious devotion. "There's Something, yes, something in your power and in your glory that will sweep over / Me" avers Shelah, asserting "I will have full understanding of this—of this— / I will! / I will be stead fast!" (76). By neither ratifying nor nullifying her certainty, the play offers Shelah as a case study in McCraney's skeptical theodicy. For although Shelah professes certainty, McCraney alters his source material to deny her the type of direct response from God found in Job. In part, the anger of Job's God serves as assurance that God is invested in human affairs.

Without that response, *Head of Passes* offers no such assurance. McCraney therefore invites his audience to interrogate Shelah's certainty and, in turn, God's attendance upon *Head of Passes*. "As with any prophet," points out David Román, "we are asked to consider: Has she gone mad? Or are her visions and voices the testament of spiritual convictions?"[12] Shelah is certain that her convictions are deep, but Román is astute in pointing out the necessity of audiences interrogating her faith, a task that McCraney made more perplexing at the Public Theater. At Steppenwolf, the actor playing the angel returned at the play's conclusion as a construction worker who soothes Shelah's anguish; he tells Shelah that he is no angel, but she disagrees. Writing about the Steppenwolf production, Román says that Shelah must "entertain doubt if not despair before finding redemption in what had originally reassured [her]."[13] McCraney revised the script for the Berkeley production, bringing the angel figure back on stage to accompany Shelah during her monologue, this time without a construction costume and saying nothing, but attending upon her for comfort. In Chicago and Berkeley, Shelah at least received some indication that God heard her. By cutting the angel for the Public Theater's production (and beyond), McCraney denies Shelah soothing company, making the question of her solace uncertain. From draft to draft, the playwright increased Shelah's isolation and decreased her solace, revealing a growing interest in religiosity laid bare. Over its lifecycle, *Head of Passes* grew into a more challenging and open-ended theodicy, with McCraney less accommodating to religiosity and forcing audiences to contribute more and more directly to the process of its theodicy.

Shelah's religiosity gives occasion to this play, and so its audience has no authority to deny the substance of her faith; but it is certainly fair to doubt. Perhaps that is the responsibility of the audience for *Head of Passes*: to doubt, interrogate, and wonder. Wooden points out that Shelah "aurally signifies on *selah*—an exclamation that punctuates many of the psalms of the Old Testament and serves as a reminder to pause and meditate."[14] This connection helpfully elucidates Shelah's role in McCraney's theodicy as a figure for speculation and critical consideration. The definition of the Hebrew word *selah* remains uncertain—"interlude" and "lift up" are possible translations for the word that could have been a liturgical instruction or a congregational response—but it is telling that psalmists prefer *selah* to *amen*, meaning "certainly" or "may it be so."[15] Rather than the certainty of *amen*, *selah* encourages reflection and deeper consideration; through Shelah, McCraney encourages the same of his audiences. By withholding resolution, the play encourages its audience to wrestle with the divine while watching a character do the same.

In recalling Hecuba, Lear, and Oedipus—"Pour. Oh, Pour" was one of Shelah's first lines at the Public Theater, addressing the raging storm as Shakespeare's king does the wind, and later she threatens to "dig my eyes out right now"—the play invokes tragedy while allowing for at least the potential of redemption for its fallen hero.[16] In Shelah's mind, her future is in God's hands, and even though McCraney proves much less convinced of this than either Shelah or Job's author, he enables its potential in a critical, investigatory manner. This approach renders *Head of Passes* skeptical, hopeful theodicy; the playwright joins his character in summoning "the strength to bear witness, to see what the end is going to be" but does not allow the play to give itself over to either blind faith or atheism. Concluding with an open question, *Head of Passes* offers its Job at the outset of her arduous journey, encouraging its audience to wonder if and to what degree her faith will find reward. Asking how fruitful a life of steadfast religiosity can be, the play dwells inquisitively in a space of uncertain grace.

Gods and Drag and Humanism: *Wig Out!*

Like Job, Shelah lives a pious life, giving herself to God and her children; for her, to live a godly life is to sacrifice the needs of the self in favor of the divine or human other. The notion guiding this brand of piety is that partaking in an excess of life's pleasures is succumbing to human weakness and ushering oneself away from divine grace. It is a concept as familiar in the modern world as it was in the ancient world. But shortly after the composition of Job, a Hebrew taking the moniker "Qoheleth"—Hebrew for teacher—offered a different tactic for the best, most holy human life. The book of Ecclesiastes (its title taken from the Greek translation of Qoheleth) is most famous for the King James Version's rendering of its central tenet: "man hath no better thing under the sun, than to eat, and to drink, and to be merry," a concept the book reiterates regularly throughout its short length.[17] Both Job and Ecclesiastes wrestle with the difficulty of understanding God's desires for humanity, but the books come to very different conclusions. Job finds that investigating God's whims is foolish, but Ecclesiastes suggests that humans need not wonder about their position in God's grace because the conditions of their lives provide evidence. Bountiful food, drink, and merriment are signs of God's pleasure, and should be enjoyed as such. "For to the one who pleases him God gives wisdom and knowledge and joy," insists Qoheleth, adding, "but to the sinner he gives the work of gathering and heaping, only to give to one who pleases God."[18] Job says close your eyes and believe; Ecclesiastes says open your eyes and know.

The wrinkle in Ecclesiastes's philosophy is the often difficult task of determining what exactly brings one the pleasure that Qoheleth suggests is so paramount to earthly fulfillment, and in the folds of this wrinkle emerges the philosophical underpinnings of *Wig Out!* McCraney's 2008 play focuses on a fraught, often contentious, occasionally joyous community of black drag performers who unite as a means for each to explore individual and collective identities that are out of sync with dominant social norms. Each character is on a unique personal journey while the collective force of constituting the drag community allows all to contribute to the journeys of others. McCraney does not cite Ecclesiastes as a source for this play as he does Job for *Head of Passes*, but the comparison elucidates the open-ended struggle of the playwright's drag performers. Much in the same way that McCraney leaves unanswered the question of Shelah's redemption, so too does he refuse a verdict on the quest for sustainable identity in *Wig Out!* Qoheleth suggests that fulfillment will come from enjoying the bounty, something which *Wig Out!*'s characters attempt by embracing their identities, forming houses, and performing at balls. But it would be difficult to claim that any of the characters in *Wig Out!* achieve fulfillment within the space of the play. McCraney at once allows his characters the opportunity to find fulfillment by exploring their identity within an accessible earthly realm but also leaves open the question of their success.

Focusing on the manifold dynamics of the drag community, *Wig Out!* takes place over one particularly charged day during which several divergent forces in the community clash. The play opens with Ms. Nina, a drag queen in the House of Light, picking up Eric, a gay man, by gradually revealing her masculine identity. While Nina is with Eric, the House of Light receives a visit from Loki, a member of the House of Diabolique, who challenges Light to compete at a Cinderella Ball, a drag competition to be held that night at midnight where various houses will compete for glory. "The stakes are higher," at a Cinderella Ball: "All the drag houses invited but half of them won't show . . . can't get it together in time. So only the / Strongest most skillful and legendary of houses / Will be there" (34–35). The high stakes of the ball put stress on all members of Light and over the course of the play several interpersonal conflicts within the house erupt while Nina eventually realizes that a relationship with an outsider like Eric is untenable: "You're not this type of gay," she explains to Eric, "It scares you . . . this little ride I am giving you" (43). Through the vehicle of the Cinderella Ball and various clashes over sex, respect, and performance, *Wig Out!* examines the individual and collective struggle of identity within all its characters. Nina characterizes the life of drag as "two souls in one," the balancing and negotiation of which the play suggests is complex, difficult, and interminable (43).

The biblical God is by no means as significant a force in this play as in *Head of Passes*, but allusions to deific forces from a broad range of religious traditions litter the play's drag community. As he does in *The Brother/Sister Plays*, McCraney signals congress with the divine through characters's names. The play's dramatis personae includes characters named Venus, Deity, Faith, Fate, Fay (these last three are designated "The Fates Three"; "Fay" may be a phonological queering of "Faith" or "Fate," an allusion to the *OED*'s archaic first definition, "a religious belief," a reference to the *OED*'s third definition, "a supernatural fairy," or could point to this last definition's derogatory use for homosexual men; it is probably best to read the name as an amalgamation capturing all these resonances), and Loki (called "Trickster of the House of Diabolique," referencing the Norse trickster god). Nina tries hard to make "Angel" stick as a pet name for Eric; and by gesturing to *diablo* in the name of the play's antagonist house, McCraney suggests Heaven/Hell and God/Devil dichotomies in the relationship of Light and Diabolique (26). The play thus offers a menagerie of religious allusions from a variety of traditions without prioritizing any single faith or even summoning godly allusions too directly. Naming in *The Brother/Sister Plays* is a form of Ifá divination, associating characters with their orisha namesakes, but such associations are looser in *Wig Out!*[19] Although a diverse pantheon of forces swirls among this play, its characters find themselves facing challenges outside the domain of godly forces.

Like most theodicies, the author of Ecclesiastes never questions God's existence or investment in human affairs; those are givens upon which the book conducts its examination of human devotion. Still, God does not appear in the book. Qoheleth presents himself as a teacher of wisdom, presumes a human audience, and concentrates entirely on how humans should conduct themselves in a world lacking God's clear presence. McCraney's naming in *Wig Out!* makes clear that forces of the divine—or at least echoes of those forces—are always present to the play's community, but, like Ecclesiastes, the play demonstrates no expectation that the divine will show itself. Humans are left to figure out their own path as best they can with the apparent goal of coming to a clear and sustainable sense of identity. Here, however, McCraney offers a more complex vision than does Ecclesiastes. The biblical text is categorical in its pronouncements: "Go, eat your bread with enjoyment, and drink your wine with a merry heart; for God has long ago approved what you do."[20] At bottom, the book argues for humans to accept their lot in life as a clear sign of the degree of God's favor bestowed upon them. In *Wig Out!*, clarity is fleeting. Characters struggle with their own identities as much as they do with relationships on levels both interpersonal and social. Every character is an open question.

Certainly, an examination of fraught journeys of self among a vibrant and tenuous community like drag could be done without a theological component, but religiosity remains important for McCraney even here. As he does in *Head of Passes* and elsewhere, the playwright invokes religion as a means of scrutinizing its force, open to a wide range of possibilities for the influence of that force, including indifference, support, oppression, partial degrees of any of those, or even total absence. Like *Head of Passes*, *Wig Out!* allows for the possibility of atheism, the notion that the echoes of the divine in characters' names are simply quaint references to powerless mythology. Most importantly, the play does not foreclose the possibility of either complete investment or utter fictionality of divinities. Instead, it allows for a critical investigation of the matter in ways quite different than *Head of Passes*. There, Shelah conducts her life with a view to God and spends the closing section of the play directly demanding recompense for her piety; the play calls God to the stage and wonders if an answer will come. In *Wig Out!* divine forces remain in a referential periphery, seemingly welcome to interject themselves into the proceedings, but not expected to do so.

Even a scene of prayer carries an air of syncretic uncertainty before shifting to a focus that is decidedly humanist (a concept Edward Said defines as "the secular notion that the world is made by men and women, and not by God, and that it can be understood rationally").[21] Before departing for the Cinderella Ball, Rey-Rey, mother of the House of Light, calls the family together for prayer:

> BEY-REY: Let us pray.
> ERIC: You pray?
> REY-REY: Honey, this is the House of Light.
> FAITH: The house that prays together . . .
> FAY: Stays together.

The emphasis is on the benefits of the performative act of prayer, not on its potential to sway the will of God. Rey-Rey is not even convinced of the Christian principles she espouses by praying, asking Venus before starting the prayer to "translate please. Just in case / God's a Lukumi after all," thereby making space in the play's religious menagerie for Yoruba and Santería cosmologies; the fact that a character bearing the name of a Roman goddess embodies an ill-defined space between Judaism, Christianity, Yoruba, and Santería exemplifies the muddled nature of the play's syncretism. Finally, although Rey-Rey begins the prayer by addressing "Heavenly fem Father," her ultimate focus is earthly and human:

> I say I walked through the Valley of the Shadow of Death,
> Fiercely.
> I fear no evil.
> A new day is coming . . .
> And the House of Light will be bringing in the dawn bitch!
> Bright as the morning star!

"Amen! Amen! Amen!" respond The Fates Three, chorus-like (87–88). McCraney says this play resulted from his becoming "over-interested in the ways that people who are marginalized set up a structure that is similar to that of the normalities around them, to the mainstream society," an urge that seems to be at work here.[22] Having constructed a domestic unit with Rey-Rey as mother, the House of Light mimics family prayer, but queers both the performance and its desires. Rey-Rey and family would probably be happy to accept divine intervention on their behalf, but the invocation here is markedly different than Shelah's, emphasizing human agency rather than a desperate need for divine intervention. To whatever extent there is religious intent here, it is the "radical humanism that claims a religious sensibility for itself" that Carol Wayne White calls "sacred humanity."[23] Employing the trappings of the religious normalities around them, Rey-Rey and her family's faith is most directly in themselves. The House of Light has every intention of slaying at the Cinderella Ball, regardless of divine favor or its lack. This suggests that the play's scenes at the Cinderella Ball are powerful moments of performative humanist ritual. Rather than waiting for a divine intervention like Shelah or interpreting the evidence of their lives like Qoheleth, McCraney's characters attempt to claim identity and community themselves on the runway in *Wig Out!* The performances are aggressive, assertive, and of the highest stakes, because for these characters, this performative rite is sacred in the utmost. Characters' prayers and names suggest that divinities might be in the audience and respond to these rituals, but the performers' primary goal is to claim sacredness for their own contested humanity.

McCraney therefore denies his characters in *Wig Out!* the certainty that Qoheleth promises in Ecclesiastes, but the playwright does offer this community access to a realm that is at least potentially broader than everyday human confines. These characters choose to wrestle with forces of earthly sociality much more ardently than with the divine forces that attend upon the play, and so the energy of McCraney's theodicy is far more subdued here than in *Head of Passes*. Here, the theodicy is more passive, perhaps even egalitarian, allowing for the influence of any number of divinities from any number of religious traditions, but not relying on them. Still, the effect of skeptical investigation remains. By not excising divine forces from this play, McCraney enters *Wig Out!* into his broader project of exploring the power and efficacy of religiosity in the lives of the disempowered. Like Ecclesiastes, the play's particular approach to that question is on the everyday lives of humans. "There is nothing new under the sun," says Qoheleth, a philosophy embraced by McCraney's drag community by eschewing the search for divine intervention.[24] Gods are welcome to contribute to McCraney's characters' difficult journeys of self-actualization, but divine absence will not deter them.

Conclusion: Theodicy as a Force of African American Community

As biblical authors concerned themselves with the plights and triumphs of the Hebrews, McCraney is particularly concerned with African American invocations of religion within projects of liberation, community, and joy. "Religious expression has been one of the key strategies used by African Americans attempting to free themselves from [racist] conceptions and the problematic cultural practices ensuing from them," argues White, insisting that "black religiosity as a people's ongoing desire to achieve self-preservation, self-definition, and self-determination [is] arguably, one of black culture's most vital productions."[25] McCraney creates a black community bound up with religiosity in the way White suggests, but the playwright is more critical than devotional. This is the attitude he brings to his engagement with the Bible, a central text throughout black American history, in part because it models resistance against oppression. "The Bible is one of the few books of world literature that looks at life 'from below,'" points out Allen Dwight Callahan. "It is replete with upsets that flout the rules of power, privilege, and prestige." Callahan is certainly correct that the "Bible privileges those without privilege and honors those without honor," a reality that he suggests speaks to the prominence of the Bible in black American life: "As modernity's most thoroughly humiliated people, small wonder that African Americans have taken the texts of the Bible so eagerly and earnestly."[26] As Eddie Glaude demonstrates, for African Americans, beginning in the antebellum period, "the image of America as New Canaan was reversed. America was Egypt."[27] As Glaude and Callahan make clear, throughout African American history, biblical stories have offered valuable models of endurance, resistance, hope, and joy; these conditions are constant concerns of McCraney's work. Indeed, in stories from the Bible and other bodies of myth, the playwright offers his characters paradigms to follow and adapt. Wooden calls this dramaturgy "an aesthetics of recycling . . . reviving and revising a classic story to dramatize the pleasures and perils of contemporary African American life."[28] One means of repurposing religious myths in this way is to secularize them; the playwright's theodicy wonders openly about the necessity of the divine in archetypal stories. Still, McCraney seems unwilling to confine the challenges of African American life to the human world and uncertain of the degree to which religion can contribute to struggles of liberation, identification, and empathetic understanding. His skeptical theodicies of hope are always as willing to allow for positive divine influence as they are prepared to accept a void of religious power.

Like most biblical Hebrews, none of McCraney's characters are in positions of significant social power. They are not utterly downtrodden, and frequently find space for joy, but all are struggling to advance or even secure their place in life and their sense of identity against the oppressive forces of a society laced with structural bigotry. It is telling that most characters with authority—the sheriff in *The Brothers Size*, the board members who breathe down the neck of *Choir Boy*'s headmaster, or the drag queens's angry family members in *Wig Out!*—exist offstage, extending their oppressive force to McCraney's characters without showing themselves to the audience. Characters subject to oppressive authority populate McCraney's stage, and in their efforts for liberation and identity, they form a broad, multifaceted community. In this regard and others, the playwright's attention to religiosity is of a piece with his focus on the people and plights that constitute a fractious community defined by struggle and endurance.

Yet, as *Head of Passes* and *Wig Out!* demonstrate, McCraney casts a skeptical eye on the role of religion in the lives of his characters and by extension in black American life. Shelah finds no release from grief in God, and *Wig Out!*'s drag performers face their struggles with identity and desire on their own quotidian terms. Certainly, none of the various religious traditions referenced in McCraney's work promise unequivocal divine protection to humans or complete support for devotees' desires, insisting instead that humans faithfully strive on their own before receiving full benefits from divine powers. In this regard, theodicy usually wonders what humans must do to receive or at least understand divine favor. This notion has caused some critics of black theology to reject theodicy; Anthony Pinn, for example, insists that arguments founded in theodicy "are unacceptable because they counteract efforts at liberation by finding something of value in Black suffering."[29] But McCraney's skeptical theodicy takes a broader approach, querying whether faith is worth his characters' efforts. His theodicy is skeptical not in that it expects a negative answer, but rather because it is unwilling to offer the benefit of the doubt to the divine, shifting the burden of proof from humanity to the divine.

McCraney's plays thus allow for the possibility of atheism while holding onto the potential of religion's benefits. In this way, McCraney proves to be a creator offering empathetic support to his characters and a cultural critic offering the same to those in his audience subject to institutionalized bigotry. For although his plays stop short of suggesting that religion is a valuable vehicle toward liberation and social or inner peace, he is nonetheless willing to broaden the community of support beyond the earthly realm to include the divine, even if only potentially. Rather than shut down any hope for Shelah's invocation of God, McCraney, as he does throughout his work, grants his character the leeway to explore the possibility. In the process, the playwright scrutinizes Shelah's decision—and that of devotedly religious people like her—to trust in the divine; for certainly Shelah and others might be damaging their quests for liberation and peace by relying too heavily on impotent or nonexistent forces. Most important, though, is the power of potential: McCraney shows an awareness of the prominence of religiosity in black liberation struggles, and although his dramaturgy seems unconvinced of faith's efficacy, he welcomes it into his dramatic world and subjects it to critical, open-minded scrutiny.

McCraney invites audiences to join him in bearing witness to the religious journeys of his characters—and in fact to constitute those journeys by allowing for performance—with the courage to allow for open-endedness. Soyica Diggs Colbert highlights McCraney's "resistance to teleology" and suggests that his theater is exemplary of how "Black performance challenges the notion that once completed events should and will remain in the past," helpfully underscoring how the open-endedness of these characters' religious journeys, like the playwright's theodicy, continues and evolves through performance.[30] None of the wrestling matches with the divine that consume McCraney's characters to various degrees conclude at a script's publication or a performance's final curtain. Rather, McCraney's theater constantly reinvestigates questions of religion, making crises of faith perpetually present, unconcluded, and potentially fulfilling to the characters. This is a dramaturgy of hope. That hope is unromantic, without delusions, and constitutively skeptical, but it is hope nonetheless. McCraney seems to want his characters' faith rewarded, but remains unconvinced that such a reward is achievable.

The Distant Present of Tarell Alvin McCraney

✦

David Román

I wrote this essay, one of the first major scholarly engagements with Tarell Alvin McCraney's plays, during the summer of 2013. I had been following McCraney's career for several years already, always eager to see his plays as they emerged in the regional theaters throughout the United States. I first experienced his work through his affiliation with Tina Landau, innovative theater director and Steppenwolf Theatre Company ensemble member, who I have long admired and whose work I had written about in Performance in America *(Duke University Press, 2006), my book on contemporary American theater. Landau and McCraney had collaborated on* Wig Out!, *which I saw at New York City's Vineyard Theatre in 2008, and on the trilogy* The Brother/ Sister Plays, *which I saw at the Public Theater in 2009 and then again at Steppenwolf in 2010. Soyica Diggs Colbert, one of our contributors and the first scholar to publish on McCraney's work, offers a compelling reading of* In the Red and Brown Water *in her epilogue to* The African American Theatrical Body *(Cambridge University Press, 2011). She argues that McCraney's theater, "questions the process of inheritance—passing down information, history, or performance from one generation to the next—and instead, uses performance to interject the present in the past."[1]* Wig Out! *and* The Brother/ Sistere Plays, *which are beautifully engaged by other scholars in this volume, made a deep impression on me on multiple levels. First, I was drawn to the playwright's artistic vision, how he was able to create a unique and specific formal structure that served the play's radical dramaturgy; second, I was drawn to the intensity of the collaborative theatrical process, which included young actors of color performing fully realized and complex characters, and, under Landau's direction, creating a unified ensemble of artistic virtuosity; third, I was drawn to the sheer beauty of the dramaturgical and theatrical collaboration between the playwright and the director, their facility in making important and relevant and visually compelling theater; and finally perhaps most simply, these were worlds I had never seen represented on the American stage.* Head of Passes *and* Choir Boy, *which premiered in 2013, only*

American Quarterly, March 2014. Photograph by David Román.

convinced me of what I already knew: Tarell Alvin McCraney was among the most important new voices in American theater and, by extension, American culture at large.

The essay was published in American Quarterly, *the premiere publication of the American Studies Association, in 2014. I wanted my colleagues in*

American Studies, scholars whose work is by definition interdisciplinary, to learn about McCraney's work. McCraney was already generating significant buzz in the world of theater, including among scholars and critics. Isaiah Wooden published a review of Head of Passes *in* Theatre Journal *in 2014 and Kathy Nigh, one of our contributors here, published a review of* The Breach *in* Theatre Journal *in 2008; others, too, were beginning to look closely and carefully at McCraney's plays.*[2] *But I felt strongly that people outside of the theater should be introduced to McCraney and his extraordinary body of work. I wanted colleagues in African American studies, critical race studies, queer studies, performance studies, cultural studies, to name only a few of the intellectual communities that comprise American studies, to learn of his work and the importance of his contribution to American theater. Placing the essay in* American Quarterly *would guarantee that exposure and also highlight the significance of American theater to American history, politics, and culture.*

Now, as I write this preface six years later in 2019, McCraney's work has deservedly reached mainstream recognition. Moonlight, *which was based on an original unpublished play by McCraney, was named Best Picture in 2017 and won McCraney an Academy Award for Best Adapted Screenplay.* Head of Passes *and* Choir Boy *have gone on to have multiple productions throughout the United States. Tina Landau's production of* Head of Passes *moved from Steppenwolf to Berkeley Rep in 2015 before arriving at the Public Theater in the spring of 2017, with Phylicia Rashad replacing Cheryl Lynn Bruce in the lead role as Shelah. This same cast then transferred to the Mark Taper Forum in Los Angeles for a limited run in the fall of 2017. Along the way, McCraney revised the script considerably, although the main themes and concerns of the play remain consistent with the version I describe here.* Choir Boy, *too, has been transformed since the initial 2013 premiere discussed below. Trip Cullman's production moved to the Geffen Playhouse in Los Angeles with most of its original cast. Other productions followed with new casts and new directors, providing multiple opportunities for young black actors to work in an ensemble setting.* Choir Boy *premiered at the Samuel J. Friedman Theatre in 2019, marking McCraney's Broadway debut. The Broadway production reunited the original creative team and producers six years after its initial premiere, but recast several of the roles; Jeremy Pope continued as Pharus, the play's protagonist. McCraney made some minor textual and plot changes in the play, but overall, except for the addition of Camille A. Brown's choreography, the production didn't depart dramatically from what New York audiences first saw in 2013. The play was well reviewed by critics and was extended due to popular demand. It closed in March 2019 after a limited run of seventy-two performances.*

My American Quarterly *essay was written primarily as an introduction to McCraney and his dramaturgy, placing him in the context of an emerging renaissance in African American theater and performance, in which he is a major artistic force and presence. There are other writers, of course, who are part of this artistic movement, including those whose plays have been produced or who have risen to critical prominence since this essay was first published: Branden Jacobs-Jenkins, Marcus Gardley, Dominique Morisseau, Mfoniso Udofia, Donja R. Love, Jocelyn Bioh, Jeremy O. Harris, Jackie Sibblies Drury, Christina Anderson, Inda Craig-Galván, and so many others who have emerged in regional theaters across the country in the past six years. What most distinguishes these writers is that they write about a wide-range of experiences and do so in artistically innovative ways. Like McCraney, they are unique in their content and creativity.*

The impulse for this essay, to call critical attention to McCraney's achievements, remains the impulse for this collection. Sharrell Luckett, Isaiah, and I agree that McCraney's work deserves a wide-readership across academic disciplines and reading communities. We started working on this anthology a few years back. The three of us were committed to creating an intellectual cohort of scholars working on McCraney's various plays. McCraney had already composed a strong and vibrant group of artistic collaborators through his plays and their productions, and we wanted to honor that group as well.

I ended my initial essay anticipating McCraney's adaptation of Shakespeare's Antony and Cleopatra, *a transatlantic collaborative production concerning the effects of power in two disparate but, for McCraney, related areas: the Roman Empire and French colonialism. That production, which I saw at the Public Theater in 2014, highlighted the collisions of French culture and the culture of Saint-Domingue, or what we now know as Haiti, and the ongoing tensions resulting from French colonial rule. Shifting the setting from Egypt to Haiti, McCraney focused on the plight of the oppressed, and the ongoing racial trauma of colonization. For this production, which McCraney directed, he worked with three different theaters—The Royal Shakespeare Company, The Public Theater, and Miami's GableStage—along with actors affiliated with each of these venues.*

This time around, I am anticipating McCraney's Ms. Blakk for President, *his latest collaboration with Tina Landau.* Ms. Blakk for President *is inspired by the true story of Joan Jett Blakk, the first black drag queen candidate for president of the United States. According to Steppenwolf, which is producing this world premiere, "[Joan's story begins in] Chicago, 1992, and with the AIDS crisis at its height, Joan and the newly formed Queer Nation Chicago have an urgent agenda. Joan sets off on an exhilarating and dangerous journey to drag queer politics out of the closet and into a future where ALL are visible and ALL have a place at the table. . . . MS. BLAKK FOR PRESIDENT takes us into the heart and mind of one of Chicago's most singular and radical citizens. Infused with music and hilarity, MS. BLAKK is part campaign rally, part nightclub performance, part confessional—and all party!"[3] McCraney himself will perform the role of Joan Jett Blakk, an unusual opportunity to experience McCraney as an actor in one of his original works. For me, McCraney continues to surprise and delight. He also continues to produce politically relevant work for politically challenging times. From Shakespeare to Joan Jett Black, McCraney invites us to revisit the hauntings of the past, bringing to the surface the stories we need to live through these times.*

At the end of the first act of Tarell Alvin McCraney's remarkable new play, *Head of Passes*, the home of Shelah Reynolds spectacularly collapses. The house, a former bed-and-breakfast in the Head of Passes (the marshlands at the mouth of the Mississippi River), had been in gradual decline. Shelah, the play's central character, has been aware of a leak on the roof for some time, but the evening's heavy rains exacerbate the damage. While the leak gets progressively worse as the act unfolds—each entering character comments on it, often amusingly—nothing prepares the audience for this stunning coup de theatre, where the play's set implodes in front of us.

This surprising and thoroughly unanticipated scene characterizes McCraney's plays, which are full of such bewildering moments. In a very short time, McCraney, who was born in 1980 in Liberty City, the inner-city region of Miami, has emerged as one of the most significant new voices in American theater. McCraney trained as an actor at DePaul University in Chicago before receiving his M.F.A. in playwriting from the Yale School of Drama in 2007. In 2008 he was named RSC/Warwick International Playwright in Residence at the Royal Shakespeare Company. Since then, McCraney's plays have been staged in regional theaters throughout the United States and London to great critical success. His artistic accomplishment is part of a larger cultural explosion in contemporary African American theater that has gained momentum in the past several years. This essay considers McCraney's two most recent plays, *Head of Passes* and *Choir Boy*, which had their U.S. premieres in 2012, in the context of this renaissance moment in African American theater. *Head of Passes* and *Choir Boy*, two uniquely unusual plays, secure McCraney's reputation as a playwright equally committed to cultural insight and artistic form. These two plays capture deep and intimate inner and interpersonal expression while experimenting with dramatic form.

Consider the collapse of Shelah's house at the end of the first act of *Head of Passes*. It is all the more striking given that the play begins in the familiar setting of the domestic drama. We are introduced to Shelah's family and friends as they gather in her home to celebrate her birthday. The play's design and direction fully commit to the realist tradition of American theater, where audiences are asked to willingly suspend their disbelief and accept this onstage world as plausible. Every aspect of the production—design, acting, costume—manipulates the audience to accept the theatrical representation as actual. It is as if we are looking into Shelah's life and home through a window. Everything looks real. There is only one violation of this convention: Shelah, and only Shelah, sees a man whom she mistakes at first as a waiter hired to work at the party and then presumes to be an angel sent from God to

Tim Hopper, Ron Cephas Jones, James T. Alfred, Cheryl Lynn Bruce, Jacqueline Williams, and Glenn Davis in a scene from Tarell Alvin McCraney's *Head of Passes* at Chicago's Steppenwolf Theatre. Photograph copyright © Michael Brosilow.

deliver her to heaven. His appearance at key moments in the first act position Shelah as a religious woman at peace with the terminal illness she has kept secret from the others. It also hints at the larger meditation on faith that the play offers as it unfolds.

As the play begins, Shelah's two adult sons, Aubrey and Spencer, worry about their mother's isolated life at the Head of Passes. They want her to move inland and rent out her home, but Shelah is determined to stay. For decades, Shelah and her recently deceased husband ran the inn for Texans working the oil barges on the Gulf. The home represents the foundation they built in a time when few "colored folks could say this piece of earth is for me and mean it round here."[4] The house embodies this history; she will not leave. Throughout the first act, McCraney delivers a play that, in the spirit of the great American playwright August Wilson, seems mostly about the quotidian lives of black people, in this case, living in the rural south. McCraney captures the rhythms and cadences of their regional vernacular, and the intimate dynamics of inter- and intragenerational exchange. Like the characters in Wilson's extensive oeuvre, McCraney infuses his characters with full lives and intricate histories.

The play's first act is filled with lightness and humor, anchored in the familiar ease of kinship among its characters. Shelah's friends and family, including her daughter, Cookie, and even the family physician, celebrate their individual and collective relationships with her, poignantly underlining their love. All the characters are African American except for the doctor, whose integration into the family is so unremarkable that it deserves mention. The doctor easily moves from his professional role as the family physician to the more personal dynamic of extended kinship. In one hilarious scene, he freely and comfortably—and much to the amusement of the assembled group—claims that Shelah needn't worry about more people showing up in her house that night given the weather: "Black people don't like rain," he explains. Later in the scene, and after having a few drinks, he dances the "hully gully" for the group, again to everyone's delight. McCraney displays this intimacy as a matter of fact.

The production at Chicago's Steppenwolf Theatre, perhaps the foremost regional theater in the United States, was directed by Tina Landau, one of today's most talented directors and a frequent collaborator with the playwright. Throughout his career, McCraney has taken risks both in the subject of his plays and in their dramatic structure. *The Brothers Size*, his trilogy based partly on Yoruban myths and southern black life, was beautifully crafted with individuated plays that immediately put McCraney on the theatrical map. They too were directed by Landau and featured members of the Steppenwolf acting ensemble, who found in McCraney such enormous talent that they invited him to join their company in 2010. McCraney's voice as a playwright varies depending on his subject matter, but each of his plays shares an interest in language and character. He finds the form necessary to move his story forward and, with Landau as his frequent director, succeeds in staging theatrically compelling drama. His plays are intricately plotted and beautifully staged. The McCraney-Landau-Steppenwolf alliance is among the most exciting theatrical collaborations of the contemporary scene.

Steppenwolf's production of *Head of Passes* beautifully presented the play's onstage world as believable and its fictional characters as real. The audience relaxes into the recognizable terrain of the family drama, unsuspecting that the world the creative team took such care to assemble would be a setup for a completely different kind of theatrical experience in act 2. The first act ends with the house collapsing in on itself, a stunning spectacle of demolition that leaves audiences aghast.

The play shifts dramatically from the conventional family drama of act 1 to a tour de force poetic monologue in act 2. By the beginning of act 2, Shelah has lost everything. Inspired by, but not reliant on, the Book of Job, McCraney's play becomes a contemporary version of the biblical story of individual loss and suffering. How much can one person endure before they stop believing? The catastrophic string of events revealed at the top of act 2 moves the play into the realm of the tragic. Shelah's three children have all died overnight—the results variously of violence, accident, and drug overdose—and the world in which she was embedded no longer exists. All she has left is her faith. And so she wonders: Is God punishing her for the sins of her past? Is her faith being tested to see if in fact she deserves salvation? The actor Cheryl Lynn Bruce skillfully captures Shelah's range of emotions. Her performance is the bridge that holds the two acts together as a play. The audience's faith is also being tested. The play shifts gears so quickly and deliberately in act 2 that audiences might lose confidence in McCraney's dramaturgical skills and Landau's artistic vision. The world of act 1 is mostly lost to us after intermission. Very little of act 2 resembles what preceded it. The house has been deconstructed, and Shelah, who has been the play's central guiding figure, seems otherworldly in her disorientation. Like Shelah, we too must adjust to the new reality with which we have been confronted.

The collapse of Shelah's house leaves her without the structure of daily life she has known all these years and leaves the audience without the realist structure of a conventional play. Shelah's faith in God is being tested even as the audience's faith in theatrical form is challenged. We have all lost our foundation. Shelah's monologue in act 2 also questions our ability to rely on her version of events. As with any prophet, we are asked to consider: Has she gone mad? Or are her visions and voices the testament of spiritual convictions? The play's brilliance lies in its audacious investigation of faith and theatrical form. While unsettling in its refusal to remain within the conventions of realism, McCraney's innovative dramaturgy succeeds in challenging audiences to invest in other forms of theatrical representations of kinship and faith. McCraney's turn from kitchen-sink realism in act 1 to Beckett-like philosophical absurdism in act 2 is artistically risky. There is no guarantee that audiences will follow him into this unexpected theatrical terrain. By the end of the play, McCraney returns us to reality when the actor playing the angel in act 1 reappears as a construction worker. Shelah once again mistakes him for an emissary of God, but the audience understands the man to be someone simply checking out the property before its demolition. In an extraordinary scene of intimate connection between strangers, the man engages Shelah on her own terms, allowing her the chance to reaffirm her faith in the midst of her tragedy. Shelah has explained to him the tragic events that have befallen her. Patiently, the man responds to her, a woman who he initially regards as delusional and mad, with kindness.

CONSTRUCTION WORKER: Lady you didn't know that your sons would die like that. How could you? Only God knows those things and who want to know all of that all the time? Seem, seem he just say to us here go your lil' piece. Make with it what you will and if you need me I'll listen.
SHELAH: "He hears you."
CONSTRUCTION WORKER: Yeah.
SHELAH: So what you saying Angel James?
CONSTRUCTION WORKER: I ain't no Angel.

Cheryl Lynn Bruce in a scene from Tarell Alvin McCraney's *Head of Passes* at Chicago's Steppenwolf Theatre. Photograph copyright © Michael Brosilow.

SHELAH: Me Neither but I need the light of God.

CONSTRUCTION WORKER: Its Somewhere.

SHELAH: I need him to reach down and . . . I need Him to . . .

CONSTRUCTION WORKER: Bring the tide in and out, sets the day to spinning. Call up and down? Things just go 'cause they go Lady. Everything else I don't know.

The construction worker's words of compassion offer Shelah the closure she needs to move forward in her life, however limited her time. And he offers audiences the path back to realist conventions and plausible encounters. No longer in doubt, but still unknowing about her future, Shelah is back in dialogue with another person, Angel James, who is both of this world and outside it. The play ends on this note.

McCraney is among an exciting cohort of new African American playwrights who have flourished since the death of August Wilson in 2005. Wilson's legacy rests on his ten-play cycle depicting the experiences of black people in plays set in each decade of the twentieth century, which he completed shortly before his death. If Wilson was the signature playwright of black life in the twentieth century, various playwrights have followed accordingly. *American Quarterly* readers most likely are familiar with some of these figures, especially Suzan-Lori Parks, the most critically esteemed and produced African American playwright of the twenty-first century, whose play *Topdog/Underdog* won the Pulitzer Prize for Drama in 2002.[5] *Topdog/Underdog* was the first play by an African American woman writer to win the prestigious honor, and Parks was the first African American to do so since Wilson's own awards for *Fences* (1987) and *The Piano Lesson* (1990). The current group of playwrights includes Lynn Nottage, who won the 2009 Pulitzer Prize for *Ruined*, a play inspired by the civil war in Congo and its effects on women, and whose perfectly crafted 2011 comedy about race and Hollywood, *By the Way, Meet Vera Stark*, was a hit in regional theaters throughout the country; Thomas Bradshaw, a talented playwright whose sexually explicit and racially charged dramas such as *Mary* (2011) and *Burning* (2011) have provoked controversy and protest; and Katori Hall, who is doing for Memphis what Wilson did for Pittsburgh, setting her plays—*Hurt Village* (2010) and *The Mountaintop* (2011), the second a play based on the final night of Martin Luther King's life in a Memphis hotel room—in the city's impoverished neighborhoods.

The first two decades of the twenty-first century are beginning to constitute a renaissance in African American theater, as the current resurgence of African American theater is not isolated to a particular region but happening nationwide. I have seen these plays staged in theaters in New York City, Chicago, Los Angeles, and Berkeley, but other cities have also staged these playwrights, often premiering their work too. The support of regional theaters across the United States has helped publicize these new playwrights and their important work while employing dozens of casts of black actors. The significance of this phenomenon is central. New playwrights need to have their work staged, and theaters need to support living playwrights writing new works for the stage.

Unlike most of these new African American playwrights whose plays focus on the historical past, McCraney's plays take place in what he names "the distant present." McCraney's anachronistic phrasing of "the distant present" forces us to consider when the contemporary moves from now to then. He is interested in setting his plays in time frames at once familiar yet somewhat removed. But he is neither a documentarian nor a historian. Consider the extraordinary work by Parks, whose most recent and current projects include her 2011 revision of George Gershwin's classic *Porgy and Bess* and her new play about the Civil War, *Father Comes Home from the Wars*, which will premiere at New York City's Public Theater in 2014. While Wilson set out to document African American life in the twentieth century, Parks has been determined to challenge the racial ideologies embedded in American history and culture. She has consistently, for nearly two decades, engaged the historical past, whether by returning to the figure of Abraham Lincoln, as she has in some of her major plays including *The America Play* (1994), or by reimagining Nathaniel Hawthorne's *Scarlet Letter* in her brilliant *Fucking A* (2000), or by revisiting the story of the Hottentot Venus and the carnival freak shows of early Americana in *Venus* (1996). Throughout her extensive oeuvre, Parks has engaged American history more effectively than any other living U.S. playwright.

McCraney, on the other hand, has kept his focus on the contemporary. The distant present—like the near future—is just out of reach, yet not quite fully in the time of the now. However, it is close enough to register as familiar. *Head of Passes* depends on that immediate recognition of time and place to lure us into its theatrical exploration of faith. In *Choir Boy*, McCraney's latest play to open in the United States, the time is "a school year, last year," regardless of when that last year was. This time, McCraney sets his play in an elite, all-black, male boarding school. Here, again, he is interested in issues of faith, particularly the role of traditional gospel spirituals in the lives of these young men. In *Choir Boy*, McCraney takes on two historically significant institutions in African American life: church and school, which is to say, religion and education. Each of these spaces is a highly esteemed location of belonging and potentiality for African Americans. But what if you are young, black, and gay? This is the dilemma facing Pharus Young, the protagonist of *Choir Boy*. A gifted singer, Pharus is bullied for defying—with relentless audacity and even flamboyance—traditional forms of black masculinity. The play follows a year in the life of Pharus and his contemporaries, a group of young black men whose differences are so obvious that one need not even make the point of their diversity. Suffice to say, they come together in song. The young men are all part of the award-winning choir, whose success drives the school's fund-raising efforts. While they are individuals of unique and disparate backgrounds, which often leads to conflict and even violence, they cohere as a choir.

The production, directed by Trip Cullman at the Manhattan Theatre Club's Studio at Stage II, intersperses traditional spirituals throughout the play to comment on the action and to foreground the relevance of these songs for contemporary audiences. The songs, as Pharus argues in his critical thinking

Jeremy Pope and Chuck Cooper in a scene from Tarell Alvin McCraney's *Choir Boy* at Manhattan Theatre Club's New York City Center Stage II. Photograph copyright © Joan Marcus.

class, have meaning and purpose to their current lives just as they had to slaves in the past. While his classmates adhere to the orthodoxy that Negro spirituals helped guide slaves to freedom, Pharus questions the evidence behind such claims, arguing instead that "these songs forged in the shame and brutality of oppression are diamonds that glint and prove true that hope and love can live, thrive and even sing."[6] The songs must have relevance now, too. The music helps coordinate *Choir Boy*'s episodic structure while providing moving theatrical moments of vocal virtuosity. The harmony of the performances stands in direct contrast to the tensions demonstrated in the play. The spirituals serve as interludes modeling a different sociality among the actors than the one often represented in the exchanges between characters. Are the actors in character when they sing, or are they meant to be viewed as the collective voice of the members of the ensemble? The fact that this remains unclear at times in the production works to McCraney's advantage. His cast unites behind his vision and helps give voice to his point of view.

Like Shelah in *Head of Passes*, Pharus is being tested. How much bullying will he endure before he breaks? And what resources does he have available to him so that he can overcome the obstacles he faces as a young black gay man? Pharus recognizes—as does everyone else in the play—his extraordinary vocal talents. What he does not yet fully know, however, is his strength of

Jeremy Pope, Kyle Beltran, Nicholas L. Ashe, Wallace Smith, and Grantham Coleman in a scene from Tarell Alvin McCraney's *Choir Boy* at Manhattan Theatre Club's New York City Center Stage II. Photograph copyright © Joan Marcus.

character. The Charles R. Drew Prep School for Boys strives to mentor young black men to be the future leaders of their community. They are expected to learn and embody the historical values of their communities while refining their own individual perspectives and points of view. Pharus struggles with this challenge to be true to himself and of value to his community in light of the open secret of his homosexuality. He is at once defiant and vulnerable. Jeremy Pope gives a beautiful performance as Pharus, capturing the boy's intense emotional journey through the play.

Choir Boy begins at the school's annual commencement program. While Pharus sings the school's anthem to the packed audience at commencement, he is taunted offstage with inflammatory comments. As a result, he turns around and momentarily pauses, causing the headmaster to doubt Pharus's focus and maturity. Rather than snitch on the boy who degraded him, and reveal what actually happened in that moment, Pharus tries to live by the Drew School mission:

PHARUS: You know the rule. A Drew man doesn't tell on his brother.
PHARUS AND HEADMASTER: "He allows him the honor to confess himself."
PHARUS: It may seem silly but ever since I was a little boy I've wanted to grow up and be a Drew man. I couldn't possibly say who *they* were.
HEADMASTER: They?
PHARUS: Have a good summer, Headmaster.

Immediately, McCraney sets up his protagonist as talented and honorable, a young gay man aspiring to be a version of long-held African American ideals of manhood. Pharus wants to be a Drew man and feels his sexuality should not be in conflict with that. As *Choir Boy* progresses, Pharus endures various demoralizing incidents that by the end of the play leave him somewhat broken. Whatever confidence he presented at the beginning of the play has been compromised by his experiences at Drew. His situation also forces the other boys to respond according to their own sense of ethics and integrity. In short, Pharus is a catalyst for everyone's growth and change at the school. Who among them—including the teachers and administrators—is actually a Drew man? *Choir Boy* insists on fronting the story of young black gay men to give voice to what McCraney sees as a dehumanizing stereotype: the effeminate choir boy of the black church. In an interview, McCraney addresses this issue with candor and conviction:

> We look at culturally effeminate boys, and we don't talk about them as human beings. We think of them as great singers and extraordinary musicians and talents, but their lives, who they are as people, is left outside of our conversations or our cultural consciousness. . . . Pharus, the main character in *Choir Boy*, speaks about his individual faith, his faith in this Negro spiritual, as hope and joy in meters, in measures, but then in the next thought about what it means to be a man, to be human. . . . I think we lose talents like Pharus because we're not recognizing their full humanity.[7]

By the end of the play, Pharus finds support in his friendship with his straight athlete roommate, AJ. It is AJ who is most concerned about Pharus's defeated disposition. And in a scene as tender as any I have seen on stage, it is AJ who reaches out to Pharus and provides him affection and love. A full year has passed since the play's first scene; the distant present that opened the play is now even more removed. Much has transpired during the past school year, and now, on the eve of their commencement, the two roommates secure their bond even more. AJ, the embodiment of black masculine heteronormativity, offers to groom Pharus for the upcoming graduation ceremony. Pharus opens up again, confiding in AJ his vulnerability and the social ostracization he has experienced as a black gay youth by other African American males. AJ, recognizing the lateness of the hour and his roommate's loneliness, invites Pharus to sleep beside him in his bed. The scene, while homoerotic, remains platonic. AJ, a Drew man if ever there was one, is confident in his identity and in his enduring friendship with Pharus. The sweetness of the scene is endorsed by the cast, who immediately take the stage to sing an old Negro work song, "Rainbow 'Round My Shoulder," which embodies the collective energy of the group to stand in for each other during times of duress.

The play essentially ends here, but McCraney adds a short epilogue where we find ourselves back, a year later, at the Drew commencement. This time, though, Pharus is nowhere to be seen. The focus instead is on the ritual of

Jeremy Pope and Grantham Coleman in a scene from Tarell Alvin McCraney's *Choir Boy* at Manhattan Theatre Club's New York City Center Stage II. Photograph copyright © Joan Marcus.

the gathering, the singing of the school song. The boy who taunted Pharus with homophobic comments the year before is now the school's commencement singer. At the point where he had interrupted Pharus's performance a year ago, the boy now turns around too, haunted by his own behavior. The security of his masculine entitlement has been challenged by his previous encounters with Pharus. He too has doubt. But the tradition of the song remains intact, and the Drew school continues to matriculate young black men into their communities.

In *Head of Passes* and *Choir Boy*, the protagonists must suffer and endure tests of their character and faith. Shelah and Pharus entertain doubt, if not despair, before finding redemption in what had originally reassured them. McCraney's gifts as a playwright are many. His dramaturgy is immersed in questions of faith without trumpeting religious dogma or condemning secular ideology. His characters are interested in individual reflection and critical engagement with their peers. They include moments of deep connection between kindred spirits unrelated by either blood or the law. His plays are uniquely composed to encompass various theatrical and performative modes, as *Head of Passes* and *Choir Boy* attest. Like Wilson, he is providing a place for African American actors across generations to perform the nuances of black life in full and spectacular contradiction, and he is supplying regional theaters with original plays to add to their programming seasons. There is so much to celebrate here.

I have been attending McCraney's plays for several years now, and while I have come to expect a unique and individuated theatrical experience, I always leave with a sense of wonder and awe. His plays are smart and engaging, moving and beautiful. They sustain interest and mystique even after multiple viewings. He is poised to become one of the most interesting and important playwrights of his generation, which is not to say that he is not both already. On September 25, 2013, he was named a 2013 MacArthur Fellow, the prestigious fellowship given to extraordinary innovators in their fields. His next project is an adaptation of Shakespeare's *Antony and Cleopatra*, which will be a coproduction between New York's Public Theater, Miami's GableStage, and the Royal Shakespeare Company. McCraney will direct the play, which is set in the 1790s in colonial Saint-Domingue on the eve of the Haitian revolution against the French.

This next venture will also be set in the "distant present," although nowhere close to the contemporary that structures *Choir Boy* and *Head of Passes*. His version of *Antony and Cleopatra* will consider the distant present of colonialism in the Caribbean, unpacking the parallels between these two disparate historical periods and cultures—the Roman Empire and the French colonial empire—in a transatlantic production produced in the Unites States and Great Britain. I, for one, cannot wait to see what other structures collapse or rise anew in his forthcoming ventures.

"My Grandmother Wore a Wig"

✦

On Tarell Alvin McCraney's Mapping of Queer Origins in *Wig Out!*

Bryant Keith Alexander

When I was growing up in Lafayette, Louisiana, in the late 1960s, my mother wore a wig. She wore a wig at times for convenience; she was a working Black mother of seven children who did not always have time to get her hair done or fix it in the morning. But my grandmother wore her wig as performance. She wore it for both style and subversion, and as a fundamental means to reinvent her way of being in the world.[1] She had three wigs of slightly dif-fering lengths and shades of gray. One was a sort of pageboy hairstyle that framed her ever-thinning face. Another was a shorter pixie cut that she wore almost like a woman's bathing cap. And the other was an in-between length—sort of a bob cut that seemed to be permanently sutured under her favorite Sunday-go-to-meeting hat. My grandmother kept all three wigs on white Styrofoam heads that lined the dresser in the bedroom of her small shot-gun house that I slept in when I visited her. My grandmother was a character. She was your average Black, Southern, trash-talking, gossiping old lady who knew everybody's business and wasn't afraid to tell it. She also served as a living repository of our family's history and the cultural history of our com-munity. I learned a lot of who I am—as a man, as a Black man, and as a Black queer/quare man—from my grandmother.[2]

I remember watching my grandmother in the process of adorning the wigs for everyday and social occasions. She wore a stocking cap to hold down her naturally short, kinky hair—the homemade type made out of a stocking with a knot tied on the top. I would watch my grandmother choose the appropri-ate wig, which was always chosen based on where she was going, who she would see, and who would see her. The wigs were always properly groomed after each wearing so that when she needed one, it was ready. She would sit in front of a small vanity that had a large mirror and hold the wig at a backward, upside-down angle; then she would lower her head, pull the wig on, then raise her head upward. And I would notice that in the moment that the wig settled on her head, and after a few twists and adjustments, something would come over her. A new posture would take over her body. A new persona would inhabit her personality. And a new energy manifested as attitude would overcome her—but it would not consume her. *You know what I mean?*

It was not like my grandmother became someone different in those moments, but maybe she became more fully alive when she wore her wigs. She was always fully present as my grandmother. *Do you know what I mean?* And as a young Black gay boy growing up watching these transformative and gendering performances, I would stare at those wigs every night—staring in part at the Caucasian features of the luminously white Styrofoam heads wearing my grandmother's hair. And although there are politics surrounding race and hair, I never thought that my grandmother wanted to wear "White Girl hair"—you know, the kind that flipped and flowed, and was often touted as some idealized femininity that made some little Black girls with naturally kinky hair feel less pretty in the public eye unless they pressed and permed their own hair. I think that the wigs simply offered my grandmother options for living, for being an imagined self.

And sometimes during those late nights, when I thought that my grandmother was sleeping, something would compel me to don my grandmother's wigs. Like my grandmother, I would choose the appropriate wig. And I would sit in front of the small vanity with that large mirror, and I would hold the wig at a backward, upside-down angle, just as she did, lowering my head and pulling the wig onto it and moving upward. Then I would stare at the image that appeared in the mirror.

Histories, Themes, and Characters in *Wig Out!*

Tarell Alvin McCraney's play *Wig Out!* was workshopped at the Sundance Institute Theatre Lab, where Kent Gash directed it. It had its debut in September 2008 at the Vineyard Theatre in New York City, directed by Tina Landau. The play won the GLAAD (Gay & Lesbian Alliance Against Defamation) Award for Outstanding New York Theater. The play is about many things, including underground drag/ball culture where families of queer performers compete against other families in the vagaries and wonders of drag performance. This culture is about artistry and the allusion of gender realness (femininity or masculinity), making a performance—if not a spectacle—of gender. It is also a performative testament to the fluidity of identity politics in the company of those who embrace that capacity, and those who have been subject to the restrictions and punishments of nonnormative sexed/gendered performances in everyday life.

It is a play about resistance to social norms, as well as a resistant commentary on the era of HIV/AIDS. The ball itself is a place in which mostly Black and Latino LGBTQ+ communities engage in queer worldmaking. The competition is about posing and posturing as stylistic movement to a beat, as well as a testament to the realness and authenticity of passing as the other and being fully alive within queer company. These performances are both socially constructed artifice and the ideal to which some strive both within and outside of particularly sexed bodies.

Wig Out! centers around the anticipation and actualization of a Cinderella Ball challenge by the rival "House of Diabolique" to the "House of Light" in the categories of style, pose, and performance. The rubric of "house" is an identifying construct in drag ball culture that defines and delineates family: membership, association, allegiance, performance style, and lineage. The play delves deeply into the politics of family and the tensions that often lead LGBTQ+ youth to run away from biological families and choose families in queer communities; communities (families) that are not without challenges but are grounded in an ethics of respect for variously gendered identities where the notion of family and house become synchronous.

In the process of developing the narrative plot, McCraney deconstructs the primary relationships and family members in the "House of Light," which serves as the primary focus of the play. Within the house, there is a focus on the relationship between the founding Father of the house, Lucian, and the founding Mother of the house, Rey-Rey. In this case, the role of father and mother are symbolic of parental roles of leadership and not necessarily relational as a couple.

The character of Lucian, a highly masculinized male figure, struggles with control of his family. He has a notorious sexual prowess that becomes both competitive and disciplinary when he sleeps with Nina's (first-child of the "House of Light" and a drag performer) new beau, Eric. Eric is a young man, and a designated sexual bottom, who is attracted to a particular masculine performativity at the time, which is the case when he first meets Wilson (aka Nina), who presents as male. He later becomes uncomfortable with Wilson's drag persona (Nina) and the whole ballroom culture to which s/he introduces him. Eric's preference for masculinity creates a suggestive tension between his sexual engagement of both Nina and Lucian. Meanwhile Rey-Rey, the Mother of the house, engages in what might be considered traditional maternal traits, as she struggles to maintain her own sense of being as an aging queen and performer. This becomes evident as she demands to perform in the ball against Lucian's wishes and jeopardizes both her standing as a legendary performer and, ultimately, her status as Mother of the house.

The other "children" in the "House of Light" add to the complexity, not only of the family structure, but of the web of significance that McCraney weaves relative to the negotiation of desire and difference and the articulation of queer sexual identities. Venus, a drag performer, is considered the face of the "House of Light" and is in a relationship with Deity, a masculine young man who serves as the House DJ. The play depicts them as ex-lovers involved in a tense negotiation of possibilities, with Deity pursuing Venus through-out. The crux of their disagreement, which is revealed by Venus, is her (his) desire to top Deity in their sexual practice. The articulation of this tension also names the multiplicity of sexual desires in same-sex couples, regardless of the presumptions and perceptions of masculine and feminine personas. The nature of this relational negotiation that McCraney offers is juxtaposed with the narrative plot of Eric's desire for the masculine. This is a particular critique that Lucian makes of Eric after discovering that Eric allowed Nina (a femme) to top him during sex. Lucian's critique oddly questions not only Eric's desire but outs broader notions of masculinity within the context of same-sex encounters and queer desire, which also reveals aspects of Lucian's own issues of being and becoming queer.

In addition to the relational dynamics that play out and promote the plot, McCraney gives each of the characters (Venus, Rey-Rey, Deity, Nina, Lucian, and Eric) a cameo moment in the play in which they deliver a "my grand-mother wore a wig" soliloquy. The soliloquies serve as moments in which the characters reflect on experiences that involve wigs, either wearing or witness-ing wigs as a performative aspect of gender identity. As the centralizing trope of the play, wigs act both as a signal to drag performance as well as the anxi-ety around queer identities. The title of the play, *Wig Out!*, is suggestive of many things: for example, becoming deliriously excited and going completely wild, or losing a sense of personal control. In short, the soliloquies serve as moments wherein each character reveals a pivotal point in their sexual and gendered becoming. McCraney strategically engages this technique to allow the characters to mark their particularity to the audience in a sea of other particularities. Their self-disclosures related to wigs as influencing origins of their gendered identities, delivered directly to the audience in cameo, offer a range of potentialities in queer-becoming. Notably, they serve as triggers for the audience to reflect on their own gendered experiences of being and becoming (queer or otherwise). Each serves as a tool of empowerment to make critical decisions that confirm identity and their desire.

The Significance of the "My Grandmother Wore a Wig" Soliloquies

While *Wig Out!* is a play that seemingly focuses on queer drag culture, the notion of queer performativity in the play is less about drag performance per se. It is about a rejection of the presumed normative expectations or limita-tions of male expressivity, or what it means to act like a boy/man especially if one identifies as queer. In this sense, queer becomes both a gendered position-ality and a strategic performance of "resistance to regimes of the normal."[3] McCraney pays special attention to issues of shame and shaming in the queer-becoming of his characters, as they discover the potential of their queer identity in and through wigs. Hence, "in this usage, 'queer performativity' is the name of a strategy for the production of meaning and being, in relation to the affect shame and to the later and related fact of stigma."[4]

McCraney variously frames the self-disclosive moments of the soliloquies in the play as preludes or invocations. They are framed mostly as such because they serve as critical insight into the gendering experiences of the character speaking, and they offer the audience an understanding of the character's motivations both as performative acts, the desirous intents that guide their decision-making process, and as a foreshadowing of their actions that motivate the plot. Each moment is staged as a cameo, delivered while the character is alone on stage with a simulated direct address to the audience. These moments are in stark contrast to the range of energetically performed dance moments with a contemporary/pop soundtrack, the glitz of elaborate costumes, and the sparkle of lights that encompass the stage in other aspects of the production. These cameos are solitary, quiet, and intimate moments between the character and the audience. They are both asides and direct discourse while in a dressing room, during a momentary pause while walking across stage, as a prelude to a transitional moment for the characters, and as a new entrance or a final exit.

In the "my grandmother wore a wig" stories, each of the key characters offers a stirring personal narrative of gendering experiences that is delivered directly to the audience. These are intimate stories that break the fourth wall of the perceived theatrical world of the play to speak directly to the audience. These are moments in the play that the audience members must reconsider their position as not just objective, partially-passive bystanders watching the unfolding of a narrative in a world different from the one they may presume to inhabit. The audience members are required to engage in active participation as they are invited into that world, a world in which they feel their way into a moment of personal discovery, a moment of triggered or discovered desire. And, while the same or not the same, the triggered remembrance in the audience forces an empathy with the character, an empathy that forestalls judgment and relates not to the actions of the character in the play, but the cultural socializing of gender itself (if gender can be considered an "it" or to have "a self"). The audience is forced to empathize with an experience of gender discovery, to recognize the socializing aspects of gender (variously performed), even in the fantastical world of queer drag performativity that the play foregrounds.

The soliloquies advance the plot and reveal the characters's inner thoughts. The soliloquies are used as a form of intimate self-disclosure that, in communication theory, establishes an interpersonal and psychic bond with the audience (receiver) to form trust. The soliloquies also establish a form of dramatic irony that gives the audience access and awareness to the inner operations of the character. Through these soliloquies, McCraney uses six characters to offer six different facets of queer gendering experience. He uses the soliloquies of each as a form of theorizing gender formation through articulated lived experience. Each character separately contributes to a queer praxis as multiple points of access and departure in queer being and becoming. In this praxis, McCraney builds a space where theories of gender formation can meet the actualization of articulated experience; where, through the use of the soliloquy, praxis becomes the "reflection and action directed at the structures to be transformed" in the lives of the characters.[5] These six characters, in fact, establish and describe a community of queerness (a queer community) that is neither monologic in its articulation nor monolithic in its performative expressivity.[6] It is a queer community that exists both within the play and in the historiography of queer drag culture to which the play signals. In other words, each character contributes to an argument that McCraney develops of queer worldmaking, without reducing each in/as the other. And while all exist in the world of the play, the diversity of characters and queer gendering experiences disrupt the reductive notions of a singular queer (gay) narrative *or* a singular queer performativity *or* queer relationality. All of which references both the presentation of queerness or the presumed sex role in queer engagement in the play (and possibly in everyday life).

Six Soliloquies of Gendered Becoming in *Wig Out!*

Six characters in *Wig Out!*—Venus, Rey-Rey, Deity, Nina, Lucian, and Eric—offer their "my grandmother wore a wig" soliloquy and do so from a specific positionality, a political positioning in the plot of the play that triggers the reflection. But, maybe more importantly, it is a location of experience that implicates family in the development of racial-gendered identities in everyday life for the audience. The fact that all of these characters are "of color," particularly of African American and Latinx descent, is also critical to the nature of the message. This is relative to the particular drag and queer world being explored and the ways in which race and culture become the alchemy of identity formation in the performativities of gender expectation on the home front, as well as to the executions of gender performance in the "House of Light." The issues of race and culture are intertwined in their narratives and in the visual materiality of the characters, but it does not foreclose; rather, it creates a space of empathy within the audience.

The narratives move through the gamut of emotions, from playful to painful memories that are both embodied and witnessed; a disciplining of the queer body and a witnessing of gender performances that both penetrated the sensibilities of their being and becoming. I believe that, while entertaining, the experiencing-witnessing dynamic forces a close examination of the constructedness of gender through what might be an *ocular epistemology* that presumes the primacy of visual perception as the dominant form of knowing. Perception, however, is never pure. It is clouded by the structure of language and culture that refuses to be anchored in the present—the site of so-called pure essence.[7] The soliloquies in *Wig Out!* challenge the audience in the artistry of the performer and the queer drag world in which the story is set, asking the audience to suspend disbelief while at the same time encouraging belief in the actuality of the happening.

Venus, "a young Latino/Black man with a beautiful face, in his early twenties, face of the House of Light,"[8] prances her way to center stage to deliver her "my grandmother wore a wig" soliloquy. She is accompanied by The Fates (Fay, Fate, and Faith) as three contemporary variations of the Greek Fates who, through song and dance, offer exposition and foreshadowing throughout the play. In Venus's soliloquy, The Fates offer echo and sass to the narrative. This is the only soliloquy offered with other entities, real or imagined, on the stage. But with the presence of The Fates onstage, there is also a curious foreshadowing of Venus's fall as a boy child and her rise as the new Mother of the "House of Light." The section reads:

> VENUS: Mi Abuela wore a wig. The fiercest wigs. Everyday: / a new wig! / Gurl, we would come down to the house on the / weekends . . . And there Grandma was, done up in a Faye Dunaway / or a short Doris Day. And when we came to the door she would be like:
> FATE: Venus!
> VENUS: Yes! She named me.
> FAITH: Venus is a girl name!
> FATE: Venus with a penis! Come in here to Grandma. Let me dance with you . . .
> VENUS: One day dancing with Grandma my mother bumped into / Me and I fell. I fell down . . .
> FAY: Ankle turned.
> FATE: Face contorted.
> VENUS: My grandma turned she looked at me and said,
> FATE: Venus, get up. Levantante, be be . . .
> FAITH: Stay down . . .
> VENUS: Eventually I got up but when I did, / My grandma had taken off her wig. (44–46)[9]

There is a beautiful and pained reality in this soliloquy, one in which the idealized feminine in the life of Venus is her (his) grandmother—a grandmother who recognized his queer particularity, naming him "Venus with a penis," and celebrated him within the framework of her own performed femininity.

The observation that his mother "couldn't dance" might be suggestive of his mother as a masculine regulator in his life. In other words, maybe the mother with the anxiety of her own racial-gendered performance as a woman of color needed to regulate the racial norms and expectations of her male child as a means of validating the success of her own performance as (biological) mother to a male child. It is his mother who bumps into him while dancing in his grandmother's shoes and causes the fall; and it is his mother's will that prevents him from getting up immediately. When he does get up, his grandmother has taken off her wig—suggesting that the wig allowed the space of play, her personal play and her play with him, outside the regulation of the social norms of his mother's intervention. The description of him as "Venus with a penis" also becomes salient in his relational negotiation of Deity; the penis becomes the literal and figurative tool of desired penetration.

Rey-Rey's (the legendary Mother of the "House of Light") soliloquy also comes as a foreshadowing of the character's fall and the dimming of her performative fierceness in a drag ball. She stands in her dressing room, which is on the second floor of the House. The audience looks, almost reverentially, up to her. She speaks:

> When I was younger the kid next door, Jay, / Was my best friend in the whole world . . . Jay had an older brother . . . Anthony. To this day / I have yet to meet a man more beautiful than / Anthony. They lived . . . Jay and Ant, with their / Grandma. Dear ole Grandmamma Alice. Grandma / Wore a wig. Sometimes when Anthony started feelin' / Full of himself, smelling himself as my mother would / Say, he would throw on old Grandmamma's wig and / Impersonate her . . . to her face . . . "Anthony, stop that!" she would say, whispering through / Shame-founded lips. "Cut that out. You do that too well." / It was true . . . / He did. / He looked so beautiful in his grandmother's wig. / Young boys in wigs can be so beautiful. / Old women in wigs save some dignity. / Old men in toupees are funny . . . / But an old drag . . . an old queen in a crown. Huh. / Well . . . (51–52)

There is a reference both to the somewhat salacious pleasure of drag performance and the ensuing shame associated with female impersonation that the grandmother projects onto Anthony's performance in the soliloquy. For in that moment, it is not only the embarrassment of the impersonation of the grandmother that may signal the phantom of her fading beauty, or even her own simulated performance of drag, but the performed and embodied feminine in the boy wearing her wig that causes both shame and envy.

The literal reference to impersonation is important in this soliloquy because McCraney takes the moment to allow the character to speak to the act of impersonation. This is in relation to the presumption or perception of what that act signifies: either mimicry or the imagined embodiment of a desirous feminine persona. Rey-Rey's closing line speaks to a typology of wigs, if not drag itself, in the social imaginary. The description that "young boys in wigs can be so beautiful. Old women in wigs save some dignity. Old men in toupees are funny . . . But an old drag . . . an old queen in a crown. Huh. Well . . ." offers a perspective on the motivations or effects of wigs. Maybe it serves as narration of her evolution in the shifting stages of her drag persona, but the fact that she is an "old queen" who will fight in performance to retain a remnant of her past glory makes suspect her own beauty and the dwindling power of the wig to transform and project the desired allusion. In some ways, while less tender and poetic, the same sentiment is later delivered by Lucian as he tries to discourage her participation in the ball. He states: "But if you want to stay a legend you won't walk this ball. I won't let you. Let it go" (68).

Deity, "a young man of colour, twenties, the DJ for the House of Light," delivers his "my grandmother wore a wig" soliloquy after witnessing Lucian's refusal to allow Rey-Rey to walk (perform) in the ball. He witnesses her dejection and disappointment in the moment. When The Fates assist Rey-Rey off the stage, Deity speaks:

> My grandmother wore a wig. She died before I ever met / Her. But my granddaddy, Pere, always kept her wig up / On a Styrofoam holder next to his bed. Sometimes when / I would sleep over my granddaddy's house / I would hear him praying, talking to God, and then he / would / In the smallest voice, / That I could barely hear, I heard 'em say, "I miss you / Mary, every day. / I miss you and I love you." / My grandmother wore a wig. It sat in my grandfather's / room. We / Would sit staring at it sometimes and he would tell me / To treat women with respect, open / Doors for them and say sweet things. "When they gone," / he say, / You miss 'em, especially in the night, but even when / it's bright / You miss them all day long. (70)

I appreciate the manner in which McCraney filters a heteromasculine desire for the heterofeminine real into this queer context. Deity's narration of his grandfather's love for his departed wife is mapped onto Deity's yearning to rekindle his relationship with Venus. McCraney forces the audience to see the relationality of desire as both the same and not the same, but real.

The depth of this moment speaks to a relationality of gender performances, not the particularity of sexed desire. The notion of treating women right, to which the grandfather speaks, invokes that gender relationality. And like gender performance, relationality requires a culturally learned set of behaviors towards the other. The wig on the Styrofoam head in Deity's narrative becomes the personification of the grandfather's lost love. It is also the supreme artifact of a desirous feminine persona that has lingered long after her death. The relational commitment is embedded in the mind and heart of his grandson, who experiences it with and for Venus.

Nina's (aka Wilson, a handsome man of color, late teens, early twenties) "my grandmother wore a wig" soliloquy is delivered in a relationally transitional space. It is delivered after Wilson and Eric's first intimate encounter, and after Nina brings Eric to the house to meet the family, including Lucian. She stands in the same upstairs dressing room where Rey-Rey stood and says:

> My grandmother wore a wig. / One night when I thought no one was looking I / Grabbed the wig and ran into my room and stood / Before

the mirror, mirror, and snug that wig behind / My heaven-kissed ears. I couldn't believe who I saw. / It was like standing there, after a long look, to find / Someone and finally seeing who you were searching / for . . . / Right there. Not who they told / You you were, not who they say you should be, just / Me. I couldn't walk away from the sight / So my father knocked me away from it. Guess he / Snuck in when I was sun self-bathing. Guess he might / Have been standing there all along. But he knocked me / Down. I fell into the mirror and it broke like heaven / From the first fall into a thousand pieces. / He called me every faggot and homo he could / Muster. And I took it. I guess I felt like I could. / Now that I knew me. / He saw that, though. / He took pieces of the mirror, snatched it up like a / work tool, / And he said, he said . . . / "If you want to be a woman so bad, I'll make you / One. I made you a boy I can remake you a lil girl." / Standing there with that piece of glass in his hand. / Gripping it so tight he cutting himself, slicing his hand, / Blood just dripping down his hand his fingers. / I remember / Worrying about him. I wanted to grab his hand and say, / "Daddy, it's okay. It'll be okay. Okay?" I just stood there. / "I'll make you one," he mumbling. / He thought he was God, I guess. Huh. I had to remind / him that / He was barely a father. (83)

This particular soliloquy makes real both the transformative power of the grandmother's wig when adorning a latent feminine queer male subject (or an emergent drag femme), and the thrust of masculine hysteria in relation to that practiced potentiality. Wilson discovers Nina (his drag persona) in the mirror under his grandmother's wig. His father knocking him down and the subsequent shattering of the mirror is an attempt to reinforce a hegemonic masculinity that is already doomed to Wilson's recognition of his real possibility (or self). The allusion to the first fall invokes the first sin and Adam and Eve's fall from heaven (grace). McCraney's use of the reference in that context of awakening seems to recognize the duality of Wilson as Adam and Eve, falling from the force of an angry father only to find themselves in the shattered pieces of a new reality. The reference also invokes what is already a form of spirituality or sacredness that is present in the play.

Yet, I am also reminded of a quote from J. M. Barrie, the creator of Peter Pan, when he writes: "When the first baby laughed for the first time, its laugh broke into a thousand pieces, and they all went skipping about, and that was the beginning of fairies."[10] The mixing of these sacred and secular texts becomes metaphorical to the language that McCraney gives Wilson. It invokes both a punitive action that bespeaks a kind of death from paradise—the fall, along with a rebirth of a figurative fairy, in the best sense of that term, in the thousand pieces of a shattered whimsy. Both the fall and the shattering of the mirror lead Wilson to a range of possibilities in his/her performative selves. Her particular relationship and attraction to Eric tests the range of that possibility—both in the literal sex of their encounter, as well as Eric's personal confusions about gender performance. And the narrative of her biological father juxtaposes the relational dynamic with Lucian, the father of the "House of Light."

McCraney also introduces and makes more salient a shift in the psyche of drag characters as they move in and out of their drag personas (reality). In this soliloquy, Nina begins telling the narrative of her personal discovery and the act of violence initiated by her father upon his discovery of her wearing the wig. The shift is referenced by the "first fall into a thousand pieces." It is at that moment in performance that Nina pulls the wig off. The script and persona then shift from Nina to Wilson. It is Wilson who then delivers the second half of the soliloquy that outlines his father's threat to castrate him with the shattered piece of mirror. It is the same shattered piece of mirror that created (or illuminated) the fairy, to which the father states: "I made you a boy I can remake you a lil girl." The rage and sentiment of this moment is a God complex as McCraney's religious reference to the biblical dictates on queer sexuality. But it might also be read as a kind of masculine panic in the father relative to the virility of his own sperm and spawn, and the performativity of his own masculinity and fatherhood—to which Wilson clearly signals.

Lucian's (a Latino man, late twenties, founding father of the "House of Light") "my grandmother wore a wig" soliloquy comes after his admonishment of Nina for entering the house late and with Eric, who was (and is) an object of his desire. After a tense conversation with Eric about his encounter with Nina and after making another sexual advance, Lucian speaks:

> My grandmother . . . wore a wig. / My mother . . . wore a wig. My father wore / A wig. No, not a man-wig. Not a rag to the hide/ His widow's peak. The nigga wore a wig. In / Secret. In a private place where he thought / No one could see. I saw. / I stumbled into him dancing around his / Bedroom for another man, dancing and prancing / Like a fucking girl, like a woman, like he was weak. / I walked into his room, I wasn't embarrassed, or scared, / I just walked right in. Curious. Not about my father. / No. Fuck 'em./ I wondered about the man my father wore a wig for. / I wondered what power he had to make my father be / A woman for him. (92)

The soliloquy that McCraney gives to Lucian pushes at the borders of the wig narratives to invoke and evoke a different orientation in desire, a search for a *masculine ontology*, "the pursuit of being and becoming masculine by the masculine subject" within the framework of queer desire.[11] So, this is not a story about a personal desire to wear a wig but the evolution of a masculine performativity and a desirous orientation, not just to men who wear wigs but to the type of masculinity (queer or otherwise) to which other men would engage a feminine response. And hence, "the concept of desire being discussed here is not primarily one of libido and sexuality, but rather production (of self)" in relation to the other.[12]

When Lucian seemingly disavows the particularity of his father wearing a wig and identifies with the man for whom his father wore a wig, this "removes the dichotomies between essence and existence, and between cognitive intent and the 'free-floating subject.' For desire can be understood as both a precondition of existence and as mediated by the conditions of its own production."[13] In other words, whether Lucian's queer identity preexists the moment of seeing his father wearing the wig or the viewing of his father wearing a wig and presumably dancing for another man, the scene triggers the desire for a particular queer performativity that is not about the father. It is about the type of man that the father desires and that Lucian wants to become, resulting in a queer and resistant Electra complex of male masculine performativity.

The soliloquy that Lucian delivers also forces the audience to see differently a plurality in masculine queer performatives within the same drag world. Lucian's performative masculinity becomes caustic when his intended conquest Eric, another presumed "masculine" queer, becomes romantically and sexually involved with Nina, a femme. The audience members are then faced with understanding a comparative relationality, both through their witnessing of the staged coitus of Nina and Eric, and through the rage of Lucian when he discovers the misdirected sexual encounter (his with Eric, and Eric's with Nina). The audience begins to see that the nature of gender performance and sexual desire is not restricted to the presumptions of masculine and feminine performativity—or, reductively speaking, that the feminine is the bottom and the masculine is the top. Nina, the drag queen (and the presumed feminine), tops Eric (the presumed masculine). This is the nature of their desire, not particularly masculine to feminine relative to the fluidity of gender that Nina embodies, but that which also becomes salient in Eric's unease toward drag.[14] These particularly relational and desirous dynamics shake and question the audience's understanding of the sometime signifiers of *top/bottom, versatile, versatile-top, versatile-bottom* that often become the language of negotiating, identifying, and referencing gay sexual positionality.

Through these characters, McCraney boldly forces the audience to reckon with the presumptions of queer sexuality and the politics of desire—a politics that operates in the regime of heteronormative framework about sex roles and identities. At the end of the aforementioned scene, Eric walks off with Lucian to have sex in his office. The sexual encounter for Lucian, the audience can assume, is more about sexual conquest and about showing Eric that sex with a "regular masculine dude" is presumably better than with the "femme dick," as he describes Nina. It can also be assumed that Lucian is making real his desire to be the *type of man that his father wore a wig for*—the type of man whose masculinity compels other men into the presumed feminine role.

In which case, the presumption of being the bottom to his top is symbolic (or euphemistic) of them wearing a wig for him. And beyond Lucian's specific intentions, maybe these are qualities of a performative masculinism, "the ideology that justifies and naturalizes male domination . . . as such it is the ideology of patriarchy."[15]

The character of Eric is presented as a crisis and a catalyst—a crisis within the negotiation of his own sexual identity, and a catalyst that invokes psychic and relational issues both within and between Nina and Lucian. He is also a variable in the overall storyline of Rey-Rey, Venus, and Deity, who are all engaged in moments of self-discovery and taking chances with differing outcomes. Eric is the outsider in the "House of Light" who actually forces characters to see themselves in relation to each other. The prompting of Eric's soliloquy comes at the very end of the play, after he has sex with Lucian, and after Nina dismisses him. The dismissal is not for the presumed infidelity with Lucian but for his inability to reconcile his own issues related to drag, sexuality, and the processes of being and becoming. The scene is worth highlighting:

> ERIC: You talking like . . . like Wilson.
> WILSON: I met you as Wilson, I should / Say goodbye the same way.
> ERIC: Goodbye? Where are you going?
> WILSON: Nowhere. Ain't got nowhere to go.
> ERIC: You asking me to leave?
> WILSON: Before he comes back.
> ERIC: Is it about . . . with Lucian?
> WILSON: No. This about us.
> ERIC: Ey, man, I like you a lot.
> WILSON: I know.
> ERIC: This whole scene, it's . . . it's . . . / I mean, don't you get confused?
> WILSON: No, I don't.
> ERIC: Oh. I guess that's how you know you belong. / Or not.
> WILSON: Yes.
> ERIC: I had a real good time today.
> WILSON: When? With me?
> ERIC: You're the only good time I've had. [WILSON puts the wig back on.] Will you tell everybody I said bye?
> NINA: They won't even know you missing.
> ERIC: Dam, that's vicious.
> NINA: You don't know the half.
> ERIC: Will you know? Will you know I'm missing?
> NINA: I always have. (114–15)

A classic breakup, send-off narrative, the scene eschews the construction of a pained breakup or the emotionality of jealousy that is most often attributed to the female (feminine) in such breakup representations. The scene begins with a reference, both in content and in the structural dialogue of Wilson, engaging Eric in the breakup, reductively speaking, man-to-man. The dialogue evolves into a confessional on the part of Eric regarding his confusions about the scene of drag culture. But Eric's reference to the culture as a scene reifies the importance of McCraney's construction of the actual theatrical scene that is projected onto the broader backdrop of being comfortable in one's own sexuality and performed gender identity.

The remainder of the scene is important for different reasons. What is telling is McCraney's construction of the second critical moment in which Wilson puts the wig back on (as in the opposite gesture of the Nina soliloquy). The relational dynamic between Eric and Wilson shifts—even as a script notation—from Eric to Nina. It is in this moment that McCraney allows Nina to *read* Eric, as in to tell him off, to tell him about himself. She says, "They won't even know you missing," which is to reinforce the recognition that Eric was never fully present, either in a relationship or in the queer drag world of that culture. The shift from Wilson to Nina in this moment is critically important because unlike the Nina soliloquy, in which Wilson pulls off the wig, moving from Nina to Wilson, this is a moment in which Wilson puts the wig on, claiming the power and authority of Nina as both voice and volition. The ability of the character to shift and claim the performative authority to do so shows a consistency in his psychological makeup. He is not confused. He is fully confluent in his identity complex.

The last scene of the play features Eric walking across the stage. He is walking, not downstage, but in an upper section of the set that crosses the space where both Rey-Rey and Nina delivered their soliloquies. After his dismissal by Nina, he walks across the area, appearing to walk toward the horizon. He stops center stage and speaks: "My grandmother wore a wig . . ." McCraney includes the ellipses but does not allow Eric to deliver the full soliloquy, only a trigger for the story. This is a critical moment, a sort of suspended ending of the play in which McCraney forces not a conflation but a confluence of all the "my grandmother wore a wig" stories: the mother's disdain of a son's queer identity as he danced with his grandmother (Venus); the witnessing of a friend impersonating his grandmother while wearing her wig (Rey-Rey); the invocation of a grandfather's remembrance and love of a biological woman who wore a wig (Deity); the father's disdain for a queer son discovering himself while wearing a wig (Wilson); and "The man who made my father wear a wig" story (Lucian).

After witnessing each of these "my grandmother wore a wig" soliloquies, performed in direct address to the audience, and after witnessing Eric's particular promiscuous and experimental engagements throughout the play, the audience is given the space of imagination. Indeed, the audience is given the space of possibilizing what Eric's "my grandmother wore a wig" story might reveal about his gendered origins, and in that process, to begin to imagine their own "my grandmother wore a wig" story and how it might reflect their own performed gendered reality.

Grandmothers, Wigs, and Quare Studies: A Conclusion

In his now germinal essay, "'Quare' Studies, or (Almost) Everything I Know about Queer Studies I Learned from My Grandmother," E. Patrick Johnson uses the word "quare" to contribute to a growing body of literature on queer-of-color critique that he refers to as "Quare Studies."[16] Johnson's contribution is an expansion of the more conventional usage of "queer" in queer studies that ignores the experiences of queers of color.[17] In particular, Johnson offers Quare Studies as a theory of and for gays and lesbians of color. For him, quare not only speaks across identities, it articulates identities as well. Quare offers ways to critique stable notions of identity and, at the same time, to locate racialized and class knowledges. Amongst many contributions, Quare Studies closes the gap of queer theories' failure to acknowledge consistently and critically the intellectual, aesthetic, and political contributions of non-white and non-middle-class gays, bisexuals, lesbians, and transgendered people in the struggle against homophobia and oppression. And Quare Studies's theorizing of the social context of performance sutures the gap between discourse and lived experience by examining how quares use performance as a strategy of survival in their day-to-day experiences.[18] Johnson's contribution joins a range of other scholars doing queer-of-color critique.[19] Tarell Alvin McCraney's *Wig Out!*—along with a host of his other plays and the smash hit film *Moonlight*—also works in powerful ways as a queer-of-color critique, and, maybe more importantly, as a focus on queer lives of color.

What is most important to my current moment in foregrounding the work of Johnson is that he also begins in theorizing through gendering experiences that he had with his grandmother. Echoing the "my grandmother wore a wig" stories, he writes:

> I remembered how "queer" is used in my family. My grandmother, for example, used it often when I was a child and still uses it today. When she says the word, she does so in a thick, black, southern dialect: "That sho'll is a quare chile." The use of "queer" is almost always nuanced. Still one might wonder, what if anything could a poor, black, eighty something, southern, homophobic woman teach her educated, middle-class, thirty-something gay grandson about queer studies?[20]

While the play *Wig Out!* is about many things, for me, it speaks to "gender-shaping moments in childhood," particularly gender-shaping moments that link grandmothers and wigs as the triggering of gender possibility, as well as the stories we tell of how family members helped shape our gender realities/identities.[21] This is not unlike Johnson's notion of his grandmother teaching him everything, or almost everything, about queer/quare studies.

Wig Out! asks us to imagine the cultural rituals of speech, language, walk, and dress that make up the environments of our everyday habitation. How extreme are those cultural patterns of performance, particularly around the complex of gender and sexuality? The play asks us to think about dating rituals, intimate negotiations, and the nature of family relationships through blood and through the ties that bind. The play also asks us to explore how strangely such answers might be critiqued on the stage, and how normative or normalized do those performances appear and feel when we are inhabiting our own drag? When we are walking and talking in community? What are the phantasms of our own performative traits that might seem atypical or abnormal to a casual tourist in our cultural communities (or worlds)?

It is evident that in writing *Wig Out!*, McCraney is doing an artistic queer-of-color critique, a critique that approaches culture as one site that compels identification with and antagonisms to the normative ideals promoted by state and capital. It examines how culture as a site of identification produces odd bedfellows and how it fosters unimagined alliances. The play offers an epistemological intervention that denotes an interest in materiality but refuses ideologies of transparency and reflection. It is a play that presumes that liberal ideology occludes the intersecting saliency of race, gender, sexuality, and class in forming social practices. It is also a play that challenges ideologies of discreteness, charts genealogies of difference within a variety of locations, and both critiques and employs disidentification.[22]

I believe that McCraney asks the audience to both sympathize and empathize with the characters in the play. But the play also promotes an environment of tolerance and acceptance as it serves as a visual metaphor for the ever-shifting and expanding nomenclature of gender identities and gender variance. The play allows for contemporary audiences to address the meaningfulness of an emerging taxonomy of terms such as gender-expansive, gender nonconforming, same-gender loving, transgender, transphobia, and genderqueer, as ways of seeing, knowing, articulating, and talking about gender. The play allows for reflection upon gender identities that exist both inside and outside the gender binary and cisnormativity of presumed everyday male/female notions of normalcy.[23] In the staged world of drag ball performance, McCraney uses the theater in general, and *Wig Out!* in particular, as a microcosm of society, a laboratory for experimentation, and a showcase for audiences to see, know, and understand the particular and plural aspects of gender identities.

And as an element of queer-of-color critique, I strongly believe that the play contributes to discourses about home and family, "tak[ing] up the critical task of both remembering and rejecting the model of the 'home' [and family] offered" in most aspects of the queer experience, "first by attending to the ways in which it was defined over and against [queer] people of color, and second, by expanding the locations and moments of that critique of the home to interrogate processes of group formation and self-formation."[24] This is evident in each soliloquy, defining and emerging moments of queer desire and identity both in relation and resistance to remembered moments within particular social formations. Each character engages in a form of *disidentification* in relation to their social construction and the politics of gender identity, and then reveals their emerging sense of self from that disempowered positionality.[25] Each character offers an account of an experience that is from a "queer of color subject's historicity"—which is both personal and political, making the queer-of-color experience visible and known in ways that are both particular and plural in relation.[26] Each character then ostensibly rejects, as they are rejected from, some aspect of home, to search for and define family on their own terms. And each character in her/his own way offers *critiques of stable notions of identity* to which the audience, as well as members of the play's world, have subscribed, thus making their performances and performativities both queer and quare.

At the end of the play, the Cinderella Ball is staged, and the confrontation between the rival houses occurs in the splendor and spectacle of drag performance competition.[27] The outcomes are clear: the "House of Light" wins, but there are changes. Each of the characters in the play experiences a form of displacement from and in the house, but also a reestablishment of roles in the family. Venus is named new Mother of the house. She and Deity reconcile with a negotiation of his care-filled departure from the house. Eric is dismissed, and life in the house and family goes on.

In so many ways, my wearing my grandmother's wigs was also a gender-shaping moment in my childhood, but maybe not as much as my seeing my grandmother wear her wigs. Same and not the same, this mirrors several of the characters' experiences in *Wig Out!* Unlike my grandmother, who assumed a new persona, a magnified aspect of her own self when she donned her wigs, in my childhood exploration I did not. She was not consumed by the power of the wigs, but maybe I was consumed in an otherness that was the me and the not me—and the *not* not me—all at the same time. And just in case you are wondering—my grandmother knew that I would try on her wigs. One evening when I engaged my curiosity she saw me staring at myself in the mirror with the wig. It was her pageboy, pixie-cut wig. And as our eyes met in the mirror she simply said, "That looks good on you. But, it looks better on me." And we laughed. She kissed me on the head, on the wig, and walked away. And we never talked about it again. I adored my grandmother.

And while I grew out of trying on my grandmother's wigs, the wearing of her wigs in those halcyon days of my childhood did offer me insight into the performance of gender in everyday life. It did offer me entrée into the playfully salacious and sometimes empowering possibilities that drag performance presents as both rehearsal and realization of particular identities. For surely my grandmother was also performing drag in her own way. The wearing of my grandmother's wig and seeing her wear her wigs allowed me to begin thinking about the plurality of femininities and masculinities—and the in-between possibilities that are thus available to all of us both within and outside of LGTBQ+ communities. And at times, how those same social constructions are always linked with presumptive expectations of the socially fixed notions of being a "real" man *or* a "real" woman (or something in between or *altogether different*); categories with attending performative expectations that I often navigate between with ease. I have come to both embody and present my own queer masculinity in the drag of everyday, as both private affair and public display that drag affords us all. To have a ball. To act up. And to *Wig Out!*

The Breach

✦

A Rupture in the National Narrative of Katrina

Katherine Nigh

One might ask what "good" a play addressing a traumatic event such as Hurricane Katrina can possibly do in the face of such devastation? Among many other things, an important function of the playwright or storyteller is to offer alternative perspectives on the dominant narratives that the media and other such meaning-making institutions, including the government, create. As Scott McKinnon, Andrew Gorman-Murray, and Dale Dominey-Howes note: "During and after disasters, critical information is supplied by the media, who are therefore capable of enhancing individual and community capacities for survival and recovery. By making choices on how to report on disasters and which experiences to highlight as newsworthy, the media also constructs and shapes public perceptions of a disaster."[1] In the case of Hurricane Katrina, the portrayal of New Orleans as a "city gone mad" had a direct impact on public opinion regarding the rescue operations (or lack thereof) following the storm. Whose stories were told and how they were told were greatly determined and divided by class, race, and sexuality.

In 2005, playwright Joe Sutton, dismayed by the physical and emotional wreckage that he witnessed on television, decided to do the one thing he could think to do in response to the devastation of Hurricane Katrina: write a play. "I am watching television images of Hurricane Katrina, and I can't believe what I'm seeing. How can we allow our own people [to] be treated like this in America? *What is happening?* . . . I have to do something. My first thought is to write a play," he explains.[2] Sutton soon thereafter contacted Catherine Filloux, a playwright known for her explorations of human rights and genocide in such works as *Eyes of the Heart*, *Lessons of My Father*, and *Lemkin's House*. The two immediately became conscious of their positions as "outside writers" trying to capture what occurred in New Orleans, so they contacted Bill Rauch, then artistic director of Cornerstone Theater, the Los Angeles company well known for its community-based productions. Rauch helped the pair develop community partnerships and guided them through the process of writing with multiple playwrights.[3] Tarell Alvin McCraney, a young—and, at the time, relatively unknown writer pursuing his M.F.A. at the Yale School of Drama—joined the duo later in the process. It was McCraney's own experience growing up in Florida, where Hurricane Andrew destroyed his family's home in 1992, that likely influenced his eagerness to join the writing team. *The Breach*, the play that Sutton, Filloux, and McCraney would go on to cocreate, is an example of storytelling that presents a critical counternarrative to the "official" and "historical" record on Hurricane Katrina.

Those who saw the play in one of its three productions—Southern Repertory Theater in 2007; Seattle Repertory Theater in 2008; and The Public Theater in 2008—particularly the ones presented outside of the city, were exposed to a more intimate portrayal of a post-Katrina New Orleans. The experience of watching *The Breach* in the theater differed from watching events unfold on television because there were bodies on stage, and because the theater afforded spectators a communal viewing experience. Whereas watching someone on television (an anonymous face of a person that we do not know) drowning in water can be heart wrenching, it can also become numbing. In watching a work like *The Breach*, however, audiences become invested in just a few people's stories, following the journey that they take over the course of a play. For a few hours, our attention belongs to them and them only—turning the channel is not an option. This challenge to the mainstream media's narrative about Hurricane Katrina is significant in terms of whose stories are heard and, thus, which communities and experiences are considered in terms of compassion and aid.

Rather than presenting one main narrative, *The Breach* comprises three distinct stories written by each playwright. Filloux's plotline concentrates on Mac, a bartender with multiple sclerosis who finds himself floating through toxic waters, taunted by Water—the natural element embodied as a sensual and seducing female—and hallucinating that his son, currently serving in Iraq, will rescue him. Sutton's plotline focuses on a journalist named Lynch who, like the playwrights, is confronted with the challenges of understanding and representing a community that is not his own. McCraney's plotline imagines the interactions between family members as they wait, stranded on their rooftop, to be rescued. Pere Leon, the grandfather, confronts his grandson Severance (or Sev) about his perceived sins (notably, his queer identity) while Quan, the youngest grandchild, watches. McCraney's story notably brings a perspective that is rarely represented in narratives about the disaster—the LGBTQ experience. That Severance, his main protagonist, is black, young, male, *and* queer is even more significant in terms of rupturing the dominant narrative on Hurricane Katrina. McCraney's plotline forces us to look at a community whose particular struggles with disasters or crises are often completely omitted from even politically liberal analyses of such events. In its attempt to highlight narratives that were pushed aside by the media, *The Breach* not only *preserves* history but also *intervenes* in history making.

The Breach shuttles between each of the playwrights's storylines—one of the plotlines might progress for twenty minutes, for example, and then switch to another—but the three are never explicitly connected; except, of course, that each plotline focuses on a group of people impacted by the storm. Although each of the plays could stand alone as individual short plays, the three plotlines in total have a running time of about two hours. The impact of the play comes, in part, from its asking audiences to listen to multiple and distinct narratives simultaneously. One cannot pick and choose which experience of Hurricane Katrina is most important to them or most reflective of their own life. The story of a white bartender with MS occupies the same stage, space, and time as the story of a queer, young, African American man. And, unlike watching the news, the audience cannot turn the channel when the story being told no longer appeals to them.

Although not directly based on testimony, *The Breach* was greatly influenced by the playwrights's trips to the areas devastated by the hurricane. In December 2005, less than four months after the hurricane, Sutton made his first visit to New Orleans:

> Landing in New Orleans is surprising. Steeled as I am for the devastation, I see relatively little of it as we come in from the airport. But once we cross into the city proper, the collapsed houses and piles of debris come into view . . . It is almost four months after the storm, but it's as if it hit yesterday . . . I am in shock. I thought I was prepared. I wasn't.[4]

On his trip, Sutton spoke with those who had experienced the events leading up to and during Katrina's impact on the Gulf Coast. Listening to these informal testimonies gave him a sense of urgency to write the play and gave him the inspiration for the format of the piece. "I start to imagine an epic tale, told in a variety of voices, turned into a collage," he explains.[5] Sutton also decided to develop the play through a series of readings across the country that would then take into account the reactions they received from audiences.

Sutton's plotline gives us insight into what I would call the function of the play: to provide a counternarrative to the mainstream media and to highlight those whose unique challenges during catastrophe often go unseen, unheard, and unacknowledged. As Sutton's plotline provides the framework for McCraney's and Filloux's, I want to briefly describe his contribution before focusing attention on McCraney's. In Sutton's plotline, Lynch is, no matter his intentions, a journalist from New York, viewed as an "outsider" in every possible way. When he attempts to interview a character named Woman about the "rumors" that the levees were intentionally bombed, he is very quickly reminded of his position as interloper. During their first encounter, Woman asks Lynch if she knows him. He says that she does not and that he is a writer. She asks him if he is from New Orleans, and when he tells her no, she tells him, "well then you can't understand this."[6] Lynch is, on the surface, not very different from the many journalists who came from outside the area to tell the story of the weather event. Woman very quickly turns the power dynamic between journalist and subject matter around by questioning *his* identity and motivations. In so doing, she inverts the relationship between the subject of the interview (and the object of media fascination) and the interviewer, whereby the latter is made to feel equally objectified and equally obligated to explain himself.

In his attempts to find out what is the "truth" or what "isn't the truth" about the possible levee bombing, Lynch encounters larger notions about the concept of a definable truth. Through his interviews, he discovers that many members in the communities that have been impacted by the levee breach believe that there is a real possibility that the levees were bombed. The *belief* that the levees could have been bombed becomes more important to Lynch than whether or not they *were* actually bombed. Lynch's interest in this theory is very similar to Sutton's, who notes, "The levees in New Orleans were intentionally dynamited. That's the rumor that many people in the region, on the Internet, as far away as Biloxi, seem to believe. What is behind that rumor? It is the question I decided to write about."[7] Sutton's words mimic Lynch's almost directly, making it easy to "read" Lynch as a veiled representation of Sutton and his collaborators.

While unsubstantiated and biased claims that massive looting and crime were taking place in New Orleans received mainstream media attention, claims that the levees were intentionally bombed did not. On the New Orleans–based website Rense.com, Greg Szymanski writes:

> Whenever the subject of the levees being intentionally detonated comes up, most mainstream commentators like ABC's Michele Martin, dismiss even the slightest possibility of foul play, appeasing Black listeners with comments like "Anybody with any knowledge of history can understand why a lot of people can feel this way, but any real possibility that the levees were intentionally exploded must be dismissed."[8]

Although Martin's ABC report provides substantial information about these claims, the framing of the article through its title (as "investigating conspiracy theories"), along with its rarity amongst the multiple reports on Katrina, demonstrate that these accusations by community members were not meant to be taken seriously within the larger narrative created about the event. Furthermore, although Martin acknowledges that there are historical reasons for people to feel the way they do about the levees (in 1927, the levees were intentionally bombed in order to save affluent and mostly white neighborhoods), as a journalist, she feels entitled to distinguish "rumor" from "fact" and to expressly instruct people to dismiss reports about a possible levee bombing. This demonstrates the power of the media to inform the American public of what they should think and feel about disasters such as Katrina.

Media coverage not only often feeds into preexistent racism and stereotypes but also creates an overall distancing effect between those who experience an event in person and those who do not. This is what Benjamin Bates and Rukhsana Ahmed refer to as the I-It relationship to survivors.[9] They contend that the person who experiences a crisis or disaster through the media is kept at an emotional and physical distance from the perceived other. They write, "Instead of seeking a deep understanding of the other, media coverage allows us to observe the other from afar and keep ourselves out of moments of relationship with them as valued others."[10] In the case of Katrina, the media portrayed the African American population as the Other, which created a sense of self for a white audience, placing them in a superior position to the "animalistic" behavior they saw on television.[11] Again, this othering process contributed to the lack of outrage over the abandonment of an entire city by the U.S. government in the wake of Katrina; if we see the victim of a disaster as Other, it is easier to turn a blind eye to what is happening to them. In this case, the media had to legitimize their portrayal of allegedly criminal African American survivors of Katrina who were framed as looters and also had to claim ownership to determine what was "fact" from what was "fiction" within emerging narratives about Katrina.

In addition to the media's misrepresentation of the financially poor African American communities in New Orleans—a misrepresentation that in many cases criminalized those who were merely trying to survive—religious leaders took it upon themselves to assert that Katrina was God's punishment for the sin that New Orleans is so famous for (just think of the most clichéd images of Bourbon Street). Shortly after the Hurricane, Pat Robertson asserted on the Christian Broadcasting Network that Katrina was a punishment (along with September 11) for legalized abortion in the United States. At a speech in Virginia, Franklin Graham (Billy Graham's son) declared, "This is one wicked city, OK? It's known for Mardi Gras, for Satan worship. It's known for sex perversion. It's known for every type of drugs and alcohol and the orgies and all of these things that go on down there in New Orleans." Reverend Graham continued, "There's been a black spiritual cloud over New Orleans for years. They believe God is going to use that storm to bring revival."[12] One has to wonder if the term "black spiritual cloud" wasn't a thinly veiled assertion that God was specifically punishing the black community via the hurricane. It would not be too difficult to imagine that Graham's comments had a racist undertone considering some political leaders and real estate developers also implied that Hurricane Katrina was a welcome scouring of the black community that came directly from God. Republican Louisiana Representative

Richard Baker told lobbyists, "We finally cleaned up public housing in New Orleans. We couldn't do it, but God did."[13] Baker was not the only public figure to imply that Katrina would bring a welcome decrease in the African American population. While water still covered most of New Orleans, Jimmy Reiss, a prominent local businessman and then head of the Business Council of New Orleans (a public-private entity that perhaps, not coincidentally, has been a key player in the privatization of public schools in the city), told the *Wall Street Journal* that the city would come back in "a completely different way: demographically, geographically, and politically," or he and other white civic leaders would not return. In fact, Katrina did dramatically and permanently change the racial landscape of the city. As of 2016, nearly 100,000 fewer African Americans were living in New Orleans than at the time Katrina hit the city.[14]

Representing the experience of the black community during Katrina, as Sutton and McCraney do via their plotlines, is important since race played such an undeniable role in the media representation of the storm and in the local and federal response to the disaster (or lack thereof). As Michael Eric Dyson asks, "How can race possibly be quarantined from a consideration of Katrina when it so thoroughly pervades our culture—the choices we make, the laws we adopt and discard, and the social practices that are polluted by its pestering ubiquity?"[15] Indeed, it seemed impossible for many to imagine that if those who were left stranded in the wake of Katrina had been white, the events that occurred before, during, and after the hurricane, as well as the narratives that attended it, would have been quite different.[16] The playwrights of *The Breach* directly intervene in the dominant narratives created by the media by prominently featuring the belief that the levees could have been bombed and explaining the historical framework and societal experiences from which these beliefs emerged.

Significantly, the play also draws attention to the experiences of those who were vulnerable before, during, and after the storm. New Orleans was a city in financial peril when Hurricane Katrina arrived. Cindi Katz notes:

> In late August 2005, for example, 27% of the population lived below the federal poverty level, the unemployment rate was over 10% citywide but 40% in certain neighborhoods such as the lower ninth ward, two-thirds of the city's public schools were labeled "failing," there was a single public hospital required to treat un- and under-insured patients, and the rickety racist legal system had produced instability and "demographic collapse" in poor black neighborhoods, to use Clyde Woods' compelling term.[17]

After Katrina, these issues were exacerbated and also taken advantage of, particularly by real estate developers who wanted to "clean up" after the storm by gentrifying and raising real estate values. As Katz observes, "In post–Katrina New Orleans (and long before it as well) it is possible to see all that is wrong with neoliberal capitalism as it works over a landscape of racialized and gendered class inequality, injustice, and enduring cronyism and corruption."[18] Indeed, over a decade after Hurricane Katrina, these issues have continued to create great inequities, including in determining who has been able to return to the city and rebuild their lives there. If a person or community of persons is financially or socially vulnerable *before* a natural disaster, it can only follow that these vulnerabilities increase during and after a disaster.

To be sure, natural disasters such as Hurricane Katrina are not experienced uniformly "because different social groups exhibit varying characteristics of vulnerability and resilience. Socially oriented disaster research demonstrates disparities by gender, ethnicity/race, class/income, disability and age, during both the impact and recovery phases of the disaster cycle."[19] During a crisis, one's ability to evacuate is impacted by one's access to a vehicle or public transportation. Further, the ability to take time off from work is more of a viable option for some than others. After a crisis, the financial resources needed to recuperate, particularly if one has damage to one's housing, is again not equal. One can presume that the family members portrayed in McCraney's plotline are included in this group of people that would find themselves vulnerable before and after Katrina.

In McCraney's plotline, Severance, Quan, and Pere Leon wait on their rooftop for help that we know will never arrive. In the time since he began working on *The Breach*, McCraney has made a career of writing about the black experience in the United States. As David Román suggests, "Unlike most of [the] new African American playwrights whose plays focus on the historical past, McCraney's plays take place in what he names 'the distant present.' McCraney's anachronistic phrasing of 'the distant present' forces us to consider when the contemporary moves from now to then."[20] Hurricane Katrina itself was an event that was immediate but also repeated historical traumas of the past, as we witness in the exchanges between Woman and Lynch. As Rodriguez notes, "Hurricane Katrina is being invoked as an exceptional episode in US history—as something already framed in the past tense," however, "the racial and racist violence that continues to unfold through this alleged natural disaster—a violence often apocalyptic in its form and staging—attests to the conspicuous normalcy of white supremacy to the everyday historical functioning of the United States."[21] The *unnatural* disaster of Hurricane Katrina, the man-made disaster, is one that the playwrights of *The Breach* attempt to highlight throughout the play.

In *The Breach*, Severance's sexual identity is never overtly revealed, and it is this ambiguity and the oblique confrontation that takes place between Pere Leon and Sev that creates the tension in the plotline. Quan, Sev's younger sister, tells the story of what happened on the rooftop that day. We learn early on that Pere Leon is frustrated if not angry with Severance for some unknown reason; he makes multiple references to the fact that Sev doesn't listen to him and that he will have to face the consequences for disobeying his grandfather. At one point, Pere slips off the rooftop into the toxic floodwaters, and Sev catches and saves him. Pere becomes more exhausted and more frantic as time progresses; he believes that Hurricane Katrina is the rapture and that Sev should be scared for his soul.[22] As he becomes more panicked, he insists that Sev go to the edge of the roof with him so that he can baptize him and save him from his sins. It is this reference to sinning that provides an indication that Sev may be gay. Another indication comes through references to Sev's friendship with a young man named Gideon. Pere refers to a conversation he overheard between Sev and Gideon and accuses them of "giggling like school girls." Quan seems to know the nature of their relationship when she tells the audience, "seem like Sev only happy when they together" (76). As is the case in the film *Moonlight* and McCraney's play *The Brothers Size*, Sev's sexuality is implied through his friendship with another boy/man—it is the happiness and bond shared between peers that conjure ideas about the characters's possible homosexuality.

Pere's devotion to the church and his references to sinning creates the implied conflict between his beliefs and Sev's implied sexuality. Pere's anxiety about Sev's sexuality also reflects religious leaders who declared the hurricane was itself a punishment for homosexuality. Some Christian leaders specifically targeted homosexuality as the cause of Katrina. Michael Marcavage, leader of the anti-homosexual group Repent America, pointed out that Katrina happened just before the annual Southern Decadence event, a six-day LGBTQ event that takes place every year during Labor Day weekend. Pastor Bill Shanks of New Orleans declared, "New Orleans now is Mardi Gras free. New Orleans now is free of Southern Decadence and the sodomites, the witchcraft workers, false religion—it's free of all of those things now."[23] The many hypocrisies of these assertions were highlighted when, after Hurricane Harvey (which impacted Houston and its surrounding area), these same religious leaders remained silent; a large number of Harvey's victims were conservative Trump supporters. Though Severance's sexuality isn't directly addressed in *The Breach*, the audience can sense these conflicts of identity in his interactions with Pere Leon who, like the religious leaders mentioned above, perhaps believed that homosexuality could be "responsible" for Hurricane Katrina. It is McCraney's subtlety in portraying characters and their relationships that makes the work so compelling.

McCraney's representation of homosexuality during the storm is significant because, although not addressed in the play, the LGBTQ community faces particular vulnerabilities during a disastrous event like Katrina. As Katrina took place in the South, amid discriminatory laws regarding the LGBTQ community, this impact was particularly pronounced. One of the ways in which Katrina's landfall had a notable impact on the LGBTQ community was in how Louisiana defined and recognized family. In New Orleans, where family is legally defined as an opposite-sex couple, those in same-sex relationships, for example, faced a harder time filing insurance claims and getting access to loved ones in hospitals. At times, because of this narrow definition of family, separation during evacuations occurred.[24] Dominey-Howes notes that, "Lesbians, bisexual women and queers of color (non-white LGBTI people), for example, were more vulnerable than most White middle-class gay men due to lower incomes, and also because the neighborhoods where they lived were subject to greater flooding. Transgender and intersex people, meanwhile, had difficulties in evacuation shelters, where their gender identity was questioned and they were harassed for using the 'wrong' bathroom."[25]

The LGBTQ community is often made invisible during disaster coverage, and coverage of Hurricane Katrina was no different. The vulnerabilities faced by this community were not given any particular attention by the media either due to downright ignorance or intentional neglect. As McKinnon, Gorman-Murray, and Dominey-Howes write, "Heteronormative reporting, which assumes the heterosexuality of both media subjects and readership, positions LGBTI lives as the absent or marginalized 'other.' . . . How then, if at all, do the media seek out non-heterosexual or non-cisgendered informants in stories where the significance of LGBTI issues is less obvious?"[26] They go on to add, "An absence of news media reports that highlight the specific needs of LGBTI populations may, therefore, mean that the broader public is unaware that these needs exist or may position the LGBTI community as an unknown 'other' that does not require consideration in the development of public policy."[27]

McCraney's focus on the queer, black, male experience, then, makes an important intervention in the narrative of Katrina. In a number of ways, a young, black male is already highly vulnerable, thus, to willingly identify as gay—an identity that can still subject one to any number of violences—could be to knowingly open oneself up to greater discrimination. Being gay in the South and being a young black gay male in the South poses its own unique set of challenges. As Sears, who did a study on the LGBTQ community in the South, explains, "[African American gay men] experienced isolation within their black communities, fewer opportunities to meet others who shared their gender and racial inheritance existed, and blacks confronted oppression from a variety of sources as they struggled with their multiple identities."[28] There are a number of contributing factors to the nuanced complications of being gay in the South: "In its unapologetic devotion to family, church, and state, the South most visibly reflects those fundamental values that represent the heartland of America and that are often associated with negative attitudes and feelings about homosexuality."[29] Although it is important to note the particular experience of being LGBTQ and a person of color in the South, Sears does suggest that the experience is different by degree, not by type.[30] In other words, the experiences faced by this community (racism, sexism, discrimination, police brutality) are not unique to the South but can sometimes and in some ways be more intense.

McCraney also uses the storm as a metaphor, creating space and time during which the truth can be exposed—perhaps without consequence or perhaps without concern for consequence—since the death of self or the world "as we know it" seems imminent. In his play *Marcus; Or the Secret of Sweet*, a storm also serves as the catalyst for the coming out of a young black man. Hurricane Katrina, of course, did indeed serve as an unwitting outing process for many queers in New Orleans. As Gary Richards writes:

> Katrina eradicated much individual agency when the hurricane concretized "the closet" and indiscriminately put on display for others—not only strangers, such as rescue workers, news crews, insurance inspectors, contractors, and curious tourists, but also family members and neighbors—thousands of individual caches of pornography, sex toys, and other sexual accouterments that had not been taken with evacuees.[31]

For a number of reasons, life and death situations such as Hurricane Katrina can lead to the voluntary or involuntary exposure of sexual identities once hidden and/or kept private. Severance does seem to be on the edge of either being "outed" by his grandfather or at least being confronted by his grandfather about his sexuality, since death appears so close for all of the characters in the play. For a young, black male who is also gay, as the play suggests Severance might be, there are countless vulnerabilities during a crisis such as Katrina. Although *The Breach* never directly addresses these issues, the presence of the young black gay male in McCraney's contribution to *The Breach* creates a disruption of assumed (heteronormative) identities within the narrative of Hurricane Katrina.

The impact and implications of *The Breach* varied greatly during its three productions, all of which I had the pleasure of viewing. The premiere took place at the Southern Repertory Theater (SRP), located in New Orleans's French Quarter in one of their temporary spaces after Katrina. The play was directed by Ryan Rilette and featured local actors and designers. Of course, the most obvious distinction of SRP's production was the fact that audience members, for the most part, did not require an "education" on the events of Hurricane Katrina. When I saw the production in 2007, it was clear to me that audience members were moved by the production because of the memories it invoked and the opportunities it afforded them to grieve, commiserate, and hold space with fellow community members who had gone through the traumatic event. For season ticket holders of the theater, coming to the play offered an opportunity to see familiar faces, something that was very important in the years immediately following Katrina. The content of the play sparked conversations between audience members who openly discussed their own experiences with Katrina (comparing notes with each other) and with me (they seemed eager to explain elements of their experience that I may not have garnered from the news or other sources). Throughout the play, I could hear audience members responding to the play with comments such as "Yes, that happened" or, "Oh, I know who they are talking about." Though written by three playwrights all from outside of the city, the playwrights's interviews and research resulted in a work that clearly struck a chord with those all too intimately familiar with the pain caused by the storm. Critical reception of the play by local journalists also echoed the sentiment that Filloux, McCraney, and Sutton had managed to capture an accurate sense of what it was like in the days and months after the weather event.

Seattle Repertory Theatre next produced *The Breach* in January 2008. Neither the production's director, David Esbjornson, nor any of its actors were from New Orleans. Esbjornson did not have performers use New Orleans accents and there did not appear to be an attempt to portray an "authentic" representation of New Orleans culture beyond what was written into the dialogue of the play. The physically striking Nike Imoru, who played the role of Water in Filloux's plotline, spoke with her own, undisguised British accent. Actor John Aylward, who is known for his success in Hollywood as well as his multiple roles at Seattle Rep, was recognized as a beloved Seattle resident. While audience members in New Orleans nodded their heads in acknowledgment and recognition of the rumors that the levees had been intentionally bombed, for audience members in Seattle this information varied from the "as seen on TV" version of Katrina.

Although the production itself was undeniably disconnected from New Orleans in terms of the director and actors, Seattle Rep, in a brilliant publicity move, invited New Orleans resident and author Chris Rose, who penned the bestseller *1 Dead in Attic: After Katrina*, to participate in multiple preshow events. Rose's celebrity status as one of the most well-known writers of post-Katrina literature brought Seattle residents to these events, where they had the opportunity to learn more about New Orleans and Hurricane Katrina and were encouraged to buy tickets to the production. Rose and all three playwrights spoke together at Elliot Bay Bookstore in Seattle, lending credibility to the playwrights' portrayal of Rose's beloved city, in spite of their status as outsiders. Rose's humorous and sometimes heartbreaking readings from his book reminded those at the events, many of whom would then be part of the play's audience, of the ongoing emotional toll of Katrina for residents of New Orleans. In a *Times-Picayune* article, Rose writes about his experience in Seattle:

> I was in Seattle. And, not long before my trip, that national poll came out showing that close to a third of Americans think New Orleans still is under water, so I guess I was prepared for my share of uninformed

inquiry. And I got just that, the now-predictable range of comments from New Orleans being unlivable and uninhabited to everything being honky-dory and up-and-running.[32]

Rose went on to say that the media would come to relegate its discussion about Katrina to a once-a-year memorial report, that art, theater included, will now be the "second wave of information" for those who did not experience Katrina in person.[33] In Seattle and New York, audience members were able, through talkbacks, to discuss some of the more contentious topics surrounding Hurricane Katrina and to ask panelists who were brought in as "experts" questions about New Orleans and Katrina.

The Public Theater did a free reading of *The Breach* in September of 2008 and also held a talkback with Nicole Bode, journalist, Robert Cary, vice president of the International Rescue Committee's Resettlement Department, and Lee Clarke, the author of *Worst Cases: Terror and Catastrophe in the Popular Imagination*. As was the case with the Seattle Repertory production, the performance in New York City and the talkback that accompanied it allowed audiences to go beyond what they might have learned about Hurricane Katrina on television.

Of the three productions, those in New Orleans and New York seemed the most successful in terms of countering the experience of watching events unfold in the media. At first, I believed that this might be the result of the play traveling out of the site of the original trauma, outside of New Orleans. But the New York reading seemed to reflect more what I experienced as an audience member in New Orleans. Though the New Orleans production was distinct in that it took place at the site of trauma, it did have a few important things in common with the production in New York that did not exist in Seattle, which may help us understand how empathy and compassion are created in the theater. In both cases, the size of the theater and audience was relatively small and the space felt intimate, whereas in Seattle the size of the house was significantly larger. The production budgets in New Orleans and New York were also small, compared to Seattle (the one in New York was quite minimal since it was a staged reading and not a full production). Whereas in Seattle the audience was drawn toward more elaborate stage and costume design, including a pool that held over six thousand gallons of water, in New Orleans and New York the staging and theater spaces focused the audience's attention on the words of the play. The spectacle of the performance in Seattle was similar in ways to the spectacle created by the media. The performances in New York and New Orleans, with their more intimate, "personal" approaches, contrasted with the experience of watching reports about Katrina on television.

Years after seeing these productions—and since Katrina's devastating landfall in August of 2005—hurricane seasons have progressively become worse and will, according to predictions, only become more devastating. The

United States is yet again facing the aftermath of a major storm, Hurricane Maria, which, like Katrina, seems to have been largely impacted by class and bigotry in regards to disaster response (or lack thereof). Much of Puerto Rico remained without electricity and clean water for months after Maria's landfall; the death toll fluctuates from the hundreds to the thousands. Just as the character of Woman points out to Lynch, the devastation in New Orleans, and now in Puerto Rico, not only comes from nature but from the neglect (and sometimes downright cruelty) of man. And just as we saw images of President George W. Bush flying over the devastation, rather than being on the ground engaging with the people effected by Hurricane Katrina (images that remain emblematic of what many feel was the gross negligence of the Bush administration), we witnessed Donald Trump fly to Puerto Rico and throw paper towels like "prizes" to the victims of Hurricane Maria. The parallels between these two storms are many. Watching the events of Hurricane Maria unfold on television, I couldn't help but feel haunted by *The Breach* as well as the thousands of victims of Hurricane Katrina and the Bush Administration.

The Breach is an important play in the canon of plays addressing disaster and trauma. The play could just as easily take place in Puerto Rico, post-Maria, with just a few changes in detail. Though the play is over a decade old, rather than fossilizing as a historical piece about one isolated event and one particular hurricane, it serves as a warning of sorts of what can happen if we as a society turn our back on those who are devastated by disaster. This is a warning that we still need to hear as a nation. It is unfortunate that the play has been rarely produced since 2008; its characters, and the lessons that come along with them, are still as relevant as ever. McCraney's particular focus on those who are the most vulnerable during and after a hurricane seems more urgent than ever. One can imagine in the days after Hurricane Maria a young queer person having a moment with a family member not unlike that of Sev and Pere Leon as they waited for help and faced their own mortality. Plays such as *The Breach* and plotlines such as McCraney's not only push beyond the narrative the media constructs about disasters but keep discussions going long after the media has turned towards the next inevitable devastating event—and that is something that remains critical as a response to major crises.

"Certainly No Clamor for a Kiss"

✦

When Black Men Touch

I. Augustus Durham

Moonlight; or, The Cinema of Sweet

My first impression of Tarell Alvin McCraney occurred in 2009 when I purchased tickets to *The Brother/Sister Plays*.[1] With the 2016 arrival of the screenplay he adapted with Barry Jenkins from his unpublished work "In Moonlight Black Boys Look Blue" to yield the award-winning film *Moonlight*, I have been a witness to how McCraney's oeuvre has an investment in synesthesia. Though these disparate works transition from an excised ear to a visual playground, his sensory attention is suggestive of a plethora of manners for charting blackness, cinematically and otherwise, as yet unseen, unheard, unsmelled, and undigested.

In an article for the *Los Angeles Times*, Tre'vell Anderson highlights this multimodal reading: "As *L.A. Times* critic Kenneth Turan said in his review, 'a film that manages to be both achingly familiar and unlike anything we've seen before'"; "'I [Jenkins] felt like the only way to do the translation and have it have the same power as Tarell's work onstage was to preserve his voice'"; "'The first time I [McCraney] saw it, I went through a pretty bad depression. The second time, I burst into tears midway through. It's hard. It's rough.'" While Anderson intimates that "the movie is quite literally his [McCraney's] life playing out onscreen . . . 'It's a palpable snapshot of memories and dreams that is difficult to sit through,'"[2] I opt to linger on that very palpability: What does *Moonlight* reflect regarding being as yet untouched?

When contemplating what work the haptic does in the film, it intrigues the viewer how certain iterations of touch between black men elicit unease, later metastasizing into pathologies of disease. People consenting to be touched, as reducible to a mode of "sickness" by onlookers, is the occasion when *we* undermine what Essex Hemphill dictates "[t]hey don't know[:] / we need each other / critically."[3] James H. Cone converges at this rhetorical juncture as a

precedent to Hemphill, leaving an affective trail for Essex to cross the Rubi-
con for his "American Wedding": "People who destroy physical bodies with
guns, whips, and napalm cannot know the power of physical love. Only those
who have been hurt can appreciate the warmth of love that proceeds when
persons touch, feel, and embrace each other." Situating this "warmth of love"
as symbolic of "the blues"—"openness to feeling and the emotions of physical
love"—and the "people" as white, Cone, in conversation with Hemphill, would,
to my mind, likely connote the prevailing distrust of touch as the event of theoretical miscegenation insomuch as the blues can be *diluted*.[4] By imposing this
(un)critical distance at the level of color-blocking, of camouflage, the prognosti-
cators of these diagnoses reveal the cause of our collective death. And yet, there
are some who, under "serious moonlight" and despite the gravity that "[w]hat is
called 'advanced civilization' / means we are all closer to death," are "still here
hanging on / refusing to be intimidated"[5] by their affinity for harmonies that
possess a sensation similar to another's caress—yes, this is the confirmation of
Hemphill as a prophet, and McCraney as the vision made plain.[6]

Seye Isikalu complements this sentience in his poem "monochrome":

> black male intimacy,
> a conspiracy,
> the africa they don't show you on TV.
>
> grey is the wonderland
> we've learned not to trek to.
> because displays of
> black male affection,
> are strategically met
> with seeds of suspicion,
> that sprout this myth that
> if black men are touching,
> it means we're either
> fighting or fucking.
> for us there is no grey.[7]

In abridgement, this poem incites sitting with what the gray sounds, looks, feels
like under *Moonlight*. I surmise that the manifold ways men touch in the film
address and extend two mutually exclusive interpretations of *sola scriptura*.
In the first instance, could the groundwork laid by Hortense J. Spillers entreat
us to look at the "maybe" of her grammar book? Reinterpreting her pertinent
formulation—"The African-American male has been touched, therefore, by the
mother, *handed* by her in ways that he cannot escape"—can the fascination
with black men's desire for and to touch provide a nascent interrogation which
exceeds her doubly: are contemporary modalities of black masculine affection
due to the act, or lack thereof, of the black male being touched, therefore, by

the *father, handed* by him in ways he receives encouragement to escape?[8] If maternal handing leads to new protocols, "a radically different text for female empowerment," does paternal handing induce possibilities for the palliative— actually *claiming* the intimacy (of a male with the potential to "care")?[9]

And secondarily, although gray is the wonderland we have been taught to steer clear of, if the consciousness to "go there" was on the table, the interlude between fighting and fucking might be a mediation postmodernly coined *friending*. A new word for a new world, digitized and overwhelmingly social, this term is a refined twist on a retrospective gesture: fellowship. That being, if a friend sticks closer than a brother, the messiness of being sticky with, stuck to, someone else is precisely what touching is or has the potential to be as shot in *Moonlight*, or adapted in screenplay form by McCraney and Jenkins. Believing that these arguments hold, I grasp for a protocol, cobbled together across variegations of disciplinarity, to register *Moonlight* as a sensorium; and to reify what my grandmother used to say to my siblings and me as we left her presence: "You be sweet now."

He Touched Me

An exposé on the "bro hug" for *CBS Sunday Morning* outlines the politics of endearment between men. In excess of what has been shared heretofore, an observation made then leads us down a path apropos to the current theme: "We have found that when men are very affectionate with their sons, their sons grow up to be comfortable with that."[10] Affect as a condition one becomes comfortable with allows us to enter *Moonlight* to reason through what happens when black men touch.

Early on, the characters Juan and Little/Chiron/Black have an encounter of which we, the viewers, may be totally unaware. In the opening scene— vertiginous in its own right when the camera circles Juan, his trapping employee Terrence, and the junkie Azu—as Juan walks back to his car, one sees boys running in and against the daylight and ponders: what color are they? At the front of the pack is Little, a child being chased by bullies in his peer group. Yelling epithets at him about his sexuality, the boys have found coloring: They are black. And white. For them, there is no gray. However, the viewer notes that Little, having escaped to a decrepit apartment complex, constructs a makeshift "closet" when he locks the door behind him to flee from the shoes and rocks and sticks that will eventually be thrown. In this space, he observes detritus— furniture, a crack vial, dirt—simultaneous to sitting down and exhaling. And then we hear a knock exterior to this insular dwelling. It is Juan.

This scene is otherworldly: "Out of the corner of his eye [Juan] sees a small boy, maybe 9 or 10, running from a gang of kids out to do him no good. On an impulse the dealer follows the boy and finds him hiding in an abandoned drug shooting gallery. Though Juan is friendly and nonthreatening, the boy does not respond. Suspicious, watchful, preternaturally quiet and withdrawn, he comes off like someone from a different planet. This is our protagonist . . . Little."[11] Alienated, one might say, the film's muse has a literal breakthrough: Juan trespasses on this closet in order to share the liminal location with the boy recently sprinting beneath the sunshine. Having entered through a window, Juan leaves through the door and keeps it open for Little. As this occurs, the big one says to the wee, "Come on now, can't be no worse out here."

In my estimation, this scaffolding riffs, through inversion, on Toni Morrison's *Beloved* when Paul D first encounters Sethe's house. While she compels him to "just step through," introducing him to the sadness he earlier conceived as evil, Juan flips those instructions, nudging Little to "come on . . . out here" because he will protect him, like Sethe does on the inside.[12] If Juan achieves this feat, one not only envisions him as a "father" to Little—"Yet an unspoken yearning has passed between Juan and Little, the need the latter has for a father and the former for a son, leading to an unconventional and quietly moving relationship that proves critical in the boy's emotional life"—but also applies some pressure, alongside Sharon P. Holland, to the making of "love," with "black" and "queer" in parentheticals.[13]

When addressing bell hooks's and Cornel West's confabulation of love and politics, Holland theorizes:

> If blackness is considered the non-redemptive partner in the two-sided coin that determines what is procreative relation and what is not, then how to approach an idea of love that can be considered transformative or generative for black being? In many ways, the very idea of black love is outside the transformative power of love itself. In their assessment, (black) love cannot be achieved without attention to the self . . . In theory, blackness, in all of its aesthetic might, has the power to mark, to make injury (to itself, to others), but it does not have the power to sustain, to create, or to participate in the world-making possibility that is love itself. This love, in hooks and West's formulation, is first and foremost, self-generating, rather than acquired through connection with another. For blackness, the very foundation of generative love proceeds from a sense that something in the self is broken and needs repair.[14]

One gleans that in order for love to rule, s/he must begin at the level of the self-reflexive. Blackness—marked and marking, injurious—only has the potential to be "transformative" or "generative" if reparation begins at home, "starts with you." But one also subtly hears that the hurdle of this endeavor is that it lets the world off the hook; which is to say, while some put faith in the world as a space for making possibility, that selfsame belief system often takes shape at the cost of forgetting the spaces the world has made possible thusly. Put another way, it brings a deep sense of melancholy when watching the film, and having grown up a little black boy, that, at a rather young age, the world creates a narrative of difference so arresting that one is awestruck at the language that comprises the juvenile lexicon. This is that hardness, that roughness. Sheltered by the abandoned building's walls, Little proves that hurled sticks and rocks and shoes are a mere pittance to the damage enacted by tongues. Breathing among minutiae, he does so because he has found respite and because he has been running for as long as his feet fit their limbs; he has been unable to breathe. Hence, when Juan beckons Little to come with him, to commune with him because the closet is no better than the outdoors, he boycotts that former logic to contend that for blackness, the very foundation of generative love proceeds from a sense that something in the *world* is broken and needs repair.

While we know that Juan is not Little's father, the exhibition of touched affection toward him is the breaking of a world broken. This is made real when they become one with the water:

> *Juan steadying himself, buttresses himself against the current as he reels Little in. The boy clings to him, gasping for air, spitting out salt water.*
> JUAN:
> Hey hey hey, I got you lil' man, I
> got you, *calmate, calmate.*
> *It's movie magic but they're a good ways out now, thirty, forty yards from shore.*
> *The water's not so deep out here, Juan standing. Little is far out beyond his height however, Juan supporting him, holding him out at arms length.*
> . . .
> *Juan going into a tread, very smooth, like someone raised in the water, born at its edge.*
> . . .
> *Little settling noticeably, gradually. It's a stretch but . . . looks passable, like maybe he could [swim] . . .*
> JUAN:
> Alright lil' man.
> I think you ready.
> *Little considering that, bobbing in the ocean as he treads. His eyes on the water stretching out before him, endless. Even in this dying light, stretching on forever.*
> *Meets Juan's gaze now. Finds compassion, hope there.*[15]

These notations suggest the plausibility of our haptic contentions. Little, clinging to Juan, wades out into the water as he steadies himself against this embodied buoy. Juan utilizes his tongue to reassure Little that he has him, that this stalwart calms in the midst of choppy conditions. That Spanish reinforcement rebuffs previous curses from puerile, Anglicized mouths.

The libretto declaims Jenkins's own excitement about what the film captures through cinematic (re)birth. The setting of this "movie magic" is not lost on McCraney, who also sounds the locative juxtaposition of whimsy and reality: "Liberty City is landlocked, and it's a strange place . . . It's one of those miracle places, where you can have storms walk towards you and you can walk across the street and not be in the storm anymore. Miami is *magical* in a way, but it also has quotidian crime in a dangerously impoverished inner city."[16] Liberty City epitomizes a *dvandva*; commingling freedom beside an incorporated spatiality signifies the unregulation of boundaries. Likewise, Jenkins and McCraney have lived separate yet equal lives, which qualify their collaboration itself as magical: "They grew up in Liberty City, blocks away from each other, with mothers under the influence. They went to the same elementary and middle schools at the same time and eventually became artists."[17] Liberty City, then, could be the southern extremity of places like West and East Egg, or Sweet Home.

This residential invocation, in combinatory imagination with the address for this cinema of sweet, brings us back to that thirty or forty yards from the filmic shore and implicates Morrison once more. The relationship of Juan with the water reminisces on the emergence of Beloved: "A fully dressed woman walked out of the water . . . Nobody saw her emerge or came accidentally by. If they had, chances are they would have hesitated before approaching her. Not because she was wet, or dozing or had what sounded like asthma, but because amid all that she was smiling . . . she sat down on the first handy place—a stump not far from the steps of 124."[18] Ostensibly produced from the water, Beloved could be the ancestor of Juan, "someone raised on the water, born on its edge." Her occupation of a stump as the unearthed extension of a tree's roots, satiated through subterranean waterways, is the landlocked mimicry of Juan, the lighthouse. He is beloved, born underwater (as one faintly hears the lyricism of "On & On").[19]

If *Beloved*'s eponymous character wants to be touched on the inside part and called by her name, could Juan's calling, his ministry, be to touch Little on the outside part in order to have his inside awakened, to have the little—the least of these—know that on this big, cruel orb he personifies the principle of IALAC, that "[t]he real tragedy is that it takes so little effort to help someone feel loveable and capable"?[20] This brings to mind Mahershala Ali, Oscar winner for his portrayal of Juan, as he offers a beatitudinal homily:

> I think what I've learned from working on *Moonlight* is we see what happens when you persecute people: they fold into themselves. And what I was so grateful about in having the opportunity to play Juan was playing a gentleman who saw a young man folding into himself as a result of the persecution of his community, and taking the opportunity to uplift him and tell him that he mattered and that he was ok and accept him. And I hope that we do a better job of that.[21]

The catalyst for the unfolding of Little as the counterintuition of his persecution, our beloved Juan calls him "Blessed." He also inculcates the blessed to love his flesh in order to portend his capability for lovability by another's flesh on the shores of a beach in his adolescence.[22] By having him bathe in the very amniotic fluid that gives him his cinematic life, Juan completes a gestational period for Little to be born again, and then again under pubescent moonlight. Hypothetically, McCraney and Jenkins invert Morrison a third time.

When Sethe viewed Beloved, her "bladder filled to capacity . . . and the water she voided was *endless*. Like a horse, she thought, but as it went on and on she thought, No, more like flooding the boat when Denver was born . . . to see her squatting in front of her own privy making a mudhole too deep to be witnessed without shame."[23] The excesses of water in these narrative accounts centralize birthing conduits with differing amniocenteses. While a test of this kind chronicles the wellbeing of a fetus, the child has already been born on both occasions, proposing the afterlife of containment. All the more, if the parents in these sagas present an analogy, Sethe voids as Juan immerses. One excretes as the other enters. As for the analogous children, "the stranger," Beloved, "drink[s] cup after cup of water" as Little learns how to tread water, presumably for the first time.[24] One swallows as the other swims. Both *Beloved* and *Moonlight* summarize these proximities to water as "endless": the shameful and the salvific.

All of this implies the haptic jump with which these screenwriters preoccupy themselves: instead of giving us an archetype of touch, they teach us a prototype for *how* to touch, and what the stakes of that affective move are in an overarching cinematic and realized lifetime. One departs from the formerly comic yet quizzical filmic inquiry—"you ever dance with the devil in the pale moonlight?"—to arrive at a new query that is undoubtedly old hat: you ever entertain angels unawares under a blackened sky?[25]

It does not seem coincidental that Juan, Spanish for "John," becomes the Baptist. One free-associates that, similar to a baptism some millennia prior, as Little floats on the water, the baptized sees the heavens splitting apart with the Spirit descending on him like a sunbeam. Akin to Beloved's smile, Juan's laughter, a delight in Little's ability to swim—to survive the vicissitudes of life's waves, or a storm in peripatetic personification—is like a voice from heaven saying, "You are my dearly loved Son, and you bring me great joy."[26] What also manufactures joy is the world Juan makes for Little within that broken space. The scene is revelatory in part because when they are on the beach, no one else is apparently there. Upon entering and exiting the water, Juan and Little occupy a residence which only invites those who look the part: black males who look blue in the moonlight, hurt people who can appreciate the warmth of love when bodies touch, a black Cuban whose "son" thinks his name is "Azul" (a signpost that, up to this scene in the film, Juan has not told Little his name).

The unseen being seen by the unnamed, and obliging the potential to "name" in return, is reminiscent of Howard Thurman who dedicates his autobiography,

With Head and Heart, to "the stranger in the railroad station in Daytona Beach who restored my broken dream sixty-five years ago." That stranger was a man who saw Thurman on his way to school in Jacksonville; unable to get his trunk, "with no lock and no handles, roped . . . securely," checked because of regulatory stipulations, Thurman cries his heart out because he does not have enough money to have his luggage sent express. A "black man, dressed in overalls and a denim cap" sees him and states, "'If you're trying to get out of this damn town to get an education, the least I can do is to help you. Come with me.'" He details, "Then he took out his rawhide money bag and counted the money out. When the agent handed him the receipt, he handed it to me. Then, without a word, he turned and disappeared down the railroad track. I never saw him again."[27] James Baldwin fictionally aligns with this feeling when Leo Proudhammer gets lost on the subway in *Tell Me How Long the Train's Been Gone*:

> The first time I realized this [that colored people disappeared past a certain point on the train ride], I panicked and got lost . . . and got on another train only because I saw a black man on it . . . He was my salvation and he stood there in the unapproachable and frightening form that salvation so often takes . . . I almost said that I didn't have any [parents] because I liked his face and his voice and was half hoping to hear him say that *he* didn't have any little boy and would just as soon take a chance on me . . . I never saw that man again but I made up stories in my head about him, I dreamed about him.[28]

This man, Charles, who tells the wandering boy to call him "Uncle," equally inserts himself into a long tradition of men touching, literally and figuratively, black boys in states of peril. Whether named Little or Howard or Leo, these "sons" are the beneficiaries of haptic incantations that enable their future quests to be touched. These touching "fathers" bequeath to their heirs the belief that no matter the circumstances—invisible, lachrymose, far from home—they are touchable and worthy of said affection.

This is the something that happens and now we know that when touched, somebody, anybody, can be made whole.

(What I Did Do to Be So) Black and Blue; or, Take Me to the Water

But what of this clamor?

The subtlety of *Moonlight,* in both the film and the screenplay, is that what one might render as "clamor" is simultaneously the compassionate and the covert at play. This filmic triangulation undoes what the screen often conveys regarding blackness because it transforms the spectacular into the simplistic, the usually unknown into the exceedingly everyday.[29] With that in mind, I aim to trouble the clamorous in that it is not solely limited to the sonic; it, too, takes on a multivalent posture, even at the level of embrace.

In her essay "Home," Morrison purports that the phrase "Certainly no clamor for a kiss," the penultimate sentence in *Beloved*, evokes a still-lingering consternation about its final word:

> I am still unhappy about it because "kiss" works at a level a bit too shallow. It searches for and locates a quality or element of the novel that was not, and is not, its primary feature. The driving force of the narrative is not love, or the fulfillment of physical desire. The action is driven by necessity, something that precedes love, follows love, informs love, shapes it, and to which love is subservient. In this case *the necessity was for connection*, acknowledgment, a paying-out homage still due. "Kiss" clouds that point.[30]

In considering what *Moonlight* relays, what is put into relief is a form of sweetness as a window into the synonym for "kiss." Nonetheless, what convicts me, and the viewer, of one's residency in the black and the blue is the circumvention of Louis Armstrong's last verse: what I did do to be hued in this way was try to get a friend.[31]

While the sight of these blemishes, psychic and corporeal, is often symptomatic of being embattled, the "necessity . . . for connection" reinscribes the epidermal markings no longer as flesh wounds but as a haptic registry for someone who is tender skinned, one who "bruises" easily, even under the guise of being touched carefully. One is a carrier of beauty marks, of love handles. Speaking about Baldwin bestowing upon her "a language to dwell in, a gift so perfect it seems [her] own invention," Morrison, and her needful connectivity, is indeed a prosaic remnant reinvented: "some moments teach one the price of the human connection: if one can live with one's own pain, then one respects the pain of others, and so, briefly, but transcendentally, we can release each other from pain."[32] Furthering the aforementioned Cone, this clamor is certainly not one. Being one's connection—a hold, a kiss—is like being under the influence because, as its own stimulant, touch is a sentiment that not only indexes mutual respect, a transaction pained yet painless, but also complicates the yen for a re-up in the healthiest of ways because the next rush can outdo the first.

McCraney himself picks up on this blue-black twinship: "It's probably under the moonlight that we see black boys *can* be blue, *can* be sad and sullen and intimate . . . It's under starlight that we see them differently, or that we get the chance to. Because we rarely see ourselves in those hues or under that gauze. We see ourselves in the harsh police light or the amber of street lights, but what is it when the reflection of the sun in the moon is sitting on these bodies. What beauty can we see?"[33] One accedes to McCraney by testifying to the sad and the sullen and the intimate here: in the movement following "Little,"

Chiron is black, and blue, just as he traffics in the gray. Having engaged in ecstasy with a friend under moonlight, the forthcoming terror is unforeseeable to the point of seeming randomness. The same could be said, or not, about his reaction—everyone has a breaking point, regardless of whether that breaking includes a chair meeting the back of someone's head. But I digress.

When we get to "Black" in the aftermath of this, he is at his bluest, partly because of his incarceration and separation from the outside world ("the harsh police light"), and partly because he has become a haptic fiend. Therefore, subsequent to watching Black reacquaint himself with Kevin and digesting a meal concocted at the hands of his long-lost fixer, the viewer cleanses his palate for the oncoming synesthetic dessert:

> *Black smiling as Kevin's eyes alight with this little ditty. Kevin rises, heads over to the small kitchen—running water.*
> *He toggles a small radio. The SOUND of Kevin rotating through the dial, finally landing on a station, late night R&B, like DeBarge's* All This Love.
> . . .
> *Black fixes him in his sights, more directly than before:*
> BLACK:
> You're the only man who's ever
> touched me.
> *The air going out of Kevin's chest, his gaze fixated on Black's lips, antici-pating the words falling from there:*
> BLACK:
> The only one.
> . . .
> BLACK:
> I haven't really touched anyone,
> since.
> *INT. KEVIN'S APARTMENT, BEDROOM—NIGHT*
> *Black sitting at the foot of the bed, fully clothed, hands clasped between his knees, leaned over slightly.*
> *Kevin standing before him, frozen.*
> . . .
> *Black stands shakily. Kevin watches him as he closes the space between them, drawing right up to him. Kevin takes a hand and lays it flat against Black's chest.*
> *A puzzled look coming over Kevin's face.*
> KEVIN:
> You shakin'.
> BLACK:
> Yeah.
> KEVIN:
> Wait.

Kevin crosses the doorway, flips a switch:
TOTAL DARKNESS
. . . only the soft thudding of feet crossing the floor.
Another beat, then, under darkness:
BLACK:
I'm shakin'.
KEVIN:
Yeah.
BLACK:
I'm still shakin'.
KEVIN:
Yeah.[34]

The lines of text and blocking directions assuredly differ from the onscreen performances; nevertheless, the insights gained from these scripted moments divulge something about darkness and moonlight that brings clarity to what McCraney, and Jenkins, is up to here.

According to physics, there are three reasons why "black boys, like everyone and everything else, look blue" in moonlight: "(1) moonlight steals color from whatever it touches, (2) if you stare at the gray landscape long enough, it turns blue, and (3) moonlight won't let you read."[35] The staging of this scene in the screenplay, and the film for that matter, is interesting because although the characters are inside, specifically Kevin's apartment, one senses that, like the baptism and the pleasure on the beach, the lunar looms over these in-house machinations and affects how love is expressed. In the confines of this domicile, channeling a "gray landscape" as "[t]hey hold each other's eyes in an interminable beat,"[36] Black and Kevin frolic in an ocular wonderland to which they have learned to trek. But seeing this "gray" allows us to discern it in turn, inasmuch as we subvert a page from *In the Red and Brown Water* and reattach the severed organ to hear McCraney's offering.

Jared Sexton describes Black as "a figure of wonder than of identification or desire. His experiences of contact . . . and his relations of connection . . . all seem to unfold without intimacy, rather than in its pursuit or preservation . . . His relative silence . . . is most nearly what defines his personae across the radical metamorphosis in physical appearance . . . And in that silence his mind seems absorbed not so much in longing or reflection as in mystery."[37] On the one hand, this reading is apposite to what one watches on the screen; barring the scene with his mother in the third act, Black is the quintessence of pensiveness. Held glares (the diner scene), self-deprecation (the car scene), and hesitance (Kevin's kitchen scene) manifest this behavioral stance. On the other hand, the script divorces us from this recent assessment because our protagonist must be cajoled to express what he feels. The musical nod to DeBarge points to the choruses unspoken: Black, in silence, as the radio toggles to an R&B station playing something like that sonorous mood, speaks to Kevin through telepathy, imbuing him with the notion that *all this love is waiting for you*, that *oooooooooooooo I like it*. This precedes the admission that he has only ever chosen to be touched by him. At the same time, notice how the former object becomes an immediate subject through superimposition: "*You* are the only man who's ever touched me"; "*I* haven't really touched anyone, since." Kevin's touch, in genealogical step with Juan's haptic sense under altogether different circumstances, engenders Black to want to touch others, even if he cannot recapture the restrained freedom he experienced on a beach in Liberty City. Is this not identification? Desire?

In a musicological frame, DeBarge becomes Beethovenian in that it conjures *Moonlight Sonata*, or propounds the Mozartean as *Eine kleine Nachtmusik*; the title track of *All This Love* as *quasi una fantasia* plays upon one's comprehension of "the reprise."[38] The tautology of "Say you really love me, baby / Say you really love me, darlin' / 'Cause I really love you, baby / Oh, I really love you, darlin'" fades out when listening to the record.[39] Thus, even if the track stops, a decision of phonographic unfreedom, the repetition continues for eternity, no different than how, when standing at the seashore, one sees forever. Perhaps this is why the film takes us (back) to the water, just as one prepares now to account for how none but the righteous shall see the divine.

If the necessity for one another is critical to our survival, the subtext certain sects of culture would apply to this textual/filmic reprisal of the moonlit beach scene is that black men are not supposed to crave touch, let alone from each other, because it is not "manly."[40] But I assert that despite the dominant strictures of limitation, said negative designation is itself freeing. Borrowing from Alice Walker vis-à-vis her "Womanist" definition, the mannish is to the manly as moonlight is to darkness, with a full understanding that the reflection of the sun in the moon is the changing same at the rising and setting of the solar.[41] Transitioning to Kevin's "BEDROOM—NIGHT," Black is indeed desirous because he, fully clothed, introduces the bed as a setting and provokes contact again, "drawing right up to [Kevin]." And when they converse as Black exhibits fear and trembling, shaking in the presence of Kevin, they imaginatively orate in mannish tongues.[42] The prospect of touch between black men, and this occurrence being touching, as in moving, signals that one prefers not to be swayed by this film as solely "a '*queer* love story' or a well-done '*black* movie.'"[43] Either characterization reduces the work of *Moonlight*: the latter suggestion adds "color" to the ongoing "dialogue," while the former categorization "clouds the point" because "[t]he root of this word, as Americans use it—or, as this word uses Americans—simply involves a terror of any human touch, since any human touch can change you."[44]

This rhetorical line occasions its own parabolic reinvention:

All that you touch
You Change.
All that you Change

Changes you.
The only lasting truth
Is Change.
God
Is Change.[45]

Mathematically, these platitudes represent the transitive property:

If a = b and b = c, then a = c.

That said, God is You is Change is touch, and in this final scene, God's name is Kevin as he entertains/touches/changes an angel named Little/Chiron/Black. The calculation to turn off the lights and bask in the darkness is twofold: Kevin convenes an act of privacy in the cause of debunking the presumption of privation, especially for those who deem black men touching as an exemplary act which illumines the ostensibly depr(a)(i)ved. Also, the godhead stages creation reversed as he determines, "Let there be dark," and there is dark. We see that the dark is good.

But seeing in that obscurity returns us to the Walker-inflected analogy because, via physics, the textual scene creates an optical illusion: "Though we noted earlier that moonlight does not allow us to read, in general, there is one final 'caveat lunar' from the good scientists that seems relevant at this late hour: 'Some people can read by moonlight' . . . 'These people have 'moonvision.'"[46] We are put upon to mannishly peruse, moonvisualize, the dark for "the sound of bodies touching, the beginning of things, then . . . another sound rising—from afar—the sound of waves crashing, rushing onto shore. And mingling with that rush of waves, the sound of lips and hands, the joining of bodies, somewhere in this darkness" as two friends relearn one another, with a cut to the ocean—the beginning of the beginning where a begotten "son" first learns that he is LAC (lovable and capable) and that his "father" is elated about it.[47] Kevin and Black, translucent in the dark, glow a shade of indigo. I imagine they appear blue-black, as in the scene in the opening of *Belly*, or Lauryn Hill in the music video for "Ex-Factor."

If all of this reveals what happens when black men touch, the (not so) clamorous clamor, maybe what I am trying to say in miniature is: Ali is onto something when he posits that the prequel to *Moonlight* is a film called *Sunlight* . . .[48]

Part 2

✦

Brothers, Sisters, and the Gods among Us

Scenes of Vulnerability

✦

Desire, Historical Secrecy, and Black Queer Experience in *Marcus; Or the Secret of Sweet*

GerShun Avilez

In his 1984 poem "Serious Moonlight," Essex Hemphill details the multiple challenges that Black gay men face by presenting a speaker with a series of concerns, from love affairs and thinning hair to "man-made" diseases and unexpected aggression on the street.[1] The speaker is so overwhelmed by this unending series of pressures that the poem ends with a scene of confusion; in the final lines, love and sexual violence are muddled together. The speaker explains that he has no concerns about being lonely because his next love might surprise him unexpectedly and rape him at any time.[2] In this context, the vicissitudes of Black gay life produce a conflation of feelings and an uncertainty about the safety of the social world. The result of this lived experience is a kind of disorientation, which produces the "peculiar loneliness" referenced early in the third line of the poem. The poem describes the speaker's difficult encounters, but it also confounds readers by challenging them to make sense of love through the frame of rape. "Serious Moonlight" documents for readers the unpredictability of existing as a Black gay man in the 1980s. The recurrence of conflict and the constant state of worry presented in the poem create a structure of experience that can be so confusing—and so lonely— that love and rape can be linked.

Hemphill was part of a generation of Black gay artists in the 1980s that were consciously incorporating issues around queer sexual identity into the realm of African American literary culture.[3] The work of some of these artists appeared in Joseph Beam's groundbreaking edited collection, *In the Life: A Black Gay Anthology*.[4] In this volume, writers such as Hemphill, Beam, Assotto Saint, Melvin Dixon, Donald Woods, and Samuel Delany describe the realities of Black gay existence in multiple art forms. This project of documenting queerness is an increasingly important element of the Black social imaginary. Contemporary playwright Tarell Alvin McCraney builds on the work of artists such as Hemphill by rooting his drama in questions of Black queer sexuality and by showing how uncertainty and confusion are valuable methods for representing the trajectory of queer existence.[5] In many ways, his 2010 play *Marcus; Or the Secret of Sweet* is an outgrowth of works such as "Serious Moonlight" that articulate through art the defining challenges and opportunities of Black queer life.[6]

In this essay, I argue that McCraney imagines Black queer experience historically as a constant negotiation of serial loss, but his drama divulges the power of intimacy to defy loneliness and vulnerability—even if briefly. The play is about a Black gay man who is coming to terms with his identity and his place in his community.[7] In this text, McCraney explores the dilemmas that can define queer existence and the difficulty of having non-normative desire. Because of social pressures, the protagonist Marcus Eshu feels isolated socially, and because he knows very little about anyone who has had same-sex desire, he also feels isolated historically.[8] This dual isolation produces states of confusion, frustration, and disorientation for the protagonist; like Hemphill's speaker, he, too, worries. However, McCraney offers his protagonist two kinds of connection to deal with his concerns and offset his loneliness: same-sex intimacy and a link to a queer past. Relationships to other men, living and dead, appear to ground Marcus and provide satisfaction, but none is able to stave off loss or protect him fully.

Throughout this essay, I do not discuss *Marcus*'s many staged performances or its production history. I consider McCraney's dramaturgy and emphasize how the play as a written document extends the work of earlier writers such as Hemphill and offers a theorizing of Black queer existence as negotiated loss. I offer close readings of the play's literary construction and situate the text within theoretical discussions of queer experience to make these points about identity, loss, and desire. In the first section of this essay, I show how same-sex desire is understood through the lens of social vulnerability and detail how McCraney presents secrecy as an essential strategy that connects Black individuals with same-sex desire across time. The second section tracks how the play uses embodied encounters to explore how same-sex desire inter-penetrates vulnerability, checking its ability to define queer life completely. Ultimately, I show that queer desire in McCraney's text—even as it introduces problems for characters—emerges as a tool that can undo alienation, work against feelings of powerlessness, and bridge the past and present.

The Secret Meaning of Sweetness

The full title of the play, *Marcus; Or the Secret of Sweet*, connects the lead character to secrecy and "sweetness" and, in doing so, conveys the challenges of a nonnormative life. Marcus's secrecy derives from his discomfort with his sexual orientation and his need for a language to express both his desire and sense of self. The language used throughout the play to describe queer sexuality is "sweet," and the references to "sweet" in the play's title and characters' dialogue reflect the practice of calling queer men and young men with non-normative gender identities "sweet," especially by Black communities in the U.S. South.[9] McCraney employs this figurative language extensively to indicate the dearth of options for talking about same-sex desire in the world of San Pere, Louisiana, the fictional setting of the play. Even as he seeks to keep hidden his sexual identity, Marcus wants a more effective way of expressing his desire, and this search for language is also a search for history. In his attempt to get information about his father, Legba, and later about the character Oshoosi, his father's male lover, Marcus is looking for a connection to the past, a connection with a forebear who also had same-sex desire. The pursuit of knowledge about his father and the nature of his romantic feelings represent Marcus's wish to historicize himself. He wants to prove that there have been others like him that existed before his time so that he can place himself in a lineage. He does not simply desire paternity or the emblematic name of the father; he seeks a queer origin to make sense of his disordered contemporary life. He is looking for a foundation or history for his present.

The actual "secret of sweet" concerns Black queer vulnerability, and most characters connect Marcus to sweetness, implicitly commenting on both the direction of his desire and his state of being. His friend Shaunta Iyun questions him, bluntly asking, "Are you sweet, Marcus Eshu?"[10] This indelicate question demands an explanation of Marcus's identity and desire, but it also has implications about his relationships and future. Her words literally stop him in his tracks and make him take a step back; the stage directions read, "Marcus stung, steps back."[11] Her interrogation forcefully redirects his body. The question is likened to a physical attack or assault that overwhelms him. Shaunta's demand for knowledge is a request that Marcus out himself, or publicly identify his sexual preference.[12] However, the question itself is really rhetorical because she is already convinced that he is sweet. His reaction to the question reminds the reader or audience of his social vulnerability as a sweet man: a mere question can make him feel assaulted or endangered even in the company of a friend. For Marcus, being out could mean sacrificing friends and family and surrendering his physical safety—the exact social pressures that create the space of the closet.[13] The taunts of other young men hurled at the protagonist suggest that his safety could be in peril. To be bullied and called sweet is one thing; to proclaim yourself as sweet is something else altogether. Historically, gay and lesbian visibility has been a trope of social advancement for the community, but such visibility has also made individuals vulnerable. Both John D'Emilio and Christina Hanhardt discuss this paradox of visibility in regard to gay and lesbian history and politics.[14] Each explains how claims to political visibility are necessary for social advancement, but such claims also inevitably endanger the lives of many individuals.

However, McCraney points to a different paradox that moves beyond claims of political visibility through his trope of sweetness. As Shaunta's question suggests, Marcus gets read as sweet, meaning that, to some, he is socially legible as sweet. His sweetness is tantamount to an open secret, one that is widely known or suspected but officially unknown or unproven. Marcus feels compelled to keep his sweet feelings secret or hidden, but his sweetness makes him visible. McCraney's character is caught in this liminal space between the known and unknown, a space that makes him susceptible to suspicion and ultimately aggression. McCraney's investment in secrecy represents an exploration of this tension between queer visibility and vulnerability.

McCraney pairs Marcus's physical movement backward on stage with a narrative turn to the past. Rather than responding to Shaunta's tactless query, Marcus wonders aloud what the origin of "sweet" is to describe a person. In response to his historical consideration, Shaunta presents a specific circuit of queer desire that she recovers from obscurity to offer a basis for sweetness. She conjures and details an invented scene in which two enslaved male lovers have stolen away from work to be together under the cover of night. In the tale, the clandestine intimacy is discovered by the master of the plantation because another enslaved person betrayed their dalliance.[15] As a punishment, the master tied them up together in front of everyone and beat them until they bled. However, the punishment does not end there. Shaunta recounts:

When the wounds right he [the master] run down get some sugar
Prolly pour it on so it sting not as bad as salt but it get sticky
Melt in the stinging Southern sun. Sweetness draw all the
Bugs and infection to the sores . . . Sweetness harder to wash.
It Become molasses in all that heat and blood and . . .[16]

In this spectacle of violence, the two male lovers are made to embody sweetness literally, and their saccharine punishment is set as the basis for calling queer men "sweet" in McCraney's imagining.

The reference of sugar in Shaunta's recounting is significant because it highlights how the men and their desires are inextricable from the web of capitalist production.[17] The use of sugar to torture them means that the very product of their labor becomes the vehicle for punishment. More important, the combining of the sugar with their injured flesh produces a *crimson* molasses. Even in death, these bodies are made commodities, and the Black body remains a mechanism for production. The punitive action conflates queer desire with the destructive and painstaking work of cultivating and producing sugar. The two lovers become visual emblems of a number of negative feelings associated with their burdensome labor: frustration, exhaustion, deprivation, pain, and betrayal. Their bodies get read through these affective lenses and through the frame of sugar.[18] In other words, sweetness has to do with how bodies are read, and this is precisely what sweetness registers vis-à-vis Marcus: not how he is identifying himself, but rather how his body and actions get deciphered and coded by people in his community. To have same-sex desire, then, is to carry symbolically in one's flesh a history of violence.

In explaining this brutal origin of sweetness, Shaunta presents a scene that reminds the audience of the transhistorical vulnerability of nonnormative individuals—even as her own actions create an experience of discomfort for her friend. She defines sweetness as deriving from an enslavement-era punishment for same-sex desire. Through her character, McCraney calls up the history of enslavement as an origin narrative but with a queer difference. In the reenactment, such desire is unacceptable because it works against enslavement's defining investment in reproduction. Because it is non(re)productive, this desire is equivalent to rebelling or running away. This account of sweetness alludes to enslavement's biopolitical character, or its role in managing the life and death of enforced laborers.[19] Shaunta's words compel her friend and the audience to do the work of reconstructing the past alongside her; she turns to speculation in place of the historical record.[20] Enacting this scene means resuscitating queer experience, which entails chronicling queer desire and proffering an account of the past based upon folk knowledge and supposition rather than recorded facts. Shaunta makes sense of her friend's secrecy by arguing for the historical necessity of concealing identity and relations since the period of enslavement. She historicizes Marcus's actions and life. In divulging the secret of sweet through a historical interpretation, she connects the present of her friend with the past of those she presumes are like him.

The historical reimagining that occurs in the scene mimics the cultural work done by neo-slave narratives. McCraney's play is not a neo-slave narrative, but Shaunta's account reflects the defining features of that genre of texts. Ashraf Rushdy explains that one of the genre's central characteristics is "replicating the acts of fugitive slaves who had originally written slave narratives in order to assert the authority of their experience"; they represent literary acts of "recuperation."[21] The enslaved lovers in Shaunta's account are not fugitives per se, but they do express what can be called "fugitive desire" in that it exceeds normative boundaries in being non(re)productive intimacy. Shaunta's scene recuperates the lovers and this desire from obscurity. Rushdy adds that the writers of neo-slave narratives "wished to return to the literary form in which African American subjects had first expressed their political subjectivity in order to mark the moment of a newly emergent black political subject."[22] These writers inhabit the slave narrative to signal the surfacing of a radical Black identity. Using a counterintuitive method, they turn to the past and an older form to articulate the new. By mimicking the key generic components of the neo-slave narrative in Shaunta's monologue, McCraney takes something that is often unfamiliar—a Black queer past—and presents it through a framework that has become recognizable within the Black historic imaginary: fugitivity.[23]

This interest in the queer subject over time and the idea of a Black queer past arguably make *Marcus* an example of what critic Matt Richardson calls "expansive historiographic" literature.[24] Richardson uses this term to describe texts that

> comment on and re-imagine the past, but without concern for historical verisimilitude. . . . They simultaneously offer reverence toward history and push back against it through rebellious narratives that insist on interfering in the familiar heterosexual and normatively gendered story of the past, creating anachronism by centering queers who "don't belong" in the historical narrative as they are currently known.[25]

These pieces of literature take up the work of historical fiction without being wedded to that which is assumed to be true or accurate. Richardson describes artistic responses to the incomplete nature of the historical record; these texts seek to validate counterhistories in place of actual recorded histories, which often erase or exclude queer subjects. The question of proof matters less than thinking through what might have been: a utopian maroon community, an undocumented insurgency, or even an illicit same-sex kiss. These literary acts of speculation are the result of the desire for historical knowledge coupled with a dissatisfaction or frustration with the historical record as it stands. This opposition is at the heart of McCraney's play. *Marcus*, like other expansive historiographic texts, cannot alter official accounts of earlier periods, but it can and does ask us to rethink what is assumed to be the truth of the past and how we write about it.

Narratives of the enslaved, these accounts of the past, do reference sexuality and nonnormative desire, as Aliyyah Abdur-Rahman attests.[26] However, these texts often use oblique references or cloak events in silence to push against the exhibitionist and spectacular nature of the barbaric institution. Neo-slave narratives tend to offer more detailed considerations of sexuality, especially sexual violation, to showcase the immoral and violent nature of enslavement. McCraney's scene of the two lovers in Shaunta's monologue not only links the violence of enslavement to Black sexual expression, but it carefully considers the experience of enslaved men with same-sex desire. Marcus does not encounter the intense brutality the two men do, but McCraney conceptually connects through diction these men to Marcus: the "sting" of the sugar in the lovers' wounds resonates with the pain and humiliation ("Marcus stung") that Marcus feels at the asking of Shaunta's question. Though the degrees of violence and the contexts are different, Marcus and the two male figures all experience vulnerability at the exposure of their sexual desire. The play offers a detailing of the particular vulnerability of the sweet subject throughout time. In the section that follows, I show how McCraney handles the question of history by staging this vulnerability as queer uncertainty and disorientation through physical interactions between male characters, offering an experimental formal strategy for redefining the social meanings of intimacy.

The Power and Parameters of Desire

One of the most compelling features of the play is that it does not rely on narrative treatments of the past—such as Shaunta's account—alone. In *Marcus*, connections to the past occur through bodily, romantic encounters. It is important to note that a performative text enables a different kind of theorizing of the historiographical endeavor: the staging of a past encounter is offered instead of a mere description of one. The experimental dramatic structure of the play sheds light on the significance of the bodily encounters. McCraney punctuates the play with seven short scenes or interval sequences that interrupt the action of specific scenes, provide insight into the protagonist's state of mind, and mark the transition between scenes. The interval sequences are titled, "Prologue: A Dream," "A Day Dream," "A Mirage," "Spirit in the Dark," "A Vision on the Waters," "A Dream of Drag," and "A Re-Collection." The intervals collapse temporal divisions and unite chronologically-separate events and individuals. This temporal collapse yields disorientation for the characters (and arguably the audience). Collectively, they set up and provide meaning for the intimate encounters that Marcus will have, and they illuminate the forces that introduce difficulties into his life.

The interval "A Day Dream," which appears at the end of act 1, scene 3, shows how McCraney uses these dramatic elements to manage Marcus's desire. It opens with Marcus thinking to himself, "Ever had so much on your mind you forget what / You wanted to think about? / That's when it's dangerous / Your mind starts playing on those / Things you want least to wander."[27] From these thoughts, the interval proceeds to recreate or remember an experience Marcus had in school when other young men are trying to get his attention because they want answers to the test. Then the course of action pivots when Marcus admits that he wishes that they were asking for his body and not his exam answers: "Move your hand" (away from your paper) becomes "Let me come over," "Let me step closer."[28] His desire interrupts and redirects this recollection of the past. What initially appears as a memory transforms into a fantasy within the interval. The past surfaces only to be altered as sexual desire emerges. Through desire, Marcus enacts on stage a history that never was. The intervals work in this way: they put the audience in Marcus's mind, showing his thoughts and fantasies and allowing him to blur the lines between fantasy and reality, past and present. His desire, which he often must keep under control to protect himself, can find an outlet in a moment like this daydream. There is an almost seamless movement from remembered, frustrating experience to a delightful, speculative fantasy.

The interval sequences that interrupt and bracket the play can be read as dramatic manifestations of Saidiya Hartman's concept of the temporal interval. In her discussion of the relationship of historical trauma to present and future injury, Hartman argues, "in the space of the interval, between too late and too early, between the no longer and the not yet, our lives are coeval with [historical figures] in the as-yet-incomplete project of freedom."[29] She describes a space of temporal uncertainty, one that features the collapsing of time constraints as we know them. By ignoring the traditional restrictions of temporal boundaries—the fact that the past and present are different moments—we can read across time and forge connections between chronologically separate events and individuals. By letting go of accepted historical understandings, we can formulate innovative conceptions of the assumed relationship between the past and the present. The impossible can happen within the interval: the inaccessible past and our present can interface. Hartman goes on to explain how two goals can be achieved in this space: "attending to and recruiting the past for the sake of the living" and "interrogating the production of our knowledge of the past."[30] Because historical knowledge can be out of reach, we might have to create it for the sake of the present and consider carefully the process by which we perform this creation. These are the tasks enacted in McCraney's interval sequences that shape the play and constitute its experimental quality. They commingle past and present in service to the present. As the "A Day Dream" interval demonstrates, this commingling in *Marcus* often happens through physical intimacy and the suggestion of same-sex desire.

The language that frames the dramatic sequences (dreams, visions, mirages, recollections) suggests imaginative and temporal dislocation. In "Prologue: A Dream," which opens the play, Marcus dreams of the character Oshoosi Size weeping in a pool of water. Oshoosi is one of the primary characters of the second play in McCraney's trilogy, *The Brothers Size*. McCraney describes him as a "spirit" in the dramatis personae of *Marcus*. Over the course of the play, the audience learns that Oshoosi had an intimate relationship with Marcus's father, Legba. Oshoosi's appearance in the dream gets intertwined with the protagonist's search for information about his absent father as well as his attempt to find the origin for his own same-sex desire. As a spirit, Oshoosi ushers the past into the play. He haunts Marcus and the play as a whole through his presence in the dream. His appearance serves two distinct purposes. First, it is through him that a circuit of queer desire initially emerges. Second, this dream returns the dead to the world of the living and reminds Marcus of the reality of loss. Making evident Sharon Holland's link between queerness and the dead, McCraney uses the dead as a tool for thinking through queer desire and physical vulnerability.[31]

The opening dream interval of Oshoosi is confusing; his presence first introduces uncertainty. Marcus does not know the person he is seeing or what it means. There is simply a stranger weeping, and the protagonist sets out on a journey to figure out what his dream means. Hemphill's poem ends with confusion, but McCraney begins his drama with a confusing scene. This dream reflects what David Román calls the "bewildering moments" that fill McCraney's plays, and we might specifically think of the opening dream as creating disorientation.[32] Through this interval, the playwright disorients a character who, as the audience will soon find out, has a nonnormative sexual orientation. There is a purposeful playfulness here in that McCraney disorients the character that has a "disoriented" orientation, from a heteronormative perspective. One can understand the play as working to undo the opening disorientation for the queer body—in other words, the play seeks to orient Marcus. In her work on queer phenomenology, theorist Sara Ahmed explains,

> orientations involve different ways of registering the proximity of objects and others. Orientations shape not only how we inhabit space, but how we apprehend this world of shared inhabitance, as well as "who" or "what" we direct our energy and attention toward. A queer phenomenology, perhaps, might start by redirecting our attention toward different objects, those that are "less proximate" or even those that deviate or are deviant.[33]

McCraney provides an artistic meditation on the queer phenomenology Ahmed conceptualizes. The sense of a redirection emerges through the dramatic intervals. Marcus's dream aligns him with a person he has never known or a memory of something that he cannot have experienced. Oshoosi Size, a dead man that Marcus has never met, is that which is "less proximate," so the dream makes the distant intimate, disorienting the character. The remainder of the play finds Marcus literally looking for meaning (perhaps orientation) that is lost after the dream. Ahmed continues, "[if] orientation is about making the strange familiar through the extension of bodies into space, then disorientation occurs when that extension fails."[34] The different ways in which Marcus's movement on stage are redirected or forcefully blocked illustrate how McCraney stages the failure of the extension of bodies into space.[35] In McCraney's drama, the strange remains just that; it fails to become familiar. Marcus does discover who the man is in his dream, but he learns very little about him. In addition, he never resolves his anxieties about the young men who populate his fantasies; in fact, as I will discuss, his encounters with these men result in misunderstandings, active struggle, and further redirections.

Why does it matter that Marcus's disorienting encounters with the past, his curious dreams and fantasies, are unable to orient him or make the world more familiar? These encounters are important because they reveal how the play explores the difficulty of documenting queer experience. Confusing dreams and fantasies become McCraney's primary modes for constructing

Marcus's life. The structure of experience here is "disoriented" by being composed of fictional compositions (dreams), false ideas (mirages), and reconstructed memories (recollections). Because the interval sequences put us in Marcus's mind, it is his queer consciousness that the play reconstructs, but it does so through devices of fiction and artifice. Accordingly, the play is a dramatic translation of queer phenomenology.[36] The experience of queerness is represented here as feeling misaligned or disconnected with the past. Spatial and temporal confusion enable the surfacing of queerness. The interrupting intervals enhance this feeling of disorientation so that the dramatic structure—the interrupting intervals—creates for the audience the experience of disorientation that the protagonist navigates. The play stages disorientation to present the experience of queer existence. In this way, the interval structure puts the audience in a queer position or at least offers the audience brief exposure to the nature of queer experience through the dramatic organization.

By way of the interval sequences, McCraney links sexual desire to a longing for knowledge about the past and the social world. He transforms the longing for a past into the expression of desire and offers physical contact with dead figures as a way to reveal the complexity of Marcus's lived experience. Marcus's dream presents such an encounter and connects queer desire to an embodied past. The Oshoosi dream in the interval gets linked to two physical interactions that Marcus has outside of the space of the intervals: a kiss with Ogun (Oshoosi's brother) and sexual intimacy with Shua (a flirtatious visitor to San Pere). Directly after an interval scene in which he questions why he has "boy-boy" thoughts and wishes the gulf's waters would rise up and wash everything away, Marcus has a conversation with Ogun.[37] Marcus questions Ogun about his brother Oshoosi and the relationship Oshoosi had with Marcus's father, Legba. Both men are moved by Ogun's description of Oshoosi's relationship with Legba, and both weep for the kinfolk that they have lost. In this emotional moment, Marcus kisses the crying Ogun.[38] Ogun's weeping is a replication and revision of the earlier dreamscape of his brother Oshoosi in the first interval. The moment returns us to the opening of the play, resurrecting an earlier enacted moment on stage. Although Marcus is kissing a different brother Size—in life instead of in a dream—he is having a physical encounter with his dream through kissing Oshoosi's symbolic double (his brother Ogun). The kiss forges a physical connection to the living brother and an imagined connection to the dead brother.

The kiss is important because of the greater cultural meaning of kissing and not merely as an expression of personal desire. Phillip Brian Harper explains that part of the social function of a same-sex kiss is to make "manifest the erotic character of a relationship previously presenting as nonerotic"; it reveals "a secret not only about the character of the relationship between the persons who kiss but also about those persons themselves."[39] The kiss, shared in a highly emotional setting, means that both Ogun and Marcus get read as gay. If Shaunta's question suggests that Marcus has same-sex desire, the kiss secures this fact publicly in the eyes of the characters who witness it. In fact, Terrell, one of the characters who wanted Marcus's test answers in the daydream, happens upon the kiss and exclaims, "Oh yall niggas gay!"[40] The intimacy establishes parameters of identity; nonnormative intimacy makes him vulnerable to confrontation. This moment results in Marcus being forced to come out to his two best friends Shaunta and Osha, the latter of whom is infatuated with him. The kiss makes Marcus gay without any word on his part. The physical encounter with Oshoosi's double, which is a revision of the opening interval, broadcasts Marcus's secret and offers him a new, public identity. Kissing Ogun symbolically links him to a queer past because it connects him to his father's lover Oshoosi, but it also makes his sexual orientation publicly visible and him open to community judgment.

Marcus's later physical intimacy with Shua enhances the notion of corporeal contact with his dream about a dead man and his public vulnerability. Shua is a visitor in San Pere from the Bronx and is taken with Marcus. Intrigued by this stranger's mysterious character, Marcus engages in an extended flirtation with Shua and ends up performing fellatio on him.[41] More important than the youthful experimentation of oral sex, Shua gets linked visually to Oshoosi. This connection occurs in the interval called "A Dream of Drag," which happens at the end of act 2, scene 8, following the sexual encounter between Marcus and Shua. In the midst of rain, Shua appears, takes off his signature Kangol hat, strips off his clothes, and transforms into the dead character Oshoosi Size. Ogun may appear in a similar context as the dreamt Oshoosi (crying in the rain), but Shua turns into him on stage. This transformation retroactively suggests that the sexual intimacy with Shua—at least in Marcus's mind—is physical contact with Oshoosi, a character declared dead. Marcus has sex with an emblem of the past, an object of lost kinship.

The intimacy with Shua may be satisfying in the moment and may provide a symbolic connection to an ancestral queer man, but it ultimately results in a threatening situation. In act 2, scene 11, Shua clandestinely returns to Marcus for more physical intimacy. However, Marcus is reluctant because he knows that his female friend Osha now likes Shua, and he feels pangs of guilt. Shua is insistent and demands another, more involved sexual encounter—more than just fellatio. During their first meeting, he told Marcus that he had sexy eyes; now he insists that Marcus's eyes are "calling" him, drawing him to the protagonist and justifying forcefulness. Recalling a familiar trope of sexual assault and victim blaming, Shua is saying that Marcus's mouth "says no, but his body says yes." Because they had already had sexual contact once, Shua feels as if he has a right to more at his will. Marcus at first pleads and then insists that Shua stop.[42] The two end up struggling, and it is only the appearance on stage of the characters Shaunta and Osha that halts the attempted forced intimacy. What begins as mutually pleasurable fellatio in the first encounter becomes aggression and conflict in the second. The intimacy with

Ogun exposes Marcus, but the intimacy with Shua ultimately puts him at physical risk and forces him to have to fight. Sexual activity with Shua connects him to the past while also introducing risk; there is a cost to this connection and to the expression of his desire. In this way, the encounters with Shua resemble the ending of Hemphill's poem: affection and sexual aggression get uncomfortably linked.

I read Marcus's moments of intimacy with Shua and Ogun as intimacy with a lost object, the primary lost object in the play: the dead man Oshoosi Size. The fact that Oshoosi appears in a dream and in the present of the play through character doubles suggests the idea of the temporal hybridity of the present.[43] Marcus's dreams and intimate actions show how he is seduced by and seduces the past. This queer figure develops a sensual relationship to the historical. On one hand, Marcus's seduction of the past revives Oshoosi, ensuring that this queer man is not forgotten. On the other hand, the sensual connection between the two men associates the living Marcus with the dead Oshoosi, signaling that Marcus could be "lost" as well. The connection suggests that he might be on the verge of social absence himself. The intimacy necessarily rewrites and reclaims a queer past, but it also alerts us to the insecurity of the queer present. The play allows us to encounter a lost object, the dead queer man Oshoosi, yet it cannot necessarily protect the living queer man Marcus. If the play performs a writing of history, it does so to shed light on the uncertainty of the current moment. In achieving this connection to the past through desire, we are forced to reckon with the instability of Marcus's present.[44]

Conclusion: Redirected by the Past

After reminding the audience of Marcus's vulnerability—but not his helplessness—the play concludes with a conversation between Marcus and Ogun. Marcus tells Ogun more about his dream of Oshoosi, and Ogun realizes that it means that his brother is certainly dead. With this confirmation, Ogun then "marches a funeral processional by himself" and leaves Marcus standing alone.[45] In addition, many community members have left in advance of an approaching storm. Death, solitude, and approaching destruction appear to bring this drama to its final moments. If the play is about presenting queer experience for the audience, does this presentation then mean that these dark sentiments come to define the totality of that experience? Relatedly, is it impossible to move beyond the state of worry that fills the stanzas of Hemphill's poem? McCraney's drama does sketch out the injurious realities that can constrain queer individuals; however, it does not propose that queer existence is primarily legible through violence and solitude. Although Marcus is alone onstage as Ogun processes away, he watches his elder leave "to make sure he gets home safe."[46] Through this gesture of looking, Marcus assumes a position of protection, securing the well-being of the older generation. His embracing of the past may not have secured his safety, but it effected a connection with a forefather and empowered him in some way. His intimacy with the dead forges an unexpected bond with the living. In the final moments of the play, a queer (and intergenerational) kinship emerges in the face of devastation and solitude. He has taken on a different relationship to the past, embodied by Ogun. Marcus is no longer in search of the past; he safeguards it. The kiss they share results in a new emotional dynamic for him: a movement away from a state of concern primarily for himself. Marcus may be vulnerable, but he is not powerless; his intimate interactions instill in him emotional strength. Queer desire in *Marcus* cannot undo states of worry, but it can create moments of connection that provide stability in an unpredictable world.

Hip-Hop Nommo

✦

Orishas for the Millennium Generation

Freda Scott Giles

In the documentary film *The Language You Cry In*, a grandmother sings a song she learned as a child growing up in the Georgia Sea Islands.[1] No one understood some of the words sung in the song, and the song was perceived as a vehicle for children's play. Eventually, through the efforts of several scholars, the song was recovered as a funeral dirge sung in Sierra Leone. There is a moving scene in the film when, after much effort to bring them together, the woman from Georgia meets the village woman in Sierra Leone who recognized the song. They embrace and weep together. A village elder comments eloquently in Mende that the language you cry in is your true language.

This story might be viewed as an externalized manifestation of what August Wilson describes as "the blood's memory": "that deepest part of yourself where the ancestors are talking."[2] The ancestors, with the help of intermediaries, connected a woman from Georgia with a woman from Sierra Leone through a song from the time of slavery—a thread that was retained through the oral tradition that, once understood, provided a new dimension of signification for the African American woman in regard to her own identity. The song connection also evokes resonant thoughts of the character Herald Loomis's loss and recovery of his song in August Wilson's *Joe Turner's Come and Gone*. In that play, an intermediary, Bynum, a connector to the ancestors, assists Loomis in working his way through his pain and confusion toward reclaiming a place in the world as a free man.

If examined through the lens of Paul Carter Harrison's dramatic theories found in *Drama of Nommo* and *Kuntu Drama*[3] as well as through recent critical theories that analyze Wilson's work in terms of Yoruba cosmology, Wilson's drama itself may be viewed as part of a continuum of paradigms for representing and re-presenting the New World African in the postcolonial era. It is possible to view this continuum as a three-stage process.

The period represented by the initial publications of Harrison's *Drama of Nommo* and *Kuntu Drama* is part of the first stage. Harrison draws a line of demarcation that closely coincides with the era of the Black Arts Movement, using the production of Lorraine Hansberry's *A Raisin in the Sun* (1959) as a turning point toward a black theater "aesthetically uncluttered by realism."[4] In the first stage, there is a concerted effort to construct a body of Afrocentric drama as an intermediary that reconnects African Americans to Africa. The aesthetic underpinnings of these dramas serve almost as an exoskeleton to illustrate Afrocentricity in the productions. August Wilson's dramas of the blood's memory, which bend realism toward the metaphysical, represent a furthering of the Nommo/Kuntu drama paradigm into a second stage, a subtler exploration of African retention in African American culture, a more internalized mediation. Wilson's works have been described by some as post-Afrocentric, but they may also be described as post–Black Arts Movement. The third stage, a Nommo/Kuntu drama for the millennium generation, I suggest, is represented by works from a more recent playwright, Tarell Alvin McCraney. As a postmodern, post-Afrocentric playwright, McCraney forgoes mediation; connections are assumed, and the spectator may or may not be aware of Yoruba cosmology at all. The African connection is there, but it is one referent among many. The extent to which it is recognized is left up to the spectator—and, indeed, to what that spectator intuits. African identity, history, and culture are ingredients in the mixture that constitutes American identity, history, and culture. Racial politics and racism complicate the mixture but the combination of ingredients creates a distinctly American syncretic tradition.

The purpose of this essay is to examine how the process of recognizing and reclaiming African identity through the use of Yoruba cosmology, specifically Yoruba orishas, in drama has evolved. I outline this evolution through a discussion of selected dramas—primarily *Shango de Ima* by Pepe Carril, *The Great MacDaddy* by Paul Carter Harrison, *Joe Turner's Come and Gone* by August Wilson, and *In the Red and Brown Water* by Tarell Alvin McCraney. Notably, I suggest that McCraney has refreshed and reconstructed the African recovery paradigm. Born into the post-1980 "millennium generation," McCraney has illustrated how African identity resonates through a generation that came of age in the era of hip-hop. Each drama under discussion in this essay, I contend, is designed to connect the New World African to historical and metaphysical Africa, with the metaphysical connection being made either directly or indirectly through the iconography, ritual, and orality of Yoruba (a people from southwest Nigeria) cosmology. In the New World, that cosmology syncretized with beliefs from other African ethnic groups—but particularly with Christianity—to become Santería (Caribbean), Vodou (Haiti), and Candomblé (Brazil). Among the numerous African cultures represented in the New World, this tangible, visible link across the Atlantic makes the Yoruba connection a powerful tool for representing Africanisms in African American life. The Yoruba connection also brings together the African diasporas of North, Central, and South America. Harrison, however, expressed his theoretical concepts for Kuntu drama utilizing terminology based in Bantu languages, which represent a wider range of African peoples throughout western, central, eastern, and southern Africa.

Kuntu drama incorporates several ideas. First, there is Nommo, the mojo, the power of the Word, expressed in word and gesture. Nommo expresses all the force fields that compose the world.[5] As the four force fields (Muntu, Kintu, Hantu, Kuntu) bring all existence and experience together, Kuntu drama brings the African continuum together through the modalities of ritual, rhythm, music, dance, and spirituality: "Song, dance, and drum are as important to the modes of contemporary black experience as they always have been in traditional African life. While the experience of the New World may have colored these expressive indices, the resonance of Africa remains apparent."[6] Kuntu drama seeks total engagement of body and spirit, and fosters a sense of community. Strict linearity and material realism are pushed aside. Harrison points to the traditional African American church, Caribbean carnivals, the blues, jazz, archetypal characters, the frequent use of a chorus to represent the community, and idiomatic language as likely elements, with "race memory," the memory of the connection to Africa buried deep within, as the source. He points to Jean Toomer, Amiri Baraka, Aimé Césaire, Adrienne Kennedy, Sonia Sanchez, Derek Walcott, and Aishah Rahman, among others, as exemplary twentieth-century Nommo writers. Western influence is acknowledged, as it must be in postcolonial drama, but Nommo, the way the Word is uttered and used, keeps the African historical and spiritual continuum flowing through the work.

The mid-1960s through the mid-1970s was a golden age for the first phase of Kuntu drama. Barbara Ann Teer and the National Black Theatre led the way in creating Afrocentric ritual performances and a significant number of African American playwrights seemed to be searching for "a common semantic iconography that suggests a consanguinity of spirit and stands as a testament to the resilience of race memory" that "reveals the collective unconscious" tied to "the specifics of the diaspora experience."[7] Two examples that are specifically pertinent for this discussion include Carril's *Shango de Ima* (1970) and Harrison's *The Great MacDaddy* (1973).

Carril's stylized ritual enactment of the story of Shango's relationship with his three principal wives, Oya, Obba, and Oshun, refers directly to Cuban Santería and its rituals. It is a religious play, translated from Spanish into English, and it begins, as tradition dictates, with an invocation to Elegua.[8] Every aspect of the original production was conventionalized to reflect the colors, rhythms, movements, and songs connected to each orisha. The orishas are represented through their conflicts with each other rather than their relationships with humankind. This play shows the "backstory" of the mutual antagonism between Shango, warrior ruler of fire, thunder, lightning, personification of male sexuality and potency, and Ogun, "orisha of power who descends from the mountains," who rules iron, war, labor, sacrifice, politics, and technology. Shango and Ogun cannot meet without joining in battle. Though Ogun is the stronger of the pair, Shango will not be satisfied until he defeats him. The drama reveals how Shango's foster mother, Yemaya, supreme mother goddess of the oceans, gave Shango a wife, Obba, orisha of marriage and domesticity. Shango is a cruel and callous husband, and his sexual prowess eventually attracts Oshun, orisha of love, feminine beauty, fertility, and art, who rules the rivers, and Oya, "Queen of the Cemetery," warrior goddess of the wind and hurricanes, who, like Shango, has a temperament suited to lightning and storms. (Oya, too, rules a river: the Niger.)

In *Shango de Ima*, Obba, desperate for Shango's love, misapprehending the advice of Oshun and Oya, cuts off her ears and serves them to him. He rebuffs her. Obatala, portrayed in this play in female form—though she is both father and mother of the orishas and the guardian of light and morality—condemns Shango to suffer the cycle of birth, life, and death that his followers must endure, in perpetuity. The performance ends with a rite for Shango followed by obeisance to Elegua, messenger between gods and humans, orisha of the crossroads, who is also described as a phallic god and an often childlike trickster. Santería rituals begin and end with invocations of Elegua. *Shango de Ima* provides a window into Santería for the uninitiated, as well as a theater experience that combines African and Cuban cultures.

In *The Great MacDaddy*, Harrison attempts to go a step further toward African American culture by adapting a Nigerian novel full of Yoruba iconography, *The Palm-Wine Drinkard* by Amos Tutuola, into an African American context, setting the hero's quest in Los Angeles during the Prohibition era. There is music and dance, mainly in the form of the blues. The end is a community celebration designed to include the audience. The goal is to bring the audience closer to its cultural heritage and the products of that heritage, translating African mythic and cosmic references as they appear in African American modes of experience. Harrison calls upon the African American church and New World mythic heroes such as The Great MacDaddy, Stagolee, Shine, John Henry, and the Signifyin' Monkey: "The intention of the ritual, then, is to identify, rather than simulate African sensibilities as perceived in the context of African/Americans."[9]

August Wilson notably takes a different route toward a similar end in *Joe Turner's Come and Gone*. As Sandra G. Shannon explains, Wilson teases out a suppressed African consciousness, constructing on the stage a relationship not with a geographical and historically distant continent, but with an inner landscape of retained knowledge and culture: "The former is a material presence; the latter is a spiritually embodied area . . . These Africanisms do not announce their presence with drumbeats, colorful costumes, or expressive dances."[10] Wilson does not so much exhibit Africa as he evokes it in his dramaturgy. The Pittsburgh Hill District he has created is as mythic as Mount

Olympus or Valhalla or the realm of the Egungun, and the male and female heroes who challenge the colonialist American past create a dialectic with American history that reconnects the audience with an African worldview. In this way, African American audiences can reimagine and reconstruct their history from their own point of view, rather than the point of view of the dominant culture. Quoting Tejumola Olaniyan, Shannon calls this process the creation of "an empowering, post-Afrocentric space."[11] Shannon recognizes that audience members may become disoriented by "reading" the action of Wilson's plays from the other side of the Eurocentric-Afrocentric divide. African Americans may appreciate the African American culture represented, but may or may not recognize the Afrocentricity in both the content and structure of the play.

Sandra L. Richards takes a similar view in her essay, "Yoruba Gods on the American Stage: *Joe Turner's Come and Gone*."[12] Richards discusses the juba dance, Bynum's rituals, and other cultural elements. However, her study is more focused on the Yoruba iconography that is drawn through analogy. She draws connections between Bynum and the *Ifa*, or "priest," and the Shiny Man in Bynum's story as an amalgam of Ogun and Esu. Richards also delves into Wole Soyinka's description of Ogun as the soul of Yoruba drama, just as Dionysus is the soul of classical Greek drama. It was Ogun who courageously leapt into the abyss that separates gods and humans, reconnecting the gods to the earth: "Thus, like the Christian god, Ogun is a divinity who takes on a collective burden and leads others to self-knowledge. The shininess that Bynum reports may be related to iron, the essential feature associated with Ogun."[13] Ogun is also manifest through Loomis, who baptizes himself into a new life, after years of unbearable suffering, with a knife, a weapon of Ogun, in Wilson's play. *Joe Turner's Come and Gone* is set in 1913 Pittsburgh. Though it has been fifty years since the Emancipation Proclamation, Herald Loomis has been enslaved for seven years by a white man, Joe Turner (historically, a real person). Loomis must find a way back to himself through closure with his past, and the recovery of his "song."

Richards also recognizes that history has complicated the traditional binary of African and European in her reading of *Joe Turner's Come and Gone*: "The binary of either/or is replaced by the principal of both/and." A multiplicity of cultural interactions has taken place, and all have been syncretized within the African American experience: "August Wilson's plays and practice speak to American audiences who are challenged to acknowledge the facticity of their national identity as a site of multicolored, cultural crossings despite its ideological construction as a white monolith."[14] Wilson has often stated that African Americans are African in sensibility and worldview, and should recognize that within themselves. Such recognition mitigates the confusion caused by having to make their way in a world that is at once not of their making and is often hostile and threatening. In effecting this change of viewpoint in full view of the diverse American audience, Wilson, as Shannon states, "is in the forefront of playwrights who are experimenting with performance techniques to usher in a new activist-artistic era."[15]

Playwright Tarell Alvin McCraney has undoubtedly crossed Wilson's bridge into a new era. In his trilogy *The Brother/Sister Plays*—composed of *In the Red and Brown Water*, *The Brothers Size*, and *Marcus; Or the Secret of Sweet*—he takes the blood's memory, Yoruba cosmology, Nommo/Kuntu drama, North American popular culture (including hip-hop), and a diverse literary heritage into the twenty-first century, richly layering and adapting each.[16] A real-life analogy for his plays, for his blood's memory, might be drawn from the television series *Finding Your Roots with Henry Louis Gates, Jr.* Gates supplements traditional methods of genealogical research with the use of DNA testing in an effort to uncover multiple ancestries, including African, European, and New World ancestries, in his research subjects. The blood remembers a complex history that further complicates the traditional black-white racial binary.

Though he does not deploy the specific term, Harry Elam describes twenty-first-century Kuntu drama this way:

> A collage, a clash, a rich diversity of representations of blackness: hip-hop flavor intersects with reexaminations of slavery and civil rights; solo performance art meets with ensemble improvisatory form; the social and cultural intersect with the spiritual . . . a fire with a new millennium swing.[17]

McCraney undoubtedly does all of these things in his dramaturgy.

Often asked in interviews about influences on his writing, McCraney names Peter Brook, August Wilson, Federico García Lorca, and fellow writers in his class at Yale, but he is also deeply influenced by dance, describing his first experience seeing "Revelations" performed by the Alvin Ailey American Dance Theater as "a life changing experience."[18] He began writing *The Brother/Sister Plays* partially as a way to explore his relationship with his own siblings, not in an autobiographical sense, but in the sense of examining the complexities and intensity of love and tension in sibling and family relationships. Though it was written after *The Brothers Size*, *In the Red and Brown Water* is chronologically the first in the trilogy. There are two major textual sources—one oral, the other literary—for the work. One day McCraney asked a *santero* priest to tell him a story. The resultant story was about Oya. Oya's story had become conflated with Obba's, so it was Oya who cut off her ears to serve them to Shango. Conducting further research on Oya, McCraney learned that she was locked in an eternal love triangle with Ogun and Shango.[19] He also learned that red, brown, and maroon are the colors of Oya's orisha beads and that her connection with wind and the cemetery is a connection with life itself: she is the first and last breath. Oya, notably, is the patron of those afflicted with madness.[20] In some stories she has children, but in most she is childless, a tragic state in African culture.[21] All of these details would eventually help animate *In the Red and Brown Water*'s dramaturgy.

Around the time that McCraney was conducting his research on Oya and Yoruba cosmology, he was also reading Federico García Lorca's Andalusian tragedies *Blood Wedding* and *Yerma*. As he explains:

> It all dropped deep into me: the yearning of this young woman, how desperate she was—and the two loves of her life, just like in the story of Oya . . . then I started to think sociologically. I said, wait a minute, the man who told me this story was of Puerto Rican descent—meaning his blood was mixed with African and Spanish. This story should be born of that same heritage. It's both African, in the Oya/Oba [sic] tradition, but it's also Yerma—very much that Lorca yearning. They're so close. They talk to each other.[22]

McCraney decided to put this historical-cultural-literary intertextuality into a contemporary African American context:

> The tradition of keeping those stories alive and using them to tell stories about African-Americans in the most urban and quotidian way is nothing new . . . we call it sampling in Hip-Hop. So I was interested in keeping the tradition in the theatre. Merging the old with the new. And listening to the discourse it created in the space.[23]

McCraney created a new mythic space for Oya's story, the housing projects of San Pere, Louisiana (San Pere may be translated as Saint Peter, the "cover saint" for Ogun), a city that lives only in myth and memory, in "the distant present." Time is handled in a non-Western way in the play:

> The moon is connected deeply to Yemoja . . . and to women, to fertility, to the phases of women. In this play it also serves as a clock . . . When Elegba goes from a sliver of a moon to a full moon, years have passed by. It's almost as if Oya is the center of the piece, and all these things are . . . orbiting around her. If you count Elegba as Mercury, he goes around the fastest. So years pass in his life, whereas it seems that in Ogun's life, everything is regular. It was to be able to play with time in a way that said, "Listen: Time is magical here."[24]

The moon, notably, is also a magically real factor in Lorca's *Blood Wedding*.

In *In the Red and Brown Water*, Oya Jean Fair is a teenage track star with great potential. Her mother, Mama Moja (Yemoja, Mother Goddess, ruler of the oceans), is loving and wise, but overworked, exhausted, and ill. Early in the play, Mama Moja is visited by Lil Legba, a mercurial, mischievous boy who is addicted to candy. He tells her of a dream he had about Oya, which turns out to strikingly engage with August Wilson's story of the bones in *Joe Turner's Come and Gone* and his City of Bones in *Gem of the Ocean*, combining those narratives with an adolescent boy's dreams of sexual awakening. Like Wilson, McCraney can easily wield the power of Nommo to transition between the modalities of visions, dreams, and reality.

The exchange between Elegba and Mama Moja also features McCraney's technique of having the characters speak their stage directions, combining methods of storytelling with those of enactment. Mama Moja has no dialogue during the telling of the dream, but space is made for her nonverbal reaction. Elegba's dream is prophetic:

ELEGBA:
It's always about the water,[25] my dreams.
Near it or around it. Sometimes I stand
In the high tide and I can't breathe but I
Can breathe. And I walk on the bottom on
The floor of the waters and they's these people
Walk alongside me but they all bones and they
Click the bone people, they talk in the click.
I say, "Where yall going?" And they say, "Just
Walking for a while." I say, "Don't you want
To go home . . ." They say, "When we walk there, it
Wasn't there no more." I feel bad for them . . .
Then they click and I come up on the mud part,
Like they send me to the land part, And I'm
Sitting there waiting 'cause I know they want
Me to wait I wait there looking and on
Top of the waters is Oya . . .
Lil Legba looks for Moja's reaction.
MAMA MOJA:
ELEGBA:
Oya girl floating on top of the water,
Looking up towards the sky and with no clothes
She hardly got no clothes on and she got her legs
Wide . . .
Lil Legba ducks . . .
MAMA MOJA:
ELEGBA:
And she holding her head on the side with her
Hand like something ailing her.
But from her legs blood coming down and it's making the pond
Red . . .[26]

In the end, Legba's dream morphs into a wet dream. Notably, the bones he dreams of are displaced, but they do not walk up from the water and take on flesh as Bynum's dream bones do in *Joe Turner's Come and Gone*. Legba's dream bones send him forward, but disappear. They leave him waiting. He turns from thoughts of them to his nascent desire for Oya. The image of blood in the dream at first appears to be a reference to menstrual blood, but it might just as well be a foreshadowing of the blood that flows from Oya's ear when she presents it to Shango, or a manifestation of the psychological pain that drove her to that act. We later learn that Elegba grows up and fathers a child with Oba, an older woman who is not seen in this play. Elegba becomes obsessed with his son, Marcus Eshu, but that does not keep him from having an affair with Egungun (ancestor), a male DJ.

Oya's dreams of college are dashed when she gives up her opportunity for a track scholarship to care for Mama Moja, who is terminally ill. Her mother's scene of transition is deeply affecting: Oya desperately begs her to stay while Mama Moja moves farther and farther away, her face resolutely and fearlessly turned toward Death, as the female cast members join her in singing the spiritual "Down by the Riverside." Oya's first condolence callers after Mama Moja's death are Elegba, who mourns elaborately and humorously, and Shango, who "curls his fingers around Oya's ear and Caresses [*sic*] the soft" (45). This is a gesture that Shango will often repeat, but as soon as they have a tender moment, Shango and Oya find a way to fight. Soon, The Man from State comes to tell Oya that he has moved on and selected another runner; Oya's opportunity is gone. Like Yerma, Oya then begins to spend her days sitting in front of her home, watching the world go by. Shango joins the army, giving Ogun his chance to court Oya. Ogun Size stutters at first, but gains assurance as Oya accepts his love. He promises her a family. Their happiness is short-lived, however, as Oya watches the other neighborhood women enjoying their pregnancies, and Shango returns on leave to taunt Ogun and Oya for not having children; it is his way of reestablishing his power over Oya.

Ogun becomes suspicious; but moving his Aunt Elegua into the house does not stop Shango and Oya from resuming their tempestuous affair while Ogun is at work. When Shango's leave ends, he throws the affair in Ogun's face as he walks away. Oya's desperation to have a life with Ogun and a child leads her, as it led Yerma, to a conjure woman. Unlike Yerma's *bruja*, who conducts a clandestine nighttime ritual for Yerma, the Woman Who Reminds You tells her there is nothing she can do for her infertility issues. Oya ends her relationship with Ogun; she cannot stand hurting him any more. Soon, Shun (Oshun), Oya's nemesis, confronts her to inform her that she is carrying Shango's child: "I'm having his baby / So I'm his woman now! You ain't shit to him." When Shango returns again, this time in an officer's uniform, Oya invites him in, to give him a present to remember her by: her ear. These events are enacted in *In the Red and Brown Water*, but they are also partially recounted in *The Brothers Size*.

The characters and characterizations in the play reveal the complexities, frustrations, comedies, and tragedies of urban African American life through the complicated psychologies and traits of the orishas. If we do not recognize the godly figures literally, we recognize them intuitively, as part of who we are. To this latter point, McCraney asserts:

> That's what I mean when I say it's an American piece. Layered. In America we may try to deny that we're a hodge podge of different cultures and influences but as a person growing up in America in a place like Miami, I'm filled with experiences from bhutto training to Suzuki training to Stanislavski but also tons of African music, African dance and the emergence of hip-hop which is nothing but fragments of old music turned into new music and then lyrically poeticised over. This notion of taking the past and recreating into new form, adding your own voice to old forms, is a heritage that comes from every-where . . . *The Brothers Size* [and by extension, *The Brother/Sister Plays*] feels clear and simple but it is underpinned by a foundation that is deep in all our traditions, not just African but western, west European, South American.[27]

Whereas earlier playwrights like Carril and Harrison—and, to some extent, Wilson—were more explicit in their efforts to reconnect African Americans to Africa through an engagement with specifically Afrocentric dramaturgical strategies, McCraney's dramaturgy assumes those connections, beckoning spectators to do the work of making sense and meaning of them. In so doing, his work expands definitions of what constitutes a "Black play."

In the introduction to their anthology, *Post-Black Plays*, editors Harry Elam Jr. and Douglas Jones Jr. reflect at length on Suzan-Lori Parks's essay, "New Black Math." Parks notes that the current definition of the term "Black drama" is marked by two catastrophic events that took place in August 2005: the announcement that August Wilson was dying of cancer and Hurricane Katrina. Each were markers of permanent change but linked to a troubled racial past—things are now "the same and different." As Elam and Jones explain, the understanding of what a Black play is is "dependent on the current contexts and conditions of African American experience but also responsive to past circumstances."[28] Wilson's presence as a dramatist loomed so large during the last two decades of the twentieth century and into the beginning of the twenty-first century that his work came to personify African American drama to many. Interestingly, McCraney, born in 1980 at the beginning of the millennial generation (ca. 1980–2004), assisted Wilson on *Radio Golf*, the final play in Wilson's monumental *Century Cycle*, during his graduate school days at Yale.[29] A torch may have been symbolically passed. Perhaps Katrina's blowing San Pere away serves as a metaphor for a new era in African American playwriting. McCraney personifies a new generation where "aesthetic interest now possibly trumps racial affinities. Yet an unequal racial playing field still figures within this equation."[30]

With *Shango de Ima*, Carril brought New World African deities from religious ritual spaces into the American theater. In his *Century Cycle*, particularly through *Gem of the Ocean* and *Joe Turner's Come and Gone*, Wilson pointed toward the orishas as a source of a distinct African American culture and a refuge for the battered African American psyche. McCraney further syncretizes the orishas into the fabric of a complex, complicated take on African American culture as a world culture. Elam and Jones hearken back to George C. Wolfe, who called for us to move away from "the mama on the couch" and those who broke toward more open fields of expression,[31] such as Suzan-Lori Parks, Marcus Gardley, Danai Gurira, and others who represent "the desire of this new generation of artists to experiment with form as well as content as they compel reassessments of how and what we label as 'black art.'"[32]

During the 1970s, *The Drama of Nommo* and *Kuntu Drama* spoke to the urgent need for reclaiming and valorizing African identity among the African diaspora. The tumultuous political and social conditions of the time spoke more to binaries than multiplicities. The drama of the blood's memories, August Wilson's dramas produced during the 1980s and '90s spoke to Kuntu drama's goals while recognizing that the African presence in the African diaspora cannot be accurately described in terms of an either-or dichotomy. Nearly half a millennium of history has intervened to build upon the African worldview that remains as a cultural foundation. That heritage can be embraced and allowed to function as a buffer against a toxic environment as well as a provider of a confident, communal presence. McCraney has taken all of this into consideration for the 2000s, the era of his *Brother/Sister* triptych. He samples the cultures and family relationships that formed him and his aesthetic, and we recognize ourselves in them whether or not we recognize their sources. When he heard the story of Oya and read the story of Yerma, he brought these stories to life in a contemporary African American community, staging them in a way that utilized his experiences with African, American (North and South), Asian, and European performance. His reconfiguration of dramatic myth and theatrical practice has shown us new possibilities for form as well as content. We are the same but different for the experience.

Black Movements and Tarell Alvin McCraney's
In the Red and Brown Water

✦

Soyica Diggs Colbert

Tarell Alvin McCraney's *In the Red and Brown Water*, the first play in *The Brother/Sister Plays* trilogy, begins "like a chant or a moan."[1] In the Public Theater's 2009 production directed by Tina Landau, you hear the central character Oya's "(sharp breath out) Ah!" and then the chorus of characters puzzles over her death (12).[2] With few observations and fewer answers, Oya (played by Kianné Muschett) confirms, "Oya in the air Oya . . ." (12). Similar to James Baldwin's *Blues for Mister Charlie*, the play begins with a dead central figure and revolves around figuring out what caused her demise. The play depicts a sequence of Oya's dreams deferred. Oya defers attending a college called State on a track-and-field-scholarship to care for her ailing mother, Mama Moja, who dies a few months later. Although she runs like the wind, State does not offer her a scholarship for the next academic year. After her mother dies, Oya begins dating Shango (performed by Sterling K. Brown) and yearns for a life with him. Unfortunately, that dream must be deferred as well; Oya is infertile and unable to consummate her relationship with Shango through the birth of a child, the prize signifier of adulthood in her community. Oya settles for another man, Ogun Size (played by Marc Damon Johnson), who provides stability but no passion. She longs for a child and spends most of her life sitting on the porch waiting. When she learns, however, that another woman in the neighborhood is expecting Shango's child, she cuts off her ear and bleeds to death, fulfilling the only event in a sequence of deferred desire.

Although McCraney's plays focus on deferred dreams, his career has not experienced postponement, boasting what many theater critics mark as a dream emergence in New York and London. The second play in the trilogy, *The Brothers Size*, was first produced as a part of the Public Theater's Under the Radar Festival in January 2007, and months later premiered in London at the Young Vic to critical acclaim. McCraney's distinctive style, unparalleled at least in recent history, his rocket-like launch to stardom, and his youth (born October 17, 1980) have made him a media darling. Besides receiving numerous awards, including the position of Royal Shakespeare Company/Warwick International Playwright in Residence, London's Evening Standard Award (for most promising playwright), a National Endowment for the Arts Outstanding New American Play Award, and the inaugural New York Times Outstanding Playwright Award, the young playwright has been lauded effusively by the theater world. According to David Román, McCraney "has emerged as one of the most significant new voices in American theater."[3] McCraney's ability to sample from traditions as diverse as Yoruba cosmology, Federico García Lorca's *Yerma*, and the sounds of Motown and hip-hop, as well as to signify on the theatrical innovations of Zora Neale Hurston in his use of bawdy comedy and folk traditions, August Wilson in his syncretism and resistance to teleology, and Suzan-Lori Parks in his formal conventions, advances black theater in a new and exciting direction.

A stunning example, *In the Red and Brown Water*, the most ritualistic play of the trilogy, foregrounds McCraney's ability to render the unfamiliar familiar and the mundane strange. Straightforward and familiar, Oya's story of loss and self-sacrifice takes a dramatic turn through the use of Yoruba cosmology. If Oya is restricted to the mandates of physical embodiment, to the mundane, to the vicissitudes of black women laboring under the mandates of self-sacrifice in a person whose life begins at birth, ends decades later at death, and is confined to being in one place at one time, then in the world of the play her infertility is her downfall. Yet Oya is a mythic figure who is absent at the beginning of the play and nonetheless present in the air, and while she never leaves her hometown of San Pere, Louisiana (a fictional town), she serves as a symbolic figure of diaspora connected to the scattering of black people that slavery causes. Other figures in the play—Elegba, Mama Moja, and Aunt Elegua—also transcend time and place, creating a "cyclic reality" tied to the inflections of Yoruba cosmology.[4] The characters have names of Yoruba deities, including Elegba, also known as Elegua (the messenger, trickster, guardian of the crossroads, and spirit of chaos), Ogun (the spirit of iron, war, technology, and transformation), and Shango (the spirit of kingship, thunder, and lightning).[5] The play, through its mythical characters, setting, staging of ritual, and spoken stage directions, places the body, place, and time on the move in order to extend the life of black performance.

This essay is drawn from the epilogue of my first book, *The African American Theatrical Body*.[6] In it, I offer several examples of the ways physical movement—a gesture or a dance—reveals the constitution of bodies and places. Instead of summarizing my argument from the book that performance renders the black theatrical body flexible and therefore radically alters conceptions of bodies and places, in this updated version I want to initiate a focused reading of a twenty-first-century African American play—McCraney's *In the Red and Brown Water*—that foregrounds how black performance moves through bodies, places, and time and, in that motion, extends black political movements. In that way, this essay anticipates my second book, *Black Movements: Performance and Cultural Politics*.[7] In revisiting this essay after the completion of *Black Movements*, I clarify how black performance has the ability to shape understandings of performance's ontology and, thus, its political possibilities. Because McCraney's play takes up the question of performance's relationship to time, this analysis enables future considerations of African American theater's role in black freedom movements.

Depictions of death and life after death (physical and social) recur in black literary and cultural representations, including Suzan Lori-Parks's *The America Play* and August Wilson's *Joe Turner's Come and Gone*. Similarly, *In the Red and Brown Water* depicts Oya continuing to live in the air after bleeding to death from a self-inflicted wound to the head. Like the uncanny chill created by a whisper along your neck, Oya (named for the Yoruba goddess of wind, storms, thunder and lightning, and rage, and known as the mother of the dead) remains present in the play and arguably in the trilogy, which ends with the threat of a hurricane similar to Katrina. "For the Yoruba, death is not the annihilation of being. It is simply a rite of passage, a transition from human to divine essence."[8] Although Oya does not recur throughout the trilogy as some other characters do, she arguably gains momentum and force, threatening communal destruction to avenge her social and physical deaths. Through death, Oya flies from a state of oppression to menacing freedom. Individually productive, her liberation also sparks the metaphorical kindling that brings forth familial relationships that transcend death. Much like Joseph Roach's description of effigies, which he argues "provide communities with a method of perpetuating themselves through specially nominated mediums or surrogates," Oya's act of self-sacrifice demonstrates the relationship between embodied and political movements, altering her body to extend the life of the performance.[9]

Oya's self-initiated rite of passage repeats other such ritualized inaugural events with a difference that reproduces the insurgent force of black performance. I use the term reproduction to describe the process of historical construction and recuperation that black performance enacts in the African American theater. Building on Fred Moten's groundbreaking work *In the Break: The Aesthetics of the Black Radical Tradition*, I argue that black performance shapes history by reproducing psychic and material traces, keeping in mind the debates concerning the ontology of performance that continue to circulate in response to Peggy Phelan's claim that "performance in a strict ontological sense is nonreproductive."[10] In *Unmarked*, Phelan explains the temporal finitude of performance: "Performance cannot be saved, recorded, documented, or otherwise participate in the circulation of representations of representation."[11] Phelan's definition of performance emphasizes its potential to resist the commodification at the heart of most modes of cultural production. Her critical insight illuminates how performance disrupts circuits of capital.

It does not, however, account for, as Fred Moten theorizes, how black people in motion distinguish American capitalism, or function as "commodity[ies] who speak."[12]

Cedric Robinson argues in *Black Marxism,* "The institution of American slave labor could not be effectively conceptualized as a thing in and of itself. Rather, it was a particular historical development for world capitalism that expropriated the labor of African workers as primitive accumulation. American slavery was a subsystem of world capitalism."[13] Black performance practices disrupt the myth of American capitalism as a model of pure accumulation and, instead, point to how racism and racialization disrupts accumulative time. Phelan would not qualify theatrical production as performance. Nevertheless, if we consider how theater stages ephemeral moments of embodiment (a glance, an embrace, or a kiss) and materiality (bodies, the set, costumes, and script), theater becomes an excellent site to examine black performance. The materiality that animates *In the Red and Brown Water*—and that I trace in *The African American Theatrical Body*—offers an opportunity to not only account for how blackness informs embodied aesthetic actions and their relationship to the accumulative principles at the heart of capitalism but also to rearrange them. Therefore, black performance, especially in theatrical production, both bolsters and complicates Phelan's impulse to locate the resistance to capitalism in performance's ontology.

The force that drives black performance belongs to a cyclic history that asserts itself in and through the body of the actor, reconfiguring the shape of that body, the location of the event, and the moment in time. While acting as sites of memory, black performances call for an engagement with traumatic events in the past so that those events do not need to be rehashed but, instead, may be incorporated into history. Exemplary of the way black performance works through traumatic history, the communal disavowal of Oya due to her inability to physically reproduce creates the opportunity for her to rupture the alignment of women's production with physical reproduction, and offer revolutionary action as an alternative. Through the physical cut she performs on her body, she produces a historical cut that rearranges lines of descent.

The play communicates the force of Oya's action through the ritualized remembrance of her sacrifice in the choric scenes of the play. Therefore, instead of focusing solely on Oya's ritualized death in the final scene of the play, I want to consider the relationship between her mutilation and the staging of her floating in the air—a performance of her uninhibited desire. The gentle caresses of Shango's fingers along Oya's ear promise her erotic fulfillment that he supplies in each encounter with her. Shango, too, finds satisfaction in their intimacy, but it does not keep him from "stepping out on" Oya or meriting Aunt Elegua's designation as a "freak" (54). According to L. H. Stallings, slave narratives establish "the origins of black freaks as the merger between sexuality and antiwork activities by black individuals who uphold the integrity of the magical, divine, and marvelous."[14] Freaks open up the possibility for modes of behavior or fugitive freedom practices. The designation "freak" is not necessarily an indictment in the language of the play, but Aunt Elegua specifies, "this boy got a wickedness in his / Stance, a driving in his pants / What a good girl doing with somebody like him" (54). The uneven exchange of desire between Shango and Oya damages Oya and therefore qualifies as a problem. In the final scene of the play, Oya gives Shango her ear—the object of his erotic desire—and through her act of benevolence frees herself from a system of disproportionate desire. She becomes a freak, gaining the ability to "uphold the integrity of the magical, divine, and marvelous." The play represents this freedom in the choric scenes that feature Oya floating.

Lying on her back and suspended in the air by a metal tub also used as a drum, Oya waves her arms and legs to simulate levitation. Her floating in the Public Theater production of the play renders Oya immune to Shango's touch and to the unfulfilled yearnings of her body to produce a child. Oya's floating draws attention to the often dangerous and sometimes deadly pursuit of freedom by black people in the Americas; a pursuit that links life in what the play calls the "distant present" to the now of the theatrical production (10). Oya's floating demonstrates the temporal unrest at the heart of what might be best described by the phrase "black movements." I define black movements as embodied actions (i.e., floating) that further political movements (i.e., the pursuit of black women's bodily freedom) that in turn rearrange time and space. Black movements, then, can be seen as political practices, but not ones whose duration can be measured solely in serial time. Rather, black movements reshape temporalities in order to reorganize the social and cultural fields that facilitate the social and physical deaths of black people.

The play opens with a prologue that establishes the choric tableaux that will structure the drama. Much like Parks's remix of ancient Greek dramaturgy, McCraney's chorus provides the disparate opinions of community members, articulating the anticipated questions and assertions of the theater audience. The chorus generates the hushed local intimacy that Toni Morrison produces in the beginning of *The Bluest Eye* with the phrase "Quiet as it's kept," and the larger-than-life expansiveness that Nobel Prize–winning African playwright Wole Soyinka calls "cosmic entirety."[15] Harkening back to the all-encompassing scope of theater according to Soyinka, *In the Red and Brown Water* creates a fusion between the heavens and the earth through the shifts among realism, choric breaks, and dreamscapes. Yet it is in the choric breaks and Elegba's dreamy prophetic monologues that the characters' powers manifest themselves. These ruptures integrate the metaphysical into the quotidian and the future into the present. References to the gods elevate the battle against deferred dreaming to mythic proportions, highlighting the importance of systems of desire and hope. The play critiques Oya's inability to locate an alternative object of desire that does not depend on heteronormativity, while it dramatizes an alternative rite of passage for black women outside of physical reproduction. Through the ritualized reenactment of Oya's transition from one physical state to the next through the ritualized cutting, and which is staged as her floating, the play "disrupt[s] the idealization of the nuclear family and the cultural logic of sexual citizenship as lodged in 'normative' sexuality."[16]

The Public Theater production opens with a man and a woman dressed in white walking out onto a bare stage (save for a few buckets and tubs) with buckets in their hands. Music fills the air while the man walks forward and pours his bucket as blue light spills onto the floor. The electric, sky-blue, liquid light consumes the entire stage floor, turning land into water in the first few heartbeats of the play. The woman, Oya, remains upstage and the man begins to chant a song that the chorus, dressed in white and cream, echoes back to the call he makes as it marches down the aisle of the theater with buckets in hand. The chorus surrounds Oya and throws its water buckets at her. She moves to center stage and white light illuminates her. As the chorus begins to discuss what befell Oya, she lies on her bucket and lifts her legs in the air to simulate floating. She holds her ear and whispers "Oya in the air Oya," "A breeze over Oya," "Oya . . . Oya . . ." as the others talk (12). The cacophony of sound, minimalist staging, references to water, and monochromatic costumes establish *In the Red and Brown Water* as ritual drama, "a cleansing, binding, communal, recreative force," according to Soyinka.[17] Paul Carter Harrison further specifies black theater in general as "the ritual reenactment of black experience."[18] While Soyinka locates ritual as central to the origins of all theater even if it is absent in contemporary works, Harrison excludes any dramatic form that does not include ritual reenactment from the category of theater. While I do not draw as strict a demarcation as Harrison, his assertion points to the essential role of ritual in black culture and the way it serves as a fundamental mode of meaning-making through performance. In McCraney's plays, ritual enables the characters to craft liberatory dreams.

Oya cuts off her ear, severing her zone of erotic pleasure, and gives it to Shango, freeing herself of the burden of normative desire. In the moment of self-sacrifice she also freed herself to commune with her ancestral namesake and become one with the air. Her ability to reorient herself comes through the sacrifice of her feminized body—a socially constituted form of gender appearance that reinstalled hierarchies—and shifts the direction of the play. Her act offers insight into how temporality informs our conception of the political potential of performance. Which is to say, performance moves through bodies, across spaces, and through times to activate the force of the fourth stage: "Commonly recognized in most African metaphysics are the three worlds . . . the world of the ancestor, the living, and the unborn. Less understood or explored is the fourth stage, the dark continuum of transition where occurs the inter-transmutation of essence-ideal and materiality. It houses the ultimate expression of the cosmic will."[19] Soyinka locates cosmic will as the particular province of African drama, which distinguishes the political power of the theatrical tradition. Similar to the drama Soyinka describes, *In the Red and Brown Water* depicts the process of moving through the fourth stage of transition because the space of transition helps to cultivate revolutionary performances. The moments of ritualized rupture in the play, Oya floating and Elegba prophesying, fill black freedom practices with ancient yet unborn power.

Although drawing from other diasporic traditions, McCraney aspires toward a distinct form of African American drama that emphasizes the transformative power of performance to change the body, geographical locations, and their conceptualization as a function of time. Although the names of his characters clearly reference Yoruba deities, he laments, "The hard part is to keep people from talking about the West African cosmology of my plays . . . Yes, you can trace the myths to Africa, but that's not how I learned them. The orisha stories I learned are American myths, not West African stories."[20] A native of Miami-Dade County, Florida, he insists on the syncretism of African American culture; he recalls seeing Yemoja (Yoruba goddess of the ocean and motherhood, known as the protector of children) for the first time "not on an urn from West Africa—it was in a painting of the Virgin Mary in the middle of Miami, and she was black."[21] With a clarity of intention and tradition, McCraney cultivates a resistance to teleology that animates the playful flow of associations in his theater and enables a "lushly streetwise mélange of homespun stories and ritual modes" that Randy Gener calls "accessible and shimmeringly theatrical."[22] His theater, much like that of Parks, questions the process of inheritance—passing down of information, history, or performance from one generation to the next—and, instead, uses performances to interject the present in the past. The temporal interruption extends the life of black performance because it troubles the logics of linear accumulation.

Through the performance of floating in the air and on the water, McCraney develops a mode of African American theater that activates political power in dispersal. His work aligns scattering with omnipresence, intertwining the materiality of Oya's body with the air and the water. Therefore, the scatterings of black people that resulted from the transatlantic slave trade and Hurricane Katrina, to name just two incidents in a long history of black people's displacement, serve as occasions that enable her repair. Oya suffers from the pain of deferred dreaming, but the play suggests that the source of her longing has as much to do with social forces outside of her control as her investment in objects of desire that lock her in place.

Further injecting redirection into the form of the play, McCraney disrupts the male-dominated imagery of the trickster figure, splitting the role into two characters, Elegba, a young boy, and Aunt Elegua, an older woman. Both have voracious sexual appetites and encourage Oya to consider alternative means of satisfying her desire besides heterosexual coupling and reproduction. At one point, Elegba invites Oya to join a threesome with him and a local DJ, Egungun, suggesting, "You been looking, right? You came to see. /

Maybe this what you looking for . . . Maybe this fix whats broke" (113). The master lyricist, Elegba, spits game (a vernacular term for courting) so fluidly one almost mistakes the aggressive sexual advance for a gentle romantic suggestion. McCraney creates line breaks that ensure the musicality of the dialogue and the appeal of Elegba's character. Unmoved by the seductive, balladic offer, Oya does not accept. Nevertheless, Elegba is the figure whom the trilogy reproduces, becoming the central character Marcus in the third play of *The Brother/Sister Plays*. Oya must lose the version of materiality that locks her into place in order to activate the subversive potential of her performance, while Esu elusively slips from Elegba to Aunt Elegua to Marcus throughout the plays. A secondary character remarks of Elegba's youthful body and yet uncanny presence, "You know that ain't no boy / This little motherfucker has been here before!" (58). His ability to transform his body marks a departure in that Esu participates in an intergenerational substitution in the person of a temporally unbound figure.

Elegba's strange familiarity bolsters another characteristic of McCraney's work, the spoken stage directions. Also a technique used in Parks's theater, in McCraney's vernacular-driven, hip-hop-inflected prose, the spoken stage directions draw audience members in instead of, as in Parks's usage, creating a Brechtian sense of alienation. The direct address, often delivered with a wink and a smile in the Public Theater production, activates the audience in the show. McCraney calls it "call and response," like the dynamic in the black church.[23] In a comment about the spoken stage directions in *The Brothers Size* he notes that actors say the stage directions, "'to invite the audience into the story—to remind the audience that they are being spoken to and are a part of the experience . . . And to allow the actor a chance to really focus on telling the story rather than pretending they are someone else.'" [24] Linguistically the play communicates mutuality through the repetition of a phrase of inevitability: "How could they not?" (29). How could the audience not laugh at Aunt Elegua's and Elegba's erotic signifying in act 1, scene 9, or notice Oya bleeding as she runs around the track in act 1, scene 3? The play mocks social mandates that ensure certain responses even as it creates a tone that facilitates uncritical looking. The mockery of the very state of being that the play encourages its audience members to inhabit creates sympathy for Oya as it marks the stunning courage expressed in moments of departure from social mandates.

With a sleight of hand, the play directs the audience through indirection and capitalizes on its use of African retentions in local contexts to create a twenty-first-century ritual theater that has much in common with Soyinka's and August Wilson's twentieth-century ones. Soyinka's theater sought to revise tragedy in spiritual terms that mine the power of temporal fluidity. Harry J. Elam persuasively argues that Wilson "refigures African American spirituality, fusing the African with the American in a distinct form that celebrates a sense of spiritual self-definition and inner self-determination, a secular, sacred, and visual expression of 'song.'"[25] McCraney marshals a similar pantheon of traditions, but his drama, unlike Wilson's, has the distinctive flavor of the American South and foregrounds the struggles of queer community members.

Wilson alludes to Ogun, one of the central figures in Yoruba theater, through the characterization of Herald Loomis in *Joe Turner's Come and Gone*. In the Yoruba tradition, Ogun performs the archetypal act of overcoming by transcending the fourth stage through an act of sheer will. He moves through the transitional fourth stage, which Soyinka describes as the "chthonic realm," "the immeasurable gulf of transition," and the "home of the tragic spirit."[26] Ogun, according to Soyinka, "plunged" into the immeasurable gulf bound for disintegration but "resists the final step towards complete annihilation."[27] Elam explains, "Ogun performed a symbolic act that reaffirmed the power of the human will to overcome" and therefore functions as the prototypical tragic figure.[28] Although a central figure throughout McCraney's trilogy, none of the plays focuses on Ogun. Rather, they appropriate his mighty will and assign it to other figures, including Oya. Giving Oya the power to resist annihilation even in the face of a deferred rite of passage transforms the theater into a space where queer theatrical bodies affirm the power of the human will to overcome.

As with *Joe Turner's Come and Gone*, McCraney's play foregrounds in-between spaces as productive ones through Oya's airy location and the setting of the play. It is set in the government housing projects of San Pere in "the distant present," although the opening scene could take place anywhere, and the Public Theater production seems to be set in the middle of a body of water. The references to water take on two connotations in the trilogy: the transatlantic slave trade and the floods that devastated the Gulf Coast in 2005. McCraney first staged *In the Red and Brown Water* in 2006, just months after Hurricane Katrina hit the Gulf Coast. While the prologue does not call for the lighting or staging presented in the Public Theater production (in fact the play calls for Oya to lie down on the ground), the director Tina Landau evokes a contemporary context that the play and the trilogy affirm, while it harkens back to an initiating site of racial dispersal. *In the Red and Brown Water*, borrowing from August Wilson's rich theater legacy, describes those lost in the Middle Passage as the bone people.

Recounting a dream to Oya's mother, Mama Moja, Elegba reveals a prophetic vision that contextualizes the prologue. As the messenger begins to describe his dream, the stage is bathed in blue light, except for Mama Moja and Elegba who are center stage and covered in white light. Elegba recalls:

> It's always about the water, my dreams . . . I walk on the bottom on
> The floor of the waters and they's these people Walk alongside me but
> they all bones and they Click the bone people, they talk in the click.
> I say, "Where yall going?" And they say, "Just Walking for a while."
> I say, "Don't you want To go home . . ." They say, "When we walk

there, it Wasn't there no more." I feel bad for them . . . Then they click
and I come up on the mud part, Like they send me to the land part,
and I'm Sitting there waiting 'cause I know they want Me to wait
I wait there looking and on Top of the waters is Oya. (22–23)

Known by several different names—"Esu-Elegbara in Nigeria and Legba
among the Fon in Benin . . . Exu in Brazil, Echu-Elegua in Cuba, Papa Legba
(pronounced La-Bas) in the pantheon of the loa of Vaudou of Haiti, and Papa
La Bas in the loa of Hoodoo in the United States"—the messenger figure,
Elegba, has access to the space in between, the crossroads, the fourth stage.[29]
Henry Louis Gates Jr. explains, "Esu is the guardian of the crossroads . . .
master of that elusive, mystical barrier that separates the divine world from
the profane."[30] His ability to cross over enables him to commune with other
transitional spirits, including the mythical bone people, those lost in the Middle Passage. Strikingly, during his commiseration with the homeless bone
people, whom he recognizes but distinguishes himself from by going "up
on the mud part," he sees Oya floating. For the second time—the first is in
the prologue—Oya floats in the middle of a scene of liminality. Her bodily
suspension transforms into erotic desire as Elegba describes her: "Oya girl
floating on top of the water, / Looking up towards the sky with no clothes /
She hardly got no clothes on and she got her legs / Wide . . . And she holding
her head on the side with her / Hand like something ailing her. / But from her
legs blood coming down and it's making the pond / Red" (23). Elegba situates Oya in proximity to the bone people and through that proximity seems
to create a visual link that joins the social trauma of Oya's infertility to the
physical violence of the transatlantic slave trade. Yet he does not describe the
spilling of enslaved Africans' blood; instead he depicts the bone people on
the move. Moreover, he insists, "she / Ain't in pain Mama Moja she ain't in /
No pain it look like just laying on top of / That water. Brown skin in the red
water" (23). Oya's ease belies the traumatic connotation of the Middle Passage and suggests that her ability to inhabit the liminal space provides some
comfort that she cannot access in the present.

Many artists, including Kara Walker in *After the Deluge*, the Classical Theatre of Harlem in their 2007 production of *Waiting for Godot*, and Spike
Lee in his documentary film *When the Levees Broke: A Requiem in Four
Acts*, have linked the devastation of the twenty-first-century disaster to the
transatlantic slave trade, but McCraney does not indict the government or
whiteness for the failures that enabled the destruction in 2005. Instead, he
focuses on the cultural rituals that sustain the community imagined in the play
and link them to a long history of insurgent power. His play suggests that the
movement offers a retreat to a temporal underground, a fourth stage where
freedom practices circulate. Performance enables an active engagement with
the past that transforms not only what will be but also what was.

The transformation focuses on interrupting the finality of death. In act 1, scene 4, the play depicts dying through movement, drumming, and chanting. Mama Moja is called out to her porch where Oya finds her. In the "near distance" (37) she hears "death calling" (38). The sound of death is Aunt Elegua singing, "Gonna lay down my burdens . . . Down by the riverside" (38). In the Public Theater production, as Aunt Elegua sings she holds a drum that emits light and leads the chorus, which sings behind her with hands outstretched. Mama Moja takes the drum and starts singing, "I ain't going to study war no more," before she announces her death, saying "Mama Moja moves / To lay her cross down" and Oya replies, "Oya sees it." Mama affirms, "How could she not?" (39). The inexorability of death that forces Mama Moja to, in word and deed, "leave this world"—with a gasp she trembles, crosses her arms over her chest while kneeling, and curls over—does not prevent her from joining the chorus and speaking from the world of the ancestors in act 1, scene 11. Aunt Elegua leads the chorus, which performs the function of "chthonic reflections (or memory)," reconstituting Oya's narrative to usher in her transition.[31]

Aunt Elegua and Elegba play critical roles at the crossroads, but, ultimately, Oya must find her own voice. On the night when Oya learns that Shango betrayed her, impregnating one of her neighbors, she greets him and tells him she has a present for him "so he remembers [her] in his new life and times!" (122). Oya returns to the stage holding the side of her head, the former space of their erotic connection. In the final scene, as Shango greets her he reaches out to touch her right ear, but Oya's hand blocks his advance. Now that this erogenous zone is inaccessible, Shango must focus on what else Oya has to offer. "In the other hand, her left . . . / Oya gives it to Shango. / I do this in remembrance of you . . . / I wished I could make a part of me / To give you but I had to take what's / Already there . . . Just give you what I got. / Oya bleeds, down her right hand" (123–24). In this act of mutilation, Oya not only disfigures herself as a sacrifice for the insufficiencies of heteronormative reproduction, she also reconfigures the body as a zone of possibility. Locating the site of her pleasure and removing it as an act of sacrifice results in the unlikely opportunity for, according to Elegba, the closing of all her wounds (124). The ritual act of cutting severs her tie to a mode of desire that places her in a perpetual state of deferment. Now freed of the burden of normative desire, Oya moves freely in the air. Serving as a cautionary tale that ushers in an otherworldly force, Oya performs her own rites of passage: a young black woman's act of self-fashioning black freedom movements.

The Brother/Sister Plays and the Black Real

✦

Omi Osun Joni L. Jones

Blackness is a wonder. The empirical evidence of our persistent aliveness and formidable imagination belies the corrosive mandates of white supremacy. Art gives us an opportunity to look closely at the wonder of our lives, to pause, to reflect by unleashing the imagination, the world of possibility, the what if. Art can also reveal what may be hiding in plain sight, particularly for those of us who are navigating multiple oppressions that may obscure other powerful truths about who we are.

In *The Brother/Sister Plays*, Tarell Alvin McCraney provides a vision of Black life that exists within intersectional oppressions while simultaneously crafting a reality beyond those oppressions. Understanding Blackness as more than the sum of resistance strategies is a way to envision Black people in our deepest humanity, to know us to be profoundly, mundanely human. McCraney's fictional world of San Pere, Louisiana allows us to experience— perhaps remember, perhaps discover—the density of Black realities, what I think of as the Black Real.[1] The Black Real makes no claim at delimiting all theatrical work created for, by, about, and/or near Black people.[2] Instead, by acknowledging the richness of Black realities, the Black Real provides an approach to works that have an investment in a complex Blackness expressed through a particular set of theatrical choices. Though amply trained in and deeply conversant with myriad theatrical aesthetics, McCraney makes a host of dramaturgical moves throughout *The Brother/Sister Plays* that reveal an understanding of Black realities, an understanding of how the "real" is constituted for many Black people. Situating a discussion of his work within manifold Black frameworks expands the rich possibilities for understanding, analyzing, and respecting his dramaturgy and, importantly, for understanding, analyzing, and respecting our own Black lives.

The dramaturgical and psychic textures of the Black Real spiral through overlapping characteristics. Three of these characteristics found most prominently in *The Brother/Sister Plays* are self-naming/self-narrating, indeterminacy, and an interanimating diaspora. These elements are mutually supporting and influencing. Self-naming is a strategy of indeterminacy, as it requires a minute-by-minute evolution of one's identity, a spontaneous dynamic shifting of relations and power. Self-naming also consciously or unconsciously draws on the multiple truths of the African diaspora. Indeterminacy allows for diasporic transtemporality that situates time and place as nonlinear, multidirectional, and spiritually available, and positions kinship as bonds beyond blood lineages. In the Black Real, the agency of self-naming, the improvisational space of indeterminacy, and the spiritual and political connective tissue of the African diaspora embedded in Black lives are quotidian. The Black Real understands spiritual logics and improvisational innovation to be a way of life—in fact, an expectation.

Self-Naming/Self-Narrating

The opening scenes of each of the plays in McCraney's triptych begin with the agential, communal process of self-narrating.[3] McCraney's inventive narrative structures are an essential dramaturgical device that reveals much about the residents of San Pere, Louisiana, where these plays are set, as well as the actual lives of many Black people.

MAMA MOJA:
Mama Moja enters the space . . .
Where you going Oya? (*In the Red and Brown Water*, act 1, scene 1, 15)[4]

OGUN:
Ogun Size enters.
Osi! (*The Brothers Size*, act 1, acene 1, 141)

OSHA:
Marcus?
MARCUS:
Ever seen a black boy stop n stare?
Like he just heard a ghost.
Or remembered a . . . (*Marcus; Or the Secret of Sweet*, act 1, scene 1, 249)

In the above examples, Mama Moja, Ogun, and Marcus establish a direct relationship with the audience/witnesses and make a distinction between themselves as characters in a play and themselves as themselves.

McCraney's self-narrating brings forth a particular brand of storytelling that troubles the notion of theater as "make believe" for, as he has asserted, it allows "the actor a chance to really focus on telling the story rather than pretending they are someone else."[5] McCraney's approach blurs the demarcation between performer and character, thereby generating a fertile indeterminacy.[6] The major characters in each play are given the authority and control of self-narrating, of naming how they relate to the other characters, how they feel, and how they fit into the story. In this way, the performers as themselves have the opportunity to speak directly to the audience/witnesses rather than solely embodying a fictional character talking to other fictional characters. The performers are more active agents rather than vessels to be filled by a playwright or a director. With third-person narration, the performer can make a host of choices that allows their *own* perspective to come through along with the perspective of the character, and, in so doing, develops a particular relationship with the audience/witnesses that can exceed the bounds of the story the character is living in. In this way, the performer can claim the story, can seize it. They actively create it.

Just after the opening moments of *In the Red and Brown Water* cited above, Mama Moja responds to a challenge Oya makes by saying:

MAMA MOJA:
Moja looks at Oya like, "What I say?"
What I say? (15)[7]

The first part of her first line, "Moja looks at Oya like," references a familiar set of Black aesthetic choices—a challenging look from an elder that might be accompanied by raised eyebrows, a cocked head, and a voice communicating incredulity. Here, the performer makes an unmediated connection with the audience/witnesses and can choose to speak the first part of the line as herself, then offer up Mama Moja's personality with the remainder of the line, or can talk to the audience/witnesses by speaking both parts of the line as Mama Moja. The performer then moves to the vernacular command, "What I say?," addressing Oya directly. These series of relational shifts amplify the storytelling nature of *The Brother/Sister Plays* and give control to the performer as they create an embrace with the audience/witnesses, an aesthetic that capitalizes on the alive nature of theater.

The use of third-person narration carries a distinctive psychic force. The self becomes both here (in the theater) *and* over there (in San Pere), becomes subject of the story in the way that dramatic characters typically assume a subjective identity, *and* serves as a subject in the actual action that is the theatrical event. The performer embodying Mama Moja does not say "I look at Oya," or "She looks at Oya." By saying "Mama Moja looks at Oya," the performer stands as herself before the audience/witnesses *and* simultaneously shows Mama Moja to the audience/witnesses in the complex layering that develops as the performer assumes multiple relationships to the audience/witnesses, the other characters, and the character they embody. The simultaneity of perspectives possible with this self-narration mirrors the multiple layers of reality or nowness that characterizes Black beingness, a reality that walks closely with history and the improvisation possible in the present moment. This generates a dynamism that resists stasis and predictability and allows varied spaces and times to commingle in the now.

The dramaturgical choice to have characters self-narrate makes room for all of the self to be present, with no required illusion of an absent self for the sake of a present character. The performer embodies trans-temporality as they move across layers of time and place—the *actual* here and now of a theatrical performance that consciously enfolds the audience/witnesses into the experience, and the *fictive* San Pere, Louisiana, in the "distant present" that is occupied by the characters interacting onstage.[8]

Storytelling in *The Brother/Sister Plays* gives space for the performer, the self, to become a subject in the story in a way that is typically reserved for the dramatis personae. In so doing, the performer crafts an intimacy with the audience/witnesses, moving them from the rather passive role of audience into the more engaged role of collaborators. There is an important community-building that is possible with McCraney's dramaturgy. There is also agency in the self-naming that comes from this brand of storytelling. As seen in the examples offered earlier, McCraney's characters frequently identify themselves when they enter a scene and declare a personal feeling before entering into dialogue with another character. The performers not only inhabit characters, they pronounce them, assert them, create them. McCraney gives the performers space to find the character outside of the confines of spoken dialogue and typically unspoken stage directions. While McCraney refers to his storytelling as "spoken stage directions," I believe something more electric and laden with potential occurs.[9]

The epic device of storytelling within the dramatic device of theater creates a productive tension—*Who is telling the story?* Performer as self? A character? A performer commenting on a character? *Who is receiving the story?* An anonymous audience? Audience/witness collaborators? Spontaneously imagined friends? The answers to these questions slip and shift throughout the productions, allowing for an energetic relational awareness cocreated in the process of performance.

In a public interview with artist/scholar Aymar Jean Christian, McCraney likened the aesthetics of *In the Red and Brown Water* to *Ifa*, a divination practice built around the structures of storytelling.[10] In Yoruba-based spiritual practices, *Ifa* divination reveals the corpus of *Odu*, the multilayered verses/stories/scripture that offer guidance to supplicants seeking assistance in following their lives' paths. *Odu* are presented as tales in the epic mode—with narration, dialogue, points of view, and perspective—and they are constructed with a conscious awareness of an audience which might include the supplicant, an *Iyalawo*, also *Iyanifa*, and/or *Babalawo* (the earthly emissaries for the Divinity *Orunmila* charged with presenting and interpreting the *Odu* during *Ifa* divination), and any community members who might be present for the reading. When *Ifa* is cast, there is often a lively exchange among all present about the metaphors embedded in and import assigned to the *Odu* that manifests from the specific position of the particular divination technology used: *opele* (divining chain), *ikin Ifa* (palm nuts), or cowrie shells.[11] Each play in McCraney's triptych exists as *Odu*, recounting the lives of the characters, providing guidance for all who are gathered, and opening up cocreated commentary ignited by directly addressing the audience/witnesses.

Self-naming/self-narrating is a Black necessity, allowing for the evolution and re-articulation of what Black might be, what Fred Moten calls "consent not to be a single being."[12] In the Black Real, Black people are simultaneously many entities that morph as time and circumstance require. To name ourselves—to understand our multifaceted selves in connection to others, to tell our stories—is the very project of Blackness as identity. This naming as an enactment of Blackness is the political reality enmeshed in our everyday lives, one which McCraney aestheticizes through the people of San Pere. Though agency, sovereignty, and self-determination are surely circumscribed by the forces of patriarchy, capitalism, and white supremacy, just as surely, there is a drive toward these states as evidenced in McCraney's theatrical choices and in the very obstinate tenacity of Black lives, what Christina Sharpe calls "an insistence on existing," an aliveness that is constrained by, but not confined to, social abjection.[13]

Indeterminacy

While McCraney's triptych makes frequent use of the material, visceral act of storytelling that creates community and gestures towards agency, it also amply incorporates intangible worlds within the frame of the characters' everyday lives. Such worlds are the space of indeterminacy where improvisation can flourish. Indeterminacy is the state of multiplicity, of the often unnameable, of that which cannot be pinned down—states in *The Brother/Sister Plays* that are most often found in spirituality, trans-temporality, and erotic autonomy.

Each play opens with a prologue. In *In the Red and Brown Water*, chronologically the first of the three plays for the characters of San Pere, the prologue begins with stage directions that indicate:

The men all begin to hum, a sad sweet hum,

Thick like the early morning mist.

. . .

The cast glows like a pantheon of deities . . . (11)

These directions are followed by the women characters in ceremony offering fragments of dialogue:

> OYA:
> (*Sharp breath out*)
> Ah!
> AUNT ELEGUA:
> I don't know all . . .
> MAMA MOJA:
> Nobody does.
> AUNT ELEGUA:
> But say she ain't even scream.
> OYA:
> Oya in the air Oya . . .
> SHUN:
> Say it sound like the wind . . ." (12)

The Brothers Size opens in a similarly ceremonial fashion:

The Opening Song

The lights come up on three men standing onstage. This is the opening invocation and should be repeated for as long as needed to complete the ritual.

> ELEGBA, OSHOOSI SIZE AND OGUN SIZE:
> (*Breath out!*)
> ELEGBA:
> This road is rough
> OSHOOSI SIZE:
> Mmmm . . .
> OGUN SIZE:
> Huh!
> ELEGBA:
> This road is rough. (137–38)

And the stage directions that open *Marcus; Or the Secret of Sweet* are:

A Dream

The lights come up on Marcus in his bed sleeping and Oshoosi Size standing in a pool of water crying gently at first until he covers his mouth, doubles over, and . . .

This dream segues into:

A Processional

> *The cast forms a funeral processional led by Ogun Size and trailed by Marcus.* (247–48)

The prologues are "the break"—the site of spirituality and creativity—and as such, the "when" and the "where" of the prologues are set in a different sphere than the two acts that follow. McCraney uses these opening "breaks" to launch us into the lush space of possibility, into the crossroads of choice, into the psychic participation in our own outcome that the plays offer up. Opening with "the break" establishes this realm as part of the natural order of things in San Pere—not exceptional, but foundational. Ceremony, ritual, song, processional, hum, and dreams are the vibrations of everyday life. Here, these are not supernatural features but natural features indeed.

The centrality of "the break" as the everyday is solidified by closing two of the three plays with epilogues that exist on a spiritual psychic plane.[14] *In the Red and Brown Water* reimagines the text from the prologue as the women reflect on Oya's self-mutilation, and Oya lets out her last breath. In *Marcus*, the epilogue revisits the opening dream with an impending storm on the horizon. While *The Brothers Size* does not shift into "the break" that bookends *In the Red and Brown Water* and *Marcus*, it creates its own spiral enclosure as Ogun's struggle to push Oshoosi to flee is the very enactment of Elegba's prologue chant: "This road is rough." All three plays are encapsulated in the fecundity of multiple possibilities, of a productive unfixedness—the very homeplace of Spirit.

In responding to the endings in McCraney's triptych, *New York Times* critic Ben Brantley writes, "And Mr. McCraney remains least assured in his endings. For all the rushing momentum of these plays, each concludes with a zephyrlike gentleness that baffles expectations." And while Brantley acknowledges that, "On the other hand, such endings aren't inappropriate for a remarkable artist who knows that stories never stop, that they are mutable works in progress for as long as we live," even this recognition misses the potency—indeed, the very expectation—that endings do not indicate cessation when situated in Black realities.[15] Alexis Pauline Gumbs captures this quality so precisely when she writes in her speculative documentary, "life was precious and could spill. / it meant spirit was sticky and could stay."[16] In worlds governed by Spirit, the end of the body or material presence does not end the "real." I am interested in the ways Blackness insists on "real" governed by its own logics, not only in terms of corporeality, but through the manifestation of that which exists beyond the body—art/spirit—therefore, an ongoing, ever-present rejection of the inclusion-exclusion binary. At the end of *The Brothers Size*, Oshoosi leaves his brother Ogun to begin a fugitive life; *In the Red and Brown Water* ends with Oya (possibly) transcending to the mysteries of the next spiritual realm; *Marcus; Or the Secret of Sweet* concludes with an impending hurricane. Some have left, some have died, some are likely to perish, but, as Spirit remains, the certainty of Blackness *is*. In the Black Real, time is not discretely segmented with acts of closure; all time is presently available, is now.

The Yoruba concept of *aiye* bears heavily on my postulation of indeterminacy as an element of the Black Real. *Aiye* references the physical world where living humans reside, along with the intangible forces that move through the world. The "real" in this worldview encompasses materiality that can be shaped by unseen forces. This "real" exists outside of an exclusively physical notion of reality. What may be understood as "magic" in one worldview is part of everyday life in *aiye*. Because McCraney draws on Yoruba worlds (among others) to animate San Pere, examining Yoruba cosmology can yield another set of truths that may be more apt than concepts most commonly associated with Western theater practice. While this understanding of "real" predates colonization and enslavement, it is powerful to consider how those horrors may have amplified these already existing phenomena, an awareness of how the unseen exists alongside the seen. Perhaps the conditions of violent oppression prompt greater acuity to the unseen as a method for navigating terror. This speculation has an intellectual logic to it but should not be emphasized at the expense of recognizing the existence of a vibrant, commingling, seen and unseen *aiye* prior to enslavement and colonization.[17] The Black Real and San Pere do not require trauma in order to exist.

The Divinity responsible for carrying human messages from *aiye* to *orun*, the realm of the ancestors and Divinities, is Legba, the Divinity of the crossroads/choice and owner of the life force. This Divine energy is the very enactment of ambiguity—traversing between spiritual realms, offering multiple paths that must be fervently considered, and reveling in diverse sexualities. Ambiguity, or, more precisely, simultaneous multiplicity, is central to the worldview that is the Black Real.

It is telling that Legba is the only Divinity who exists as a character in each play of the triptych. Regardless of age or circumstance, in each play the Legba figure is a catalyst for change and pushes other characters to make tough decisions, to choose a road. Through Legba, the characters confront a "Legba moment," which requires them to address life choices. Legba is commonly understood as a trickster; however, I understand Legba as providing opportunities for humans to exercise good character when presented with choices and challenges. This understanding foregrounds the role of one's *ori*—one's head, destiny, or first *Divinity* in making decisions, rather than featuring the presumed capriciousness of a Divinity. Conceptualizing Legba as a bearer of choice connects this Divinity to agency and good character. In *The Brother/Sister Plays*, Oshoosi must examine his sexual desire when Elegba works to seduce him; Oya must consider the bounds of friendship when Elegba seeks refuge at her home; and Marcus Eshu tests the San Pere residents' ethics and commitment to secrets as he pleads for information about his father, Elegba. Marcus Eshu further prods the characters to choose sound ethics and exercise good character each time a character says his name. Said out loud, Marcus Eshu is a plea to "mark us Eshu," to guide us. In a powerful way, each time they call him, they are asking him to help at the crossroads of decision making.

Not only do McCraney's Legba characters place the other characters in the unstable space of decision making, his Legbas also reflect the Divinity's role as the owner of the life force which manifests in the plays as an exuberant erotic autonomy—Elegba in *In the Red and Brown Water* as Oya's randy, pansexual, mischievous confidant; Elegba in *The Brothers Size* as Oshoosi's mercurial, sexually ambiguous friend and former prison mate; and Marcus Eshu, the gay sixteen-year-old son of Elegba and Oba in *Marcus; Or the Secret of Sweet*.

In *The Brothers Size*, a sexual relationship between Elegba and Oshoosi is not made explicit, but the sexual undercurrent between them is palpable, in part, because of its hints and innuendoes that point to some measure of sexual consummation between them. When Elegba enters in act 1, scene 2, he tells Oshoosi that he shouldn't have told his brother Ogun about everything that happened in prison. The scene continues:

OSHOOSI SIZE:
I spoke it all man.
ELEGBA:
You say it all?
All about the pen?
OSHOOSI SIZE:
ELEGBA:
OSHOOSI SIZE:
Nah. I ain't tell him all that.
ELEGBA:
Yeah that shit ain't nothin . . .
OSHOOSI SIZE:
. . . Had to hold your own self tight at night.
ELEGBA:
You didn't want nobody to do it for you.
OSHOOSI SIZE:
Nah. Hell nah.
Nigga's always offerin.
ELEGBA:
Or trying to take it.

OSHOOSI SIZE:
That shit crazy, crazy shit.
I didn't think they would get like that.
ELEGBA:
Man when you in need, your mind . . .
OSHOOSI SIZE:
Man . . .
Sometimes I had to remind myself,
That I wouldn't gon be there that long.
ELEGBA:
Yeah you only had a year,
OSHOOSI SIZE:
Two.
Man . . .
ELEGBA:
We was like brothers.
OSHOOSI SIZE:
Yeah.
ELEGBA:
Brothers in need. (151–53)

Later, in Ogun's dream, Elegba manipulates Oshoosi into singing a seductive duet, telling Oshoosi, "My brother . . . / Can you walk with me? / I am your taker. / I am here to take you home" (177). Then, in Oshoosi's memory of the events that led to the police hunting him at the end of the play, Elegba "Slides down onto his thigh." Oshoosi responds, "What you doin?" After Elegba says "Elegba smiling. / Nothing brother . . . / Just singing to you like I used to. This nice ain't it?"—Oshoosi is silent as Elegba sings (220).

The young Elegba in *In the Red and Brown Water* is more playful than the adult Elegba in *The Brothers Size*, though no less provocative. The younger Elegba has male and female lovers. He eventually becomes a doting father even as he continues to grind with the male DJ and flirt with the women of San Pere. O Li Roon notes that Elegba "ain't no boy / This lil motherfucker been here before," suggesting an understanding of time that is nonlinear and untethered to familiar notions of birth and death (58).

In a similar, mischievously erotic way, Aunt Elegua of *In the Red and Brown Water* transgresses social boundaries by boldly flirting with Oya's boyfriend, Shango:

SHANGO:
Enter Shango.
AUNT ELEGUA:
Who this?

OYA:
Shango this Elegua.
AUNT ELEGUA:
Huh.
Yousa phyne thang ain't you.
Yes sir looka here looka here.
This here your friend Oya girl?
OYA:
Yes Shango is my friend.
AUNT ELEGUA:
Yall lovers and friends?
OYA:
Aunt Ele!
AUNT ELEGUA:
Oh honey I'm just asking ain't judging
Nah nah. Just asking. I wouldn't mind if I do . . . (52)

Moments later, Aunt Elegua and Legba engage in the verbal repartee expected of the Divine force overseeing communication and the energy of bodacious sexuality. It is a moment when kindred seem to recognize in each other the excitement of flaunting sexual and social taboos:

AUNT ELEGUA:
Who lil boy this is?
ELEGBA:
Who big woman you is?
AUNT ELEGUA:
All right now you got slick with the white man
I beat the snot out your ass and tell yo mama!
Elegua smiles.
I like him! He full of something. Like light . . .
You got pretty eyes boy. Who you leading
With them eyes? You gon be my husband
When you get grown. I promise you. (62)

This flirtation gives way to Elegba singing prophetically about Oya's death as he tells the audience/witnesses "A spell comes o'er Legba" (65). Aunt Elegua and Elegba, through their positions as social trangressors, as threshold crossers, bring the vision from *orun* to *aiye*. The sexual vibration conjures the path of indeterminacy, allowing for communication between realms.

Marcus Eshu of *Marcus; Or the Secret of Sweet* is gay, or "sweet," like his father Elegba. He senses this truth about his identity from his dreams, from the evasions he meets when he asks about his father, and, ultimately, from his unmistakable gay desire when he is with Shua. His sexuality is the very public secret that bursts forth alongside the impending storm, the natural world mirroring/guiding Marcus's erotic upheaval.

In considering the queer sexualities of McCraney's Legbas as powerful demonstrations of indeterminacy, Yoruba language provides a way of amplifying this understanding. In Yoruba, *daudu* is the first male child born into a family. This child inherits the family's wealth and holds high social status. Among the Hausa of northern Nigeria, however, *daudu* is a derisive term that refers to males who perform their identities in female-identified ways.[18] *Daudu*, then, is simultaneously valorizing and condemning; it exists in "the break," in a malleable space where competing truths can coexist.[19]

An Interanimating Diaspora

In my mapping of the Black Real, the diaspora is its own unifying organism born of direct and imagined relationships, forged through shared practices and understandings that do not mute the distinctiveness of each. This porous nature of the diaspora relates to Richard Iton's assertion that Black politics and culture do "not posit the nation-state as the only or final frontier."[20] Indeed, African diaspora dwellers share, borrow, offer, and take among each other, ensuring an ever-transforming and conjointly defining set of realities.

McCraney crafts San Pere from the diasporic remnants found in names and traditions of Cuba, Yorubaland, Miami, Louisiana; this amalgam is the "real" of Black lives, the quilt, the collage, the sampling, the sometimes-unconscious synergistic absorptions. The character names speak to the ways that the African diaspora reshapes itself through saturation of interaction. Set in the United States, with characters bearing names primarily from Nigeria but also from other parts of the diaspora, the San Pere residents are evidence of the way that diasporic locations meld, so that there are no bounded locations but a diaspora of traditions, beliefs, and practices.[21] While Legba and Esu are the manifestations used by many Yoruba-based spiritual practitioners in the United States, Esu-Elegbara is commonly found in Nigeria, Exu in Brazil, and Ellegua in Cuba. The pronunciation of Marcus Eshu's name reflects the Brazilian Exu along with an Anglicized spelling commonly used in the United States. In *Marcus; Or the Secret of Sweet*, we also encounter Elegua, here suggesting a Cuban inflection. In *The Brothers Size*, McCraney names the energy of the crossroads as Elegba, a spelling with a close kinship to the Nigerian conceptualization of Esu-Elegbara and the U.S. Legba. In *In the Red and Brown Water*, there are multiple manifestations of this energy—the male Elegba and the female Aunt Elegua.

Each of these Legba variants is found in *The Brother/Sister Plays*, so that the interconnectedness of the diaspora is established as these characters intermingle on the page and the stage. Fashioning the Yoruba *Orisa*, or

Divinities, as everyday Black folk with everyday human concerns encourages an experience of diaspora as being always here and there, then and now, and on the move to next, which is also now, as next lives in the present imagination.

The Brother/Sister Plays tilt towards this interanimating diaspora in the sequence in which McCraney wrote the plays. Although *In the Red and Brown Water* is chronologically the first of the three San Pere tales, McCraney wrote *The Brothers Size* first—the play populated only by Ogun, Oshoosi, and Legba. In many of the Yoruba-based spiritual traditions in the United States, Legba, Ogun, and Oshoosi (aka Ochoosi) are collectively known as The Warriors. They are among the first Divinities presented to practitioners; they guide and protect, and they are the required foundation before consecration to other *Orisa*. In ceremony, Legba must be propitiated before the ceremony can proceed.[22] From a spiritual vantage point, McCraney wrote the play of The Warriors before writing the stories of the other *Orisa*, thereby satisfying these Divine forces in the sequence required for successful ceremonies. The development of this triptych of U.S. life followed a mandate established long ago and far away. This (perhaps) chance sequencing of the plays is exactly what is required for a diaspora—the crossroads must be satisfied, the *ori* must be prepared to make sturdy ethical choices if the spiritual lineages are to continue.

Near the end of *In the Red and Brown Water*, Oya makes a psychic turn just after Egungun as DJ calls down a party with diasporic ritual methodology. In Yoruba cosmology, Egungun is the ancestral masquerade for a family's lineage. As the long cloth panels that encase the Egungun stir and swish the air while the masquerade swirls through the community, it demonstrates its kinship with Oya, the Divinity governing air, wind, and breath. The ancestors appear near the end of the play to offer up the ritual that will close this moment of the story:

SHANGO:
It's that bass drop . . .
O LI ROON:
So hard, thumping.
EGUNGUN:
Dum da da, dum da da!
OGUN SIZE:
It calls late, as soon as the sun downs
EGUNGUN:
And again out of nowhere . . .
ALL:
A crowd . . .
EGUNGUN:
The Egungun assumes the position.

DJing and spinning tha hottest earth
Thumping melodies invoking sex and
Heat.
Goddamn look at the girl in the green! (107–8)

After igniting the energy for the party/ritual, Egungun goes on to propose a sexual liaison with Legba and Oya while the other partygoers continue to flirt and grind. The vigor of dance and passion is part of the enactment of Spirit inside of ritual, adding to the psychic and physical transformation that ritual evokes. The residents of San Pere are not in a sacred grove or a church, but they sacralize the street with the use of spiritual technology—sonic vibration, the sweat of physicality, and the open space of the erotic. This party/ritual unhinges Oya, who then firmly rejects her partner Ogun Size, learns that her lover Shango is having a child with Shun, and presents Shango with a very personal remembrance of herself as a parting gift. The ritual methods of the African diaspora are shaped into the contexts where they are employed.

"How Could He Not?"

In this essay, self-narrating/self-naming is understood as building agency and community; indeterminacy is understood as "the break" (space of creativity and spirituality), choice, trans-temporality, and erotic autonomy; and an inter-animating diaspora is understood as a spiritually and politically constructed community. *The Brother/Sister Plays* illustrate the power of the Black Real to name and embody truths that are rooted in Black sensibilities. Reviewers of August Wilson's productions frequently describe aspects of his work as "magical realism" or "supernatural." In *American Theatre*, writer and director Isaac Butler described the ending of August Wilson's *Joe Turner's Come and Gone* as "a magic-realist act of healing."[23] Critic Terry Teachout described Wilson's *Piano Lesson* as "a domestic drama with supernatural overtones."[24] Rather than solely use traditions and cosmologies outside of Black sensibilities to discuss and experience work by Black artists, we can turn to many everyday African diasporic truths that reveal spiritual and political realities undergirding aesthetic decisions.

Throughout the triptych, different characters express a version of the rhetorical question "How could he not"—at once reflecting a Black vernacular linguistic flourish associated with Zora Neale Hurston's discussion of the "Negro's will to adorn"[25] along with posh British grammar of the highest social class. This haunting question is most present in *The Brothers Size*. When Elegba offers his hand to Oshoosi, Oshoosi replies with self-narration that can be confidentially shared with the audience: "Oshoosi takes it, how could he not." There is no question mark on this question, suggesting the inevitability of the erotic, the compelling nature of the choice Elegba presents, and the certainty that feels like no choice at all.

The African diaspora provides an abundance of traditions, cosmologies, and politics for us to employ when discussing and experiencing Black art. These analytical strategies give us the "Legba moment" of choosing non-Black constructs as the sole tools for our understanding, *or* drawing from the rich, fertile powers of the African diaspora. Why would we not.

One *Size* Does Not Fit All

✦

Voicing Black Masculinities in a Pursuit of "Freedoms"

Jeffrey Q. McCune Jr.

In the opening scene of Tarell Alvin McCraney's *The Brothers Size*, we see three men working together—in sound, in body, and in movement. The stage direction literally instructs: "the lights come up on three men standing on stage. This is the opening invocation and should be repeated for as long as needed to complete the ritual."[1] The use of invocation indicates ritual as a site of "coming together"—a meeting of people, ideas, and these three variant black bodies. While there is no set place of work given, in the use of sound and symbolic gesture we can imagine that they are building something together; we are asked to read beyond what is given, to see a world of sonic and physical transgression. This kind of clockwork machine—produced in their performative bonds and execution of movement and sound—provides a spotlight on what many black viewers know: black men often work together and work hard. What is clear—as this serves as the first spectacle for the play's audience—is that McCraney is also allowing us to witness a sort of ideological invocation about the "hardness" of black men's realities, the work of repetition, and the necessity of exhalation. This essay is an exploration of the different ways McCraney teaches us to read Black masculine performance and space, as well as challenge what I call *canonical black masculine narratives*, which have historically guided the larger public imaginary both within and outside black communities. These narratives, written historically across the bodies of black men to cast some gross universal, a one-size-fits-all model, capture the diversity of black masculine expression and conjure a way of knowing black men which configures masculinity as a singular production.

McCraney, I argue, provides us with a set of renderings that teach us to read better, beyond the gross universal, moving toward a dynamic and holistic exhibition of black masculinities which is at once flawed and fluid, limited and capacious. Through the use of Yoruba cosmology, dramatic expression, and dislocation of what Isaiah Wooden calls the "psychological realism" commonly found in dramatic renderings, we witness a treatment of black men and masculinity that demands versatility on stage and flexibility in our spectatorial practice.[2] McCraney particularly uses the stage directions in *The Brothers Size* to execute the most important element of dramaturgical choice for me: speaking and giving action in a way that enables an imagining of black men beyond the script (of drama and life). Consequently, the play, through its originality, not only takes us on a journey between brothers but also their interior struggles while simultaneously instigating a richer imagining of what black brothers can be in the American theatrical landscape. Indeed, I do not pretend that the readings that McCraney channels are novel or available to all audiences. Instead, I am suggesting that he offers a narrative practice, or a rendering, which employs the theatrical to make visible a corpus of subtexts and plain text, thereby producing a productive tension between what has been established as the "fictions of black masculinity" and a more dynamic, robust, and rigorous display of black masculinities.

Voicing Masculinities: Mapping the Road to a New Brotherhood

The opening of *The Brothers Size* is its own study in masculinity, from its commitment to silence, pausing and breathing, and spoken articulations of the turbulent road on which black men must walk, while also expressing the exhilarating force within release and reflexive ritual. Here, at the top of the morning, we are allowed to experience an invocation, which introduces us not only to affective display but also to the larger artistic thesis:

ELEGBA, OSHOOSI SIZE, AND OGUN SIZE:
(Breath Out!)
ELEGBA:
This road is rough . . .
OSHOOSI SIZE:
Mmmm . . .
OGUN SIZE:
Huh!
ELEGBA:
This road is rough.
OSHOOSI SIZE:
Huh!
ELEGBA:
This road is rough and . . . hard. (137–38)

Through breaks and breaths, coupled with "rough-hard" consonants, McCraney demonstrates through the text and in the scripted performance of it a recognition that black men face hardship while simultaneously breathing through it. McCraney shows us here that these men aren't necessarily hard, but the space of both work and masculinity is labor intensive—"rough and hard." Each person makes his own introduction, a signature pattern within McCraney's work; he draws attention to the self-awareness of each character in terms of his role in a larger narrative. Unique to his dramatic voice, actors speak their own stage directions and even sometimes narrate their own emotions—illuminating an organic storytelling tradition while also drawing attention to (un)conscious choice.

In the first version of the play I witnessed—at the Studio Theatre in Washington, D.C., in 2009—Ogun, an auto mechanic named after the deity known for ironwork, began this opening with a shovel, working on the driveway. Ogun introduces the play as the elder who opens up the path on which both Oshoosi and Elegba will travel. As they open in song and verbal chant, we understand what James Baldwin reveals in *The Fire Next Time*: "you are tough, dark, vulnerable, moody—with a very definite tendency to sound truculent because you want no one to think you are soft."[3] Rather than allowing this moment of articulating the "rough and the hard" to be the stand-alone representation for these men's gender performances, McCraney uses the rest of the play to show the very complexity Baldwin suggests in his quip to his (historic) nephew. In addition, the unique use of stage directions spoken by the performers, self-conscious speech such as "Ogun smiles," enables a reading of black men's acts as being intentionally placed and having a politics of complexity. McCraney announces these men's departures from a customary black masculine rubric—easily dismissible as "standard," "hyper-masculine," or even "gangster"—in order to interrupt and reprimand conventional audience theatrical readings.

In *The Brother/Sister Plays*, McCraney chronicles contemporary black experiences while drawing from elements of ancient West African traditions (Yoruba cosmology). Performance is a site where multiple bodies onstage can contest our spectatorial tendencies to have unifocal vision. Through a poetic, somewhat staccato tone and a highly minimalist aesthetic, McCraney forces his audiences to not only understand the beauty and complexity of blackness but also to craft their own imaginings within the almost barren set on which he plants diverse black bodies. In *The Brothers Size*, one of McCraney's first plays to receive public recognition, he introduces the world to three black men: Ogun Size, Oshoosi (pronounced "o-choose-see") Size, and Elegba. McCraney carves out a space for rich, complex black masculinities through the deployment of new dramatic language, an emphasis on "brother-ness," and the use of a small-scale set that allows for spectators to activate their own imaginings in the play. Like August Wilson, McCraney "decenters singular characters by dramatizing communities of black men to depict their various phases of identity formation."[4] This approach enables *The Brothers*

Size to erect different reading practices for its audience, wherein black men's personal stories escape the metonymic trap and act as filters to the intersections of black men's lives and their unique departures.

Ogun and Oshoosi are biological brothers, while Elegba is Oshoosi's "brother from another mother." In the play, from the beginning (as Elegba and Oshoosi have been released from prison and subjected to Ogun's fatherly wisdom) to the end (where Oshoosi is set up by Elegba and disappears with Ogun's help), we see a struggle for freedom and independence. The play poses a challenge to contemporary constructions of black masculinity— always sustaining a tension between the conventionally good, bad, and ugly. It is this productive tension that makes McCraney's *The Brothers Size* a compelling and instructive work. All three men occupy complex positions, never conceding to easy constructions of any one character as good or evil. While McCraney clearly plays with our classic dramatic expectations of good vs. evil, he confounds us through his constant disallowing of these men to be offered as exceptional, ideal, or wholly anything. Together, they are brothers sized up by American culture who embody the complex personhoods that move the spectator away from a damage-centered reading toward richer readings of black men's real lives and representations. McCraney carves a space where he radically imagines black masculine bodies that not only operate in different ways but also defy common expectations. Through the dialogic performance—the exchange between the spectacle (play) and the spectator (us, the audience)—we experience something akin to a representation of the everyday. For what McCraney includes in *The Brothers Size* is familiar, and what he does not include, we can gather within our imaginary or personal encounters.

As I have noted elsewhere, one of the unique elements of McCraney's work is his construction of a new dramatic voice through which black male subjectivity is choreographed. In other words, he makes black men speak as poets, masters of linguistic twists and turns—which allows the spectator to not only understand these men as creators of new language but also the architects of a new world. Consequently, we as audience members have to spend time with the characters, figure out their vernacular, in order to gain a fuller understanding of not only what they say but also what McCraney is teaching us.[5]

In contrast to the "rough and hard" opening, McCraney later shows us the love of Oshoosi and Elegba:

OSHOOSI SIZE:
Oshoosi size on lunch break,
Drinking a Coke Cola,
Singing a song.
(He sings.)

ELEGBA:
Elegba enters . . .
Sang that song, nigga!
OSHOOSI SIZE:
Huh? Ey, Elegba! . . .
OSHOOSI SIZE:
You crazy.
ELEGBA:
It's true brother!
Where you get a voice like that?
I been wondering since lockup,
"How Oshoosi get his voice?"
OSHOOSI SIZE:
Ah hell Legba you got a voice.
ELEGBA:
But my voice clear,
I know that, I was born a choirboy.
But you? You a siren.
OSHOOSI SIZE:
What?
ELEGBA:
A siren!
You open up your mouth an everybody knows where the pain at.
Your voice come out and say, "the pain right here.
It's here, see it? See?"
OSHOOSI SIZE:
C'mon man . . .
ELEGBA:
You don't like nobody to brag on you . . .
OSHOOSI SIZE:
Nah man.
ELEGBA:
That's all right, I ain't scared to,
Everybody needs somebody to brag on him.
You like my brother man . . . I ain't scared to brag on you.
Ain't embarrassed about my brother.
Nah, too cool to be embarrassed.
OSHOOSI SIZE:
My man Legba! (148–50)

This scene maps the importance of improvisation in McCraney's careful and committed carving of a space for the potential and possibility of a black masculine subject of rich complexity. First, McCraney opens this scene with

Oshoosi's improvisational singing. Oshoosi, as a deity who wonders and wanders, is perfect to embody improvisation. Improvisation, the performance that spontaneously erupts within a moment without warning, disrupts all that the audience may anticipate in any given moment. Here, Oshoosi bursts into song, sitting and singing solo in a play that is not a musical, foreshadowing the "tenderness" that will later be performed in the play. His act of tender singing not only calls the audience to understand him outside the "rough and hard," but also calls forth his brother and friend Elegba. Because of the depth of his singing, his ability to sing so we "know where the pain is," Elegba wanders into the space fixed by Oshoosi's song. Elegba, the protector-trickster figure in Yoruba lore, gives attention to the musicality, richness, and magic of Oshoosi's voice and clearly enlivens his spirit. Anaya McMurray refers to this as the "improvisation zone."[6] Oshoosi and Elegba are allowed to find a balance between cultural identity and individual creativity and complexity. While both have been given various scripts according to their names, which are aligned with Yoruba culture and practice, McCraney allows them to have greater fluidity. McCraney makes real here what I propose in this essay: namely, that *The Brothers Size* allows for fluidity and flux to be the nature of things, rather than activating some static construction of these black male characters for the intelligibility of the viewing audience. As the average audience engages these bodies, in this moment of the unexpected, they are offered an opportunity to read these men as comfortably contradictory.

In this zone of improvisation, we also see a space where male bonding is not predicated upon what Eve Sedgwick calls the "erotic triangle"—the "use of women as exchangeable, perhaps symbolic property for the primary purpose of cementing the bonds between men."[7] This moment, along with several like it, does not erase but rather offsets all the other moments that would be recognized as "typical" or even misogynistic performances of homosocial bonding predicated on female presences. This move, in many ways, is one that forces us outside of dominant modes of understanding black manhood in narrow ways. In this space, Marlon Riggs's revolutionary quip is sound: "black men loving black men is the revolutionary act."[8] And, as if McCraney is reading from this playbook, in an almost unnoticeable slip, Elegba calls Oshoosi "a siren." The erotic enters the space of brotherly love, and neither indicates a response to this pronouncement. Indeed, *The Brothers Size* uniquely conjures this love between brothers (Ogun and Oshoosi), while also calling forth a friend-lover dynamic (Elegba and Oshoosi). The absence of punishment of either subject for their homoerotic exchanges disallows the dramatic distractions of homo panic or a simplistic modern masculinity that has been overly enunciated as wholly homophobic. Instead, with Elegba and Oshoosi, McCraney unveils the raw potential of black male bonding, often untapped within the cacophony of discourses that are always dueling within black male humanity. McCraney writes a scene that can be staged not only to show love but also to display layers of complexity in male-male relationships in the context of prison, poverty, and inner struggle.

McCraney's gift for tapping into the everyday lives of black men is most clear in his command of black male vernacular phrases and his attention to geo-spatial issues that black men face. The most memorable moment is where he illuminates what Rashad Shabazz has called the logics that emerge from "carceral mise-en-scene."[9] In these spaces—where continuity between prison and urban space is salient—men often feel as if confinement is a built-in landscape. Prior to the following scene, Ogun, Oshoosi, and Elegba remarkably fill in each other's sentences as they narrate their experiences with the police. In what follows, all three men recall their encounters with the sheriff of the town:

ELEGBA:
He say "Where you going Legba?"
OSHOOSI SIZE:
He remember your name?
OGUN SIZE:
He call me Size.
OSHOOSI SIZE:
Call me Size too.
OGUN SIZE:
Like we twins.
OSHOOSI SIZE:
Or the same person.
OGUN SIZE:
Like its only one of us.
OSHOOSI SIZE:
Like we the same. (189)

McCraney calls our attention to the easy way that the sheriff reduces the Size brothers to be one and the same, as if one size fit all. This representation on stage calls forth a history of police profiling within black communities, whereby black men are, without reason, too often targets of crime. McCraney's emphasis on this "one size fits all" formula connects to his previous illustration of how predictive policing and surveillance is within the Sizes' community. This coupling, tied with Oshoosi's "like we the same," not only draws our attention to the surveilling mechanisms of neighborhoods, but our own policing practices. The audience must now begin to recognize not so much how the Size brothers are alike (or like us)—the traditional identification questions—but how this visual image signposts and illuminates difference. Here, *The Brothers Size* moves from a remark on last names to a recognition of how black men are subjected to canonical prejudices that pigeonhole them as ready for incarceration. McCraney disallows for such easy marks and shows us the agency found not only through black men's awareness of carceral structures but also the rich treasure of realizing our own discourses of containment.

"You Fucked Up": The State of Black Masculinity
in the Public Imaginary

While McCraney teaches us how to read black men and masculinities with greater rigor, he also presents us with the error of public imagination. In *The Brothers Size*, he offers us the inside of brotherhood to explore black men's tendency to believe, as Baldwin states, "what the white world calls a nigger."[10] When Ogun Size realizes his little brother Oshoosi Size is being sought by the police for possession of illegal drugs, he snaps. Though Oshoosi assures him "it wasn't mine," Ogun Size confesses that all of Oshoosi's "sins" have been his for years. For Ogun, it is his "life sentence" to be accountable for his brother's wrongdoings (212–16). In frustration, without full knowledge of this particular instance and Oshoosi's actual innocence, Ogun exclaims "You Fucked Up!" sixteen times. This verbal attack is to be read without breath, like bullets shooting into Oshoosi's body. The more he repeats "You Fucked Up," the more the exclamation turns into a concretization wherein Ogun transforms the logical question "Did you fuck up?" into an ontological truth. Mistaking becomes a part of the *being* of black manhood, regardless of the innocence, context, or frame. This positioning of Oshoosi mirrors what I see as a phenomenon in academic discourses around black manhood, which can sometimes function as prescriptive, overdetermining truth which does not afford black men what Simone Drake has called "grace."[11] While this essay is not rooted in an affirmation of Drake's concept, the absence of "grace" for all black people under white supremacist constraints produces what might be called a double negation. A double negation, for me, is a process by which there is no way out of the negative prescription within and outside the subjects' communities. This positionality is one where white supremacist logics can be reinforced through a carceral containment, whereby black subjects are neither layered nor made complicated in sites of discourse between and among communities. To be "fucked up" here is not temporal but evidenced in blackness. Here, Calvin Warren's framing of blackness as a "function of nothing" makes the most sense.[12] When we have settled into a dominant discourse within our own communities and outside of it, where blackness functions as negative and nothing else, we have resigned blackness to "nothing"—an empty signifier to be always demonized and discarded.[13] *The Brothers Size* affords us a space for thinking through this process of negation while also marking the layered complexity of intersectionality, sexuality, and what I want to refer to as the "what might be." And while this play takes up black men and manhood mostly, such an idea has utility in conversations which might explore black women and/or trans realities wherein the reader always declines the insignificance of possibility, never being unwilling to see beyond the so-called "givens."

McCraney provides a lens to see black men whom the world has deemed "fucked up." I am most interested in how McCraney takes what has been deemed "toxic" and conjures the tender, the touching, and the tacit. He provides a space—in terms of the space of a play—for an archive or reservoir of black masculinity, where black men negotiate this "truth" and work within and outside this prescribed notion. For me, "the distant present" that McCraney marks as the temporality of the play (and many of his plays) is an opportunity to queer the script completely; an admission of the "not here yet; the not quite known," a recognition of the "what might be" in all characters, all spaces, and blackness itself.

McCraney's aforementioned prologue shows father/brother Ogun, standing in the early morning sun with shovel in hand, as a reminiscent gesture to plantation life or chain-gang work, or even farming. But whatever the remark here, it is a manhood of truculence which opens the play. But before we can get caught there, the play moves to a resting Oshoosi, Ogun's younger brother who, in his wonderworld of sleep, cannot be still; he stirs in a nightmare that we later find is born of prison, but also becomes a framework for what can be reductively read for "lazy" but, indeed, is evidently the work of working out trauma. Here the contrast between Ogun and Oshoosi is clear. However, there is no clear stock figuration, as we see both Oshoosi and Ogun exchange roles in the play while also being accompanied by and complicated with Elegba, who in the opening scene performs the fluidity of gender. Elegba, much like the Yoruba deity who he is named after, wanders and enters "drifting, like the moon . . . Singing a song." But the song he sings does not match the mood he sets; the wanderer chants "this road is rough," while Oshoosi expresses "Mmmmm" and Ogun Size punches "Huh." Together they form a circle of lamentation that activates a spatial-cultural critique of the ground on which black masculinity is made—that which is tough, hard, untenable, yet the space in which many live and "sharply breathe out," as McCraney's prologue concludes.

The prologue provides us the backdrop for reading through and into the "fucked up." The State is fucked up for McCraney. Its offerings to black men and black people conjure some fucked-up realities, but he denies a black masculine nothingness, where black men are imagined as "nothing" more than fuck ups. He does not deny the ability for black men to traffic in problematic performances of gender or to perform gender in ways that produce problems in the lives of women and others; rather, he disallows for the function of black men (any black man) to rest in their "fucked-up-ness." This inability to allow black men to rest here—in character or life—is a creation of masculinity which I argue is an intentional practice of "reading" that McCraney draws upon in several of his works that take us beyond the given or the canonical imagination.

As *The Brothers Size* ends, Elegba implicates Oshoosi in a drug crime that would resituate him within the confines of prison. Throughout the play, Oshoosi's only focus has been on independence, freedom, and escape from carceral structures. His only escape, according to McCraney's plot, is to travel to a world where no one knows him, or his brother(s)—where the name "Size" disappears. As the police come for Oshoosi, Ogun tells him to go to Mexico and says, "I'm gon say nah, just one. Only one . . . I'm a deny you" (237). Inadvertently, Ogun attempts to excise any problematic framing of Oshoosi by erasing his profile altogether. For Ogun, the only way to offer black men freedom is to disconnect them from "home" and to produce new ones. While the easy reading may be that Ogun believed his brother was better off in another place, or that he was better off with another name, his persuasive last speech to Oshoosi says otherwise:

OGUN:
Man, don't let them put you back in there.
I wanna know you still my brother somewhere . . .
Anywhere in the world.
You still my brother . . .
I swear.
Out there you will still be a Size, Oshoosi Size,
Brother to Ogun. (239)

In this moment, Ogun suggests that it is not environment or name that makes him a Size brother per se but rather his existence in an ecological and cosmological system that allows him to wander free. In other words, Oshoosi—the Yoruba deity who is known as a wanderer—is made to roam and know the air. Such a rendering not only draws links between the play and its Yoruba inflections but also between McCraney's imposition of necessary breaths and black men's lives throughout the play. Breath represents the pursuit of life, even when the air is thick. The appeal in Ogun's framing, "I wanna know you still my brother somewhere," is to mark how Oshoosi's return to prison would be like a return to death. Thus, we watch Ogun work on Oshoosi— hard, metallic work. He convinces him to choose life elsewhere and otherwise. For Ogun, the carceral confine of prison is death. Here, I argue that McCraney, through Ogun's character, returns us to a discourse which centers actions and individual composition over a given name. In the beginning of *The Brothers Size*, Ogun is stuck in the quagmire of the Size name, wanting Oshoosi to shine light on their family legacy and be who he "fathered" him to be. This moment of reading beyond this expectation offers us Ogun's growth in thought, wherein he is moved beyond the significance of names toward the importance of action and spirit. To say that Oshoosi will still be a "brother Size" no matter where he goes is to turn the audience toward the substance of the self that is untethered to narrow frames produced through given names. Here, we watch Ogun move from patrilineal, patriarchal father figure to elder brother and liberator as he works on his masculine projections and opens up a space for freedom, one found in the recognition that black male freedom is an opportunity to be more than the canonical script. *The Brothers Size*

offers us a space to watch this work out, inadvertently giving us an opportunity to read across masculinities, gather knowledge about black men and
their doings, and attend to their negotiations in scenes of high sociocultural
constraint.

The Brothers Size: A Lesson on Masculinity and "Other Freedoms"

Another reading available for Oshoosi's "escape" to Mexico—an escape
from the police and his own scheme to take flight—is emblematic of what
Rinaldo Walcott calls "freedom's violence of a settlement with unfreedom."[14]
As the beginning of the play is focused on freedom through masculinity and
freedom outside the confines of prison, when Oshoosi escapes imprisonment
to go to Mexico—as advised by his brother Ogun—we see a writing of freedom
as destination. Walcott cautions such quick moves, as notions of "freedom"—
especially tethered to state release—are always contingent and relative.
While one reading is that he escapes or takes flight—an embodiment of
fugitivity—I would like to suggest that the ending is darker. The size of
unfreedom surrounds, meaning that the move to Mexico, as contemporary
asylum-seekers and seekers of freedom on the other side of the border illustrate, is a move into another unfreedom. A space of unknown language, a
space of its own state-regulated rigidity, and still connected to the U.S. state
and its demands. In this way, the play does not offer freedom as denouement.
The modicum of freedom we witness in the play, the play's text, and onstage
is expressed in the joy of Oshoosi, his desire to know another world. Oshoosi
ultimately desires to practice freedom in another land, to move into another
space, and to embark upon something new. Yet this travel to a "space on the
horizon" could still be equally, if not more, dangerous. And as the play closes,
we never can forget that Oshoosi is still running. If we take Rinaldo Walcott's suggestion that black people are in a "long emancipation"—freedom
has never truly been conferred—then black life and black men's life in this
play and elsewhere can be understood as a perpetual routing of escape.[15]

The excitement over flight discourse seems to always presuppose and anticipate a landing. But what is perpetually frustrating is the never-ending state
of the black actor's run. This is not only a dilemma for the characters in the
The Brother Size but a characteristic of black life. Oshoosi, "the wanderer,"
is always running, from prison, into his brother's care, and to Mexico and
beyond. Elegba is always running between truth and lies, between a yearning
for intimacy with men and a contested sexual desire, which manifests in a perpetual need to perform as trickster. Ogun is running from the past and into
a new future of economic independence, caught between being father and
brother, attempting to run from the police state through policing and protect-
ing Oshoosi. Each man is attempting to escape capture; each is a magician
manifesting new routes that lead to new routes. This is the exhausting state of

black living. In this sense, such yearning for "freedom" is a pronouncement of black men's real unfreedom. McCraney gives us an ending that reiterates the limits of freedom while demonstrating the joy found in the pursuit. The play refuses the scripted narrative of black men's lives. Instead, it opens a conversation about the processes of discovery and masculine development, the practice of freedom, and the pursuit of worlds where we are not always rewriting scripts.

Part 3

Art, Creation, and Collaboration

Backstage Pass

An Artist Roundtable on the Work of
Tarell Alvin McCraney

Edited and introduced by Sharrell D. Luckett

> Tarell's work is always *about* community, and always *requires* community.
>
> —Tina Landau

As Tina Landau observes in the above epigraph, Tarell Alvin McCraney's work "*requires* community."[1] When reflecting upon this requirement in the context of an academic text on McCraney's oeuvre, the editors understood this to mean that the voices included in this volume should not be limited to academic scholars. Rather, this text should serve as an example of the ways that McCraney's work bridges the academy and the public spheres, as well as how one might understand insight from diverse theater communities as invaluable data. Though the voices in this section are certainly central to theater making outside of the academy, direct input from professional theatre practitioners (practitioner-scholars) is often marginalized in academic spaces. Indeed, academic theater scholars and professional theater makers rarely convene.[2] Here, we bridge that gap—both for readers of the volume and for doers of McCraney's work. We aim to uphold the values of community and connection often engendered by theater making. Just as McCraney's audiences extend beyond academic institutions, performing arts conferences, theater houses, and other insular locations, so does the collective community featured in this roundtable.

"Backstage Pass" brings together the voices of twelve professional theater and entertainment practitioners who have worked closely with McCraney over the years. They include: Tea Alagić, McCraney's peer at the Yale School of Drama and an early director of *The Brothers Size*; Jabari Ali, music supervisor for the Oprah Winfrey Network's *David Makes Man*; Alana Arenas,

McCraney's childhood friend and fellow Steppenwolf ensemble member who has performed in several of his projects, including *David Makes Man*; Michael Boyd, former artistic director of the Royal Shakespeare Company who commissioned *American Trade* and several of McCraney's Shakespeare adaptations; Cheryl Lynn Bruce, who originated the role of Shelah in *Head of Passes* at Steppenwolf and Berkeley Repertory Theatre; Teo Castellanos, a mentor and former teacher who has directed and been directed by McCraney; Trip Cullman, the director of *Choir Boy* on and off Broadway; Oskar Eustis, artistic director of the Public Theater who coproduced premiere productions of *The Brother/Sister Plays* and produced the New York premiere of *Head of Passes*; Shirley Jo Finney, director of the Los Angeles productions of *The Brothers Size* and *In the Red and Brown Water* at the Fountain Theatre; Tina Landau, McCraney's longtime collaborator and director of the premiere productions of *The Brother/Sister Plays*, *Wig Out!*, *Head of Passes*, and *Ms. Blakk for President*; Carlos Murillo, playwright and McCraney's professor at the Theatre School at DePaul University; and Robert O'Hara, playwright and director of premiere productions of *The Brother/Sister Plays*.

As an accessible narrative archive, Backstage Pass invokes the power of storytelling to increase possibilities for connectivity, reflection, and transformation for anyone interested in McCraney's artistry.[3] Myriad fields—including Black feminist studies, sociology, communications, theater, and performance studies—have long espoused the rich benefits of collecting narratives. Within these disciplines, narratives have served to honor lived experiences as sites of theory-making, scholarship, and epistemological advances. Narratives, written and embodied, are also essential to surviving, thriving, and building community.[4] As scholar-practitioners whose work is often situated at the margins, David, Isaiah, and I understand that narratives can often serve as the most generative form of evidence and critique available to the critical researcher.[5] Sarojini Nadar emphasizes this idea in her essay "'Stories Are Data with Soul'—Lessons from Black Feminist Epistemology" when she writes: "Stories are not just told for the sake of telling a story, but for their power to invite us all to call deep on our courage to transform. The research we do is never solely for the sake of theory building but for the sake of community building."[6] In this spirit, I open Backstage Pass with the story of my first encounter with McCraney, a brief reflection that evidences his deep commitments to community and collaboration—and a story that perhaps serves as the catalyst for my continued engagement with his work.

Los Angeles was sunny, as usual, as strangely always. I had only lived in L.A. for a year, but already knew that I did not like the weather. Sharisa, a good friend of mine, had recently moved to L.A. as well. Besides her many acting accolades and performance experience, she was also pretty funny. We were having one of our regular, lengthy phone conversations, because sadly, even though we only lived twenty miles from one another, it was always a nightmare trying to hang out. The traffic added two to three hours to the drive.

"How do you like your job?" Sharisa asked.

"It's going OK. The students are great. They mainly Latino and Black, so that's cool." I was an assistant professor of acting and directing at California State University, Dominguez Hills.

"Do you get to direct?"

"Yes, I *have* to direct. We're going to do *In the Red and Brown Water*. Weren't you in it?"

That question was an understatement. Sharisa Whatley originated the role of Nia in the 2008 world premiere of *In the Red and Brown Water* at the Tony Award–winning Alliance Theatre in Atlanta, Georgia. Tarell had won the Alliance's esteemed Kendeda Playwriting Competition in 2007. The winner is awarded a staging of their show at the Alliance. Oskar Eustis was one of the competition judges, and Tina Landau helmed the production.

"Yes, I did it," Sharisa said in her usual soft, breathy tone.

Like a good director would, I asked: "How did y'all handle the ensemble elements and dream sequences?"

"We used buckets and moved the buckets around."

"Buckets . . . ?" Thinking, with eyebrows furrowing. Now, I have read this play several times and no buckets have come to mind. "Buckets?" A pause filled with more thinking. "And what did y'all . . ."

Sharisa interrupted me. "You going to see *Brothers Size* before it closes?" In an instance of synchronicity, the Los Angeles premiere of *The Brothers Size*, directed by Shirley Jo Finney, was playing at The Fountain Theatre.

"I hope to see it. I need to do all the dramaturgical stuff I can to direct this play. I love it, but it's complex. Gotta crack it open."

"He gonna be there tonight."

My breath came loose. I sat up off the couch. "Who gonna be where?"

"Tarell."

"What?" My eyes darted around my living room, then to the bookcase, and landed in the kitchen on the bright green digital microwave clock. I was a fan. It was already late afternoon. Could I make it in time? In this L.A. traffic? Hell, I had to try. "Ok, Sharisa, gonna go. Gonna call you back. You think I can make it?"

"Ok." Laughing at my frenzied state. "You betta leave now girl. Tell him I said hello." Click.

Yes, I will, and then I must tell him thank you. And to keep writing. We need more plays like his. With representation. I wanted to make sure he knew that Black kids in L.A. were grateful. That my student cried when she found out she could possibly be a lead because Oya was dark-skinned; that the light-skinned girls were mad. And I was secretly happy that they were mad. That several of my hetero-identified male students informed me in auditions that they were uncomfortable playing a gay dude, but then after reading the entire play, they all were like, "Dr. Luckett, put me where you need me. These are like *real* gay people." And thank you for writing roles for primarily young adult Black actors. Good roles. 'Cuz these students can't keep doing August. And more than that, I really just wanted to ask him if he would Skype with my cast. Just a quick ten-minute Skype. Just so they know that they can make it in life. Maybe Tarell could be a "question-answerer" who could address his nuanced stage-direction thingy; and he could talk about his Yoruba influences and the god-human thingy, and we can ask him why Mama Moja had to die; and maybe he could leave them with some sound advice. Yes, cast Tarell as a distant collaborator in the present, if only for ten minutes . . . nah, impossible.

Finney's production was loud, with foot stomping, hand clapping, and good singing. After the performance Tarell gave major props, bowing to the actors, and sat with them and the director on the stage. The Q&A began, but I wasn't fully listening because I noticed my friend and former Juilliard acting student Amari Cheatom sitting in the distance. It's so good to see people you know from Atlanta trying to make it in L.A., too. After the Q&A the line to talk to Tarell was crazy long so I made my way over to Amari, giving up on meeting Tarell.

Big hugs. "Shaarrrelll."

"Hey, Amari. Good to see you. What you doing here?"

"Awe, I know these dudes."

I wasn't surprised. He cheerfully asked or invited, "You coming up?"

"What you mean?"

"We 'bout to all go upstairs and just chill when everybody leaves."

There I was, sitting next to Tarell on a bench that was upstairs in the green-room. The cast, director, and a few other folks were chatting with Tarell. I was nervous, breathing all hard and slightly afraid of talking to him. Just turn to him and ask, Sharrell. Just ask him. What's the worst that could happen?

Finally, "Tarell . . ."

He looked over at me. Big doe eyes that set apart from one another like my brother's, friendly smile, not looking at me like, "somebody get this girl away from me." Not celebrity-acting-saddidy at all.

"Tarell . . . I know you don't know me. But my name is Sharrell and I'm a professor out here in Los Angeles and we are doing your play. And I wanted to know . . . to know . . ."

Him still looking at me, quiet . . .

". . . just wanted to know if you'd be willing to Skype with us, with them, just for like ten minutes . . . or whatever time . . . or whatever, you know?"

"Sure."

Sure? I was excited. "And I promise we won't take up too much of your time, it will be a quick convo and . . ." Tarell interrupted me.

"I'll just come out to the school."
Speechless.

✦

McCraney's visit with my students made me interested in learning more about his collaborative ventures and artistic processes, but more importantly, it allowed me to witness his commitment to *his* community. He spent nearly two hours with my cast in which he led a playwriting exercise, answered questions, and took many pictures.[7] I'd like to think that McCraney's interactions with student artists who *look like him* is a direct response to James Baldwin's declaration that in America the artist is often isolated from the people, and this effect on Black artists is "absolutely fatal."[8] Here, Baldwin is alluding to the problematic isolation that often occurs when American theater institutions award Black art, while undervaluing input from culturally Black people in the artistic process.[9] Thus, there becomes this isolation of Black artists in white spaces, which is both a threat to the art and the person. However, McCraney enacts resistance to the structural racism that exists in professional theater entities by staying connected and grounded with(in) *his* communities in person, in text, and in spirit.[10] And he does this while still successfully building and sharing space with professional artists and producers from all walks of life and diverse theatrical lineages. Notably, several of those professional artists are featured here.

Pedagogically substantive, Backstage Pass is divided into three sections: "In Process," "In Performance," and "Specials." Here, several artists involved with McCraney's work share their unique, varied stories as they respond to questions compiled by David Román, Isaiah Wooden, and me. "In Process" highlights McCraney's ways of doing and being as a theater artist, while "In Performance" centers the collaborators' experiences and reflections on what it means to produce, direct, or perform in McCraney's plays. "In Performance" also includes a section where his former teachers and a peer offer narratives about McCraney during his formative, undergraduate, and graduate years. Finally, "Specials," alluding to the function of a "special" in theater lighting, features interviews with Michael Boyd, formerly of the Royal Shakespeare Company (providing a transnational scope) and Jabari Ali, music supervisor for *David Makes Man*.[11] In addition, longtime collaborator Tina Landau shares actual rehearsal notes and instructive suggestions on how to approach McCraney's texts.

In the essay "The Art of Collaboration: On Dramaturgy and Directing," cowritten with Anne Bogart, theater director Jackson Gay observes, ". . . when you get into the room with your collaborators, you have to have the courage to let all your research, intellectual understanding, and homework go. You have to be fearless to go somewhere you don't know and play around in there."[12] The qualities listed by Gay are found throughout the collaborators' responses as the reader learns about pivotal, deep moments shared with

McCraney via conversation, meals, and even silence.[13] In totality, Backstage Pass serves as a critical resource for rehearsal halls and classrooms, providing a glimpse into what professionals value in a playwright, how one might work with a playwright, possibilities of new play dramaturgy, information for theatrical collaboration research, and ideas about how to engage with McCraney's work. Biographies of the collaborators are included in the contributors section in this volume. Enjoy.

In Process

Q: What is Tarell like in the rehearsal room?

ROBERT O'HARA: Tarell is very giving and yet extremely specific. When we were working on the world premiere of his *Brother/Sister* plays there was one moment when I asked the actor to say the stage direction that was written for him to say and then deny it through his action. I think it was a stage direction for the actor to "Exit." I told the actor to say it and then don't leave. This was a powerful moment of decision making and this direction added a special tension to the moment between the two characters in the scene. Tarell allowed this moment to happen and then said, "Well, if we're going to do that, then we need the final moment of the play to come quicker." He knew instinctively how much space the story needed to take. That moment of collaboration worked wonderfully.

ALANA ARENAS: Tarell is a gracious collaborator, which is a testament to his character because he's a meticulous craftsman. When you see an actor come into rehearsals suggesting that the *word should be this* or the *line should go that way*, it's endearing to watch Tarell effortlessly relent— "Whatever works for you"—because I know that nothing Tarell writes is happenstance.

TINA LANDAU: He's an open book. A shy one sometimes, but open nonetheless. He is startlingly candid about his own life and experiences. He often brings the room to tears. But then he's hilarious, too. And he loves to "perform" and quote obscure texts and pop songs and get up and dance on ten-minute breaks. He's also the oddest mixture of self-possessed and utterly humble. He's beautiful. I love him.

MICHAEL BOYD: Theater is the quintessentially collaborative art form, and Tarell the consummate collaborator. At his most successful with the Royal Shakespeare Company, he was a deeply principled artist who would always listen with grace and care, and then take what was useful from what he heard.

CHERYL LYNN BRUCE: Tarell is widely read, sentient, and a blindingly articulate thinker/writer/philosopher who, to his lasting credit, cannot dissemble. Conversations with him are genuine, considered, and can explode like a firecracker. His experiences are myriad and he generously shares them, no matter how painful or revealing. This is an enormous blessing, for what more can a truly serious collaborator do but bring *everything* to the table?

One of the most searing collaborative experiences with Tarell occurred during a workshop rehearsal for *Head of Passes* in which Alana Arenas (who played Cookie in the Steppenwolf production) and I (who played Shelah) investigated a deeply disturbing scene in the play. It was late in the day, and the room had darkened. I remember only Tarell, director Tina Landau, and the stage manager present as Alana and I improvised. We were "workin' without a net."[14] In the scene, Shelah's deeply troubled and addicted stepdaughter Cookie is suspected of having stolen from Shelah while in her bedroom unattended, and announces she is leaving. In an effort to heal the rift, Shelah offers Cookie money from her purse; however, stung and furious, Cookie refuses it. Whenever I managed to push bills into Alana's hands, she'd crumple them and fling them to the floor. Each time she did, I quickly gathered them up and tried to press them into her clenched fists. The struggle between Alana and myself was searingly real. Her tears rushed out with her bitter words. My tears rushed out with my pleading. We ran the scene several times, and I think, at some point, Alana relented and snatched up the bills in one triumphant and scornful gesture. Then a piercing wail cut through the air. Tarell was weeping, his body wracked with sobs.

We fell silent. We ended the day. We were spent.

TRIP CULLMAN: Tarell is the consummate collaborator—while his wisdom is infinite, he is always open to the creative input of actors and directors. He is kind and supportive as well.

OSKAR EUSTIS: Tarell is one of the most thoughtful, diligent collaborators I have ever known. My most precious memory is working through the third act of *Head of Passes* with him, working line by line through Shelah's extraordinary dialogue with God after the agonizing death of her children. Along with Tina Landau, the amazing director, we were able to plunge deeper into that terrifying experience than I would have thought possible.

Q: Tea, what do you remember most about the process of developing *The Brothers Size*?

TEA ALAGIĆ: When we worked on *The Brothers Size*, we agreed that we would first talk about the play, and then later we could talk about production. We spent a lot of time reading and talking. We had a lot of time, because we were students. We had no money and no designers.

I was striving to best represent the musicality of his writing in *The Brothers Size*. So, we talked about how we could do this without a budget. We created an empty space that could transform into his magical world and bring in the West African roots that were important to him. We had three actors, and every time one of them was not in the scene, they would play a beat, a rhythm. That was how the sound was born.

Also, at the time, I was very strict about text analysis, so I strove to physicalize and vocalize those beats. Everything was created out of the text and physicality in his script. The play's Yoruba influences made it more spiritual. People thought these characters were gods. I put them in minimalistic clothes. It became an iconic production, even though we had no designers or design budget.

Q: Trip, what was it like to work with Tarell in preparing *Choir Boy* for Broadway?

TRIP CULLMAN: Tarell rewrote about thirty to forty percent of the play in anticipation of its Broadway debut. Part of this stems from wanting to fix things that he wasn't happy with in its earlier incarnations, but a lot of the rewrites come from the radically altered world we are living in now as opposed to five years ago. Five years ago, Obama was in office, and I tried to mine a vein of hopefulness about the future of these kids at Drew Prep; tried to see a way for Pharus to be accepted and seen. In today's America, this optimism is much harder to discover. So, the play—under Tarell's incredible rewrites—is more despairing, more tragic, more dangerous as a result.

Q: Are there any special memories that you have of Tarell during the process of directing his show(s)?

SHIRLEY JO FINNEY: Yes. They say there is no greater reward than when the author/ playwright witnesses something they have written and may have seen a hundred times, turns to you at the end of a performance (*Brothers Size*) weeping and says something to the effect of: *I have seen this show many times but this is the first time I was so moved. I have never cried in performance.* Afterwards, when Tarell walked onstage for the talkback, he got on his knees and bowed to the actors (Gilbert Glenn and Matthew Hancock). He did this as a testament to their work. I was pleased that the conjurer had a transformative ancestral experience with his own words.

TRIP CULLMAN: One of my favorite memories occurred during the rehearsal period for *Choir Boy* (2013). During one of our ten-minute breaks, I walked out into the hallway of Manhattan Theatre Club's rehearsal space and discovered Tarell dancing with two of the actors (Jeremy Pope and Nicholas Ashe). They were teaching each other the exact dance moves from a particular

Beyoncé video. They slayed. Also, Tarell didn't think it odd when I saw his gorgeous play *Wig Out!* four times during its run at the Vineyard Theatre because I was so compelled by it.

TEA ALAGIĆ: One time, Tarell prepared food for us. I'll never forget how good it was. It was a chicken dish with macaroni and cheese and corn! I never had such rich food like that. Delicious! And that sparked my love of dining with my collaborators.

Also, he tends not to tell me when he is coming to rehearsal. He shows up in the back of the theater. I hear him, like he cries or something and I look around. I hear his voice and I know he's there.

When we did *Brothers Size* in New York, we were in this tiny room of sixty people. It was a hot summer and we were sweating. The show was sold out and we stood in the back, sweating as we watched everyone. I'll never forget standing there with him.

Q: Tina, you helped to develop several of Tarell's scripts. What were those processes like?

TINA LANDAU: It's less a memory than a continually developing process, as Tarell and I have ongoing and upcoming projects together. Thankfully!

I've been fortunate in that I've done so many premieres of Tarell's works. So, he is in the room. We are a team. It's not about my executing some vision or directive he has. It's about us discovering together what is there on the page and us experimenting together on what can be there on the stage.

On many productions we've done together, Tarell has even been on his feet with the actors, or standing in for an actor, as we rehearse. On *The Brother/ Sister Plays*, Tarell once spent a whole day being another "storyteller" with us in rehearsal, on his feet, moving, helping me and the cast find the physical vocabulary for our stories. On *Wig Out!*, Tarell often rehearsed with us as a fourth Fate (there are only three in the script). He's a dancer too, so that background influences both how he writes and how we rehearse. And then too, he's an actor, and a brilliant one at that. So, for instance, on *Head of Passes*, in its various productions, when we were missing an actor due to conflicts or illness, Tarell would regularly step in for that person for an entire day's rehearsal. He is never prescriptive. Only inspirational.

Q: And Tarell reads the whole play to you aloud?

TINA LANDAU: Yes, for every show we have worked on together, Tarell always reads the whole play aloud to me. Well, more like "embodies" the whole play for me. Acts it. *Lives* it. It started on our first production together, *In the Red and Brown Water*, at the Alliance Theatre in Atlanta, Georgia. The language and style seemed so particular to me—and I wanted to know how the *playwright* heard it. So, we sat alone in a room, at a conference table, and he started reading. But he got up and fully inhabited all the characters, and railed, and cried, and made me laugh and gasp and cry with him. It was revelatory, and also one of the greatest "performances" I've ever experienced. From that first production onward, I believe I've had Tarell "read" the play aloud not only to me but to our whole cast at some point. In some cases, sure, the actors might initially balk—they're understandably worried about being spoon-fed line readings or character choices. But it never fails. The actors end up astounded and grateful. What Tarell gifts them is not a series of prescriptive choices but an entry point into his universe and a world of possibilities that resides there. Through his reading, they're not shown how to *do* the piece but, rather, its very DNA.

Q: Teo, you enlisted Tarell to direct your solo show. What are his strengths as a director?

TEO CASTELLANOS: Having Tarell as a director is like having a family member direct me. That does not mean it is a walk in the park. Quite the opposite. With family we tend to push harder than with anyone else, and he pushes hard! Tarell and I have a long history of working together, first I as his director and mentor, then years later, the flip side of that. We have not only worked together for over twenty-five years but we have also developed a creative language. Tarell was the director of my last solo show. The subject matter of this play digs deep into my family. The pain of that excavation was at times unbearable. He held me when I thought I was going to lose my mind.

Additionally, Tarell directed me in *The Brothers Size*. I played Elegba. During this process, I learned what it was like to fall in love with a character all over again. I actually remember telling Tarell that, out of all the characters I've ever played, Elegba was my favorite. That is something I'm sure he's heard before. I relearned the joy of acting when my only responsibility was to breathe life into a character, trying to find a unique interpretation. And what a joy it is to work with a good director. I also learned how nerve-wracking it can be, being directed by the playwright himself.

Tarell's strengths as a director are not unlike his strengths as a writer. Tarell understands a world where rhythm supersedes language or text; a world where the esoteric or the subcultural is extremely vibrant and palpable. Many times, we communicate and understand through essence, mood, environment, and rhythms. Trust also plays a big role in the actor-director connection. Our relationship is full of that.

Q: What do you think other artists or playwrights could learn from Tarell?

OSKAR EUSTIS: Ambition and vulnerability. Tarell is able to be agonizingly personal about his work, and yet at the same time use the raw materials of his life to debate the gods. He achieves a remarkable universality through his granular specificity.

TEO CASTELLANOS: One time, Tarell showed up to a *Brothers Size* rehearsal drenched in sweat because he had ridden his bike twelve miles in the Miami August sun to get to rehearsal *on time*. He made it. I tell this story to young artists as an example of the type of commitment and professionalism that is expected of them.

In Performance

Q: What is the most challenging aspect of directing Tarell's work?

TINA LANDAU: Finding actors who can bring the material to life in all the various ways it demands. It's a tall order. They must be honest, authentic, deep, vulnerable. But they must also be facile, performative, theatrical, large. They must be able to live inside the naturalistic mode and the theatrical mode and go between them on the turn of a dime—over and over, without losing believability or clarity. They must be good with language, as you would need to be in speaking Shakespeare, and yet they need to make it sound like it's completely organic. Then, on top of all that, they need to have great humor and timing.

The required range is enormous and I always find the most difficult part of working on one of Tarell's plays to be the casting. You can't work with actors who do or are *one* thing; they have to be honest and emotional but they can't get lost in their emotion—they have to negotiate and perform extreme switches of intention and speed but they can't be mere technicians. You need them to be and do *everything*, and sometimes all at once or in back-to-back seconds—*and* be good at it. And be team players too.

Q: In several of Tarell's plays, the characters speak the stage directions before delivering their lines. Any advice for directors and actors who are working through this convention?

ROBERT O'HARA: I'd say what I say to all actors working on any play: "Invest in Yes." But especially for Tarell's work. It's so intelligent and complete. All that you need is there and the convention of speaking certain stage directions allows you to connect your character to the legacy of storytelling itself. It makes you a storyteller or rather an owner of the story. It invites you and the audience into the mythology of it all, and it adds that extra sense of fable. That's what makes Tarell's work so beautiful. So, let go of the "why" and "Invest in Yes."

TINA LANDAU: Know why each one is there and play the intention of it. They are not as purely descriptive as they seem and there's no point in narrating what the audience can already see or know. What do you need to draw attention to and why? What added color or nuance? Are you able to expose how the spoken stage directions serve the story? Why is this detail or action underlined and how does it add to the overall story? And most importantly, every time there is a direct address to the audience, the actor needs to make sure she or he really reaches out and connects to the audience. They are not asides—they have need in them. And it helps not to speak to the audience as a whole but to individuals within that audience—so there is connection. As with everything in this work, it is all about eliminating the general in lieu of the specific. And it is all about connection, in the moment. As E. M. Forster famously wrote (albeit in a different context), "Only connect! That was her whole sermon. Only connect the prose and the passion, and both will be exalted . . ."

In general, when working on Tarell's texts, one must honor the punctuation. Understand how it maps out changes of thought and intention, then really embrace and sometimes even exaggerate that in the acting.

Get to know how he uses ellipses. It's sometimes confusing, and certainly different than any other writer. Hint: ellipses are usually interruptions (by others or the self), more so than trail offs . . .

Q: Are there particular formal or dramaturgical qualities found in Tarell's plays that make them challenging, compelling, or exciting for directors and/ or producers?

SHIRLEY JO FINNEY: McCraney's style is poetic and rich in the ancestral elements of drum, dance, and song that evoke spirit, so that the witness is forced to reckon with a visceral, spiritual experience that is familiar; an experience that transcends the straightforward Western storytelling into African American myth.

When I directed *In the Red and Brown Water* and *The Brothers Size*, I felt like a conductor with a great score. I was fortunate that, with both productions, I had assembled the actors and musicians who could play all the right emotional notes. This allowed the Orishas to move in and through them to be a transient vessel.

I had to familiarize myself with and honor the Yoruba religion, each of the Orishas and their nature. I did not realize that what I was embracing was forcing me to take a personal journey through my own history. Often times, I felt as if I were Oya, and at other times I embodied the other Orishas, which were different emotional sides of me: participant-observer-dreamer-me-Woman-girl-child-baby-one-one me. I was on a spiritual roller-coaster ride, one that crescendoed as I led the cast home to understanding Tarell as wordsmith-conjurer. I realized if I, and then my cast, were experiencing this, then Tarell as *wordsmith* could also be understood as conjurer.

OSKAR EUSTIS: Tarell's work is miraculous in a host of ways, thematically, linguistically, theatrically. What first drew me to *The Brothers Size* was the extraordinary fusion of realism (depicting impoverished African Americans in the South) and grandeur (viewing these men through their avatars as Yoruba gods). The result was emotional and breathtaking. What Tarell was doing, as he has done in all his work since, is take some of the most marginalized people in our society and give them heroic stature, both comic and tragic.

ROBERT O'HARA: Tarell's plays operate on the level of myth. Beginning with the characters' names, he weaves a full and complete world with his plays and that's exciting. As a director, you get to build a world when you do his plays. Also, his plays don't depend on props or location as much as they depend on the texture and language. You can set his plays easily in the abstract and fulfill the gifts of their stories.

TINA LANDAU: Every time Tarell writes a play, it has its own unique theatrical universe. That is always a gift, an invitation. The world must be discovered or built from scratch.

And what Tarell writes for the theater, I think, are *events* as much as *plays*. And by that I mean they are meant to engage an audience through acknowledgment of the here and now as opposed to losing the audience in something that is "then." They ask us to immerse in, rather than look at. They ask for direct engagement with the audience. *You* talk to *me*.

Tarell's work is alive, pulsating, vibrating, demanding, embracing—awake. That is all he cares about in the theater (just as I do): that something actually *happens*.

TEA ALAGIĆ: Tarell's work is always talking about sexuality. It's elegant. Seamless. When we worked on *Brothers Size*, we discussed what the desire is in the play. These characters do love each other, but they don't know who they are. Conflict is always present. Tarell points at love, and questions what love is. *Moonlight* is similar. Love and sensuality. That is what is powerful in his work.

Also, he always has rhythm in his writing. It's very alive. Coming from acting and dancing, we shared a language when creating *Brothers Size*. We both appreciated the aesthetic that less is more. There's a beauty to that.

TRIP CULLMAN: All great dramatists are humanists. Tarell is the sine qua non of such. His plays are empathy machines for those whose stories are too often marginalized. I truly believe he is ushering in an era where the traditionally voiceless and unseen are invited to sing out and be regarded with dignity—because of the plays that he writes.

Q: Are there particular formal or dramaturgical qualities found in Tarell's plays that make them compelling or exciting for actors?

CHERYL LYNN BRUCE: Tarell's elliptical passages, oblique cultural references, reconstituted language, and torqued grammar create a challenging kind of frisson. He dares the "technician" in me to crack the code, but rewards me handsomely for the effort.

Tarell's technical-textural "rabbit holes" force me to surrender to a "New World Order" and initiate me into a vibrant, exuberant alternate universe, rich and complex. It is serious, exhilarating work untangling the web of references and images he conjures. The player must become conversant with them, and sling them comfortably like vernacular.

ALANA ARENAS: *The Brothers Size* is one of my favorite plays. It is a story about love and teaches me about a particular love that can be shared between siblings, specifically brothers. I was so proud to witness this story. It's an excellent play in form but I was also given the gift of seeing black men fight for each other onstage. I had never really seen *that* in theater, especially when the characters are young black men. It was a rare portrayal of what I believe is a common truth but, given the American narrative of black men, I didn't realize how much we desperately needed this play until I saw it. I am truly thankful for it. So much of Tarell's work is like that; it becomes glaringly apparent that before he wrote, there was a void.

Q: Did working on Tarell's play(s) teach you anything new about yourself as an actress or director?

ALANA ARENAS: When I trained and practiced acting as an undergraduate, the material was culturally dominated by a white perspective and reference. My relationship with this circumstance was tricky because, during that time, I hadn't fully articulated my experience in my mind. I knew at times I felt uncomfortable, but I didn't talk about it because I was in an academic setting. It felt taboo to openly challenge the subject of our work because that would inadvertently challenge the validity of the curriculum and maybe inadvertently the institution and the American theater heritage. The point is this: When I worked on Tarell's plays, it was the first time I felt like it was okay to be fully me in the theater. It was the first time I felt my experience as a Black woman from Carol City was just as stage-worthy as the classics. Up until that point, I never felt like it was okay to be unapologetically black. I had never seen the people in my neighborhood on stage. So, Tarell's work and the way he navigates space taught me that who I am and the particulars of my black experience should never have to cower to anyone else's existence.

TINA LANDAU: Always. And more. And to this day. That I am more capable than I knew of understanding, feeling, getting inside of characters and worlds that I thought were too far from me to represent. That I am larger than I knew. That we are more alike than I even dared dream. That all of us—regardless of color, class, religion, and so on—can find common ground through Story.

CHERYL LYNN BRUCE: I was immensely fortunate to have workshopped Tarell's masterwork *Head of Passes*, and perform in both its Steppenwolf Theatre premiere and subsequent Berkeley Rep remount, both sensitively directed by Tina Landau.

Tackling the monumental role of Shelah, the matriarch, remains, for many reasons, the zenith of my career. Working with Tarell reminded me just how exhilarating it is to dig deep, push beyond my limits, crawl right up to the edge, tempt Fate, and risk Failure.

The *Head of Passes* workshops (which spanned more than a year) were arduous, engrossing, and revealing in all directions. There was much reading and discussing of plays and treatises and even the writings of Saint Augustine.[15] There was much listening to different kinds of music, deeply soulful singing, and each others' intimate thoughts and terrors. There was much seeing, too. There was a board filled with pictures and maps and such. It was grueling, psychologically. It was thrilling, emotionally. It was challenging, technically. There were also many sessions that addressed the spiritual in ways that were refreshing, and while many religious positions were represented among the assembled cast and creatives, there was also room for the seeker and the unbeliever.

There was much analysis in those workshops. Deep, hard questioning never fails to invigorate. It's a burn I can never get enough of. *If* it is true, it will support me, carry me from the page to the stage, keep me charged all through the life of the production, and, if I'm lucky, far beyond.

I gave life to Shelah eight times a week. I walked with her through agonizing travails, stumbled, cried, prayed with her. That journey threw so many aspects of *my* life as a Black woman, Black mother, Black artist, and everseeking soul under the microscope that I was breathless at evening's end. Humbled and grateful, I remain profoundly and forever changed by it.

Beginnings

Q: Carlos, you feel that you witnessed the "birth of a writer" when you taught Tarell in your solo performance course at DePaul. Can you talk about that experience?

CARLOS MURILLO: I first encountered Tarell when I saw him in a production of Naomi Iizuka's play *Polaroid Stories*, which was directed by my wife Lisa Portes at the Theatre School of DePaul University. Iizuka's play crashes Ovid's *Metamorphosis* with the lives of young, homeless teenagers Iizuka interviewed as part of her research for the play. Tarell, at the time a third-year student at the Theatre School, played D, the Dionysus figure in the play—a charismatic drug dealer who delights in luring young lost souls into a world of chaos.

Tarell's performance was mesmerizing. The play was performed at the Merle Reskin Theatre at DePaul, a 1,300-seat venue (formerly The Blackstone) that once served as a tryout theater for Broadway-bound plays (including Lorraine Hansberry's *A Raisin in the Sun* in 1959). It's a huge space that many young actors struggle not to get swallowed in. Tarell filled that space—his powerful voice, his command of his body sent a jolt through the audience every time he made an entrance. His performance embodied what the play is attempting to do—propelling the very real lives and struggles of homeless youth into the realm of mythology. He not only inhabited the role with power, detail, and profound expressiveness, he captured the totality of the play and its aims, as well as the conceits of the production itself. I immediately sensed I was not only in the presence of a gifted actor, but also witnessing a first-rate story-teller of the theater.

The following year, Tarell enrolled in my solo performance workshop, a course I teach for advanced acting students who are interested in develop-ing original work. The course, which is an elective, tends to attract students who are seeking to stretch beyond their training as interpretive artists into discovering the generative artists within themselves. Tarell was at a place in his training where he hungered for this kind of exploration—to break out of the acting conservatory mold and find a larger canvas on which to articulate his vision.

Tarell not only brought a voracious curiosity to the proceedings—a qual-ity I think is absolutely vital for performing arts students—he was and remains dogged in pursuing the lines of his curiosity to their furthest ends. I was struck by the depth and breadth of his knowledge, certainly uncom-mon among young twenty-somethings, coming into class; he could talk with facility about Shakespeare, mythology, dance, music, religion—which few undergrads can do. I quickly realized that his pursuit of knowledge ran deep. Exposed to something new that piqued his interest, Tarell would do the work to learn as much as he could about it and absorb it into his creative vocabu-lary. Tarell's unquenchable thirst was not just the stuff of a gifted student striving for that A—for him, knowledge acquisition was a matter of survival, a quest to overcome the tribulations of an unimaginably difficult childhood.

Watching Tarell's work develop over the solo performance course was to witness the birth of a writer. In his weekly showings he brought the world of his childhood to life—embodying the characters and voices of people from his neighborhood, his family, and his younger self. In doing so, he not only rendered them truthfully and compassionately, he did to them what Naomi Iizuka did in *Polaroid Stories*—elevated them into a mythical realm. Myths contain truths and insights into reality that transcend their time. Watching Tarell's work come to life, I saw an artist who understood that within the raw material of his own life existed a window into understanding the mystery and heartache of being human in the face of chaos. I believe this lies at the heart of most of Tarell's work—from *The Brother/Sister Plays* to *Moonlight*. In the former, Tarell foregrounds the interplay between Yoruba mythology and autobiography; in the latter, he draws on autobiography to create a new mythology that shatters traditional notions of masculinity by showing us what masculinity could mean when it's endowed with the possibility of tenderness and love.

Q: Cheryl, you also taught Tarell at DePaul University in his undergrad years. What was he like as a student?

CHERYL LYNN BRUCE: I was an acting teacher and directed an "Intro" course (the first performing experience for underclassmen there), and Tarell was a member of that class. To some students' dismay, I chose to tackle my favorite play, *Antigone*. That humble but stirring production still fills me with pride and joy, and may be the strongest, purest production I've ever directed. Tarell was at the table as my stage manager and handled the lights. Even though he did not perform, he worked hard with the rest of the class to understand *Antigone* because, as I explained, the entire ensemble was duty bound to understand the arc of the story so well that one member could step into another's role and continue on without any discernible disruption—and I believe that class achieved that synchronicity. We read the play together at least three times. I later learned that infuriated some students, but not Tarell. He was an enthusiastic participant in every single aspect of that production. Eager to join the exercises and discuss (he was never shy), Tarell was usually one step ahead, antennae bright as "all get out," even as he found his way. His intellectual appetite for discovery and invention, coupled with an unbridled curiosity, made Tarell incandescent. Still does. He was and is an avid student of life. His thinking and writings bear out that incontrovertible fact.

Q: Tea, you were a peer of Tarell's when you both attended the Yale School of Drama for your graduate studies. What do you remember most about working with him?

TEA ALAGIĆ: Tarell was very young when he came to Yale, and he was always special. His writing was already distinctive and accomplished. It seemed as though he always knew his path; always knew what he wanted to write about, and always had his voice. When I started working with him in my second year, I got to know Tarell very well. He's actually a shy person. He's private, so it takes time for him to open up. But eventually, he will tell you everything. When we did *The Brothers Size*, I learned so much about him and from him. I had never worked with an African American artist before, and it shocked me to learn about police brutality and racism. I was shocked that police officers would stop him because of his skin color. This was new territory for me. As a foreigner, I didn't know anything about this. He opened my eyes. I also can't forget that he is an incredible actor as well. He would fill in for an actor if they were sick or couldn't be at a part of tech [rehearsal]. He's more than a writer. He's an actor, dancer, and all-around artist.

Q: Teo, you've actually been working with Tarell since he was a teenager. Are there any special memories that you have of him?

TEO CASTELLANOS: Oh my. There are so many. One time in his adolescence, Tarell was playing a crackhead. He made a woman in the audience cry until she couldn't stand it anymore. She had to get up and leave. And once, we performed in a detention center (still in his adolescence). I asked him to walk up a stairwell, on some "site specific" improvised direction. He went up there and when he began to deliver his monologue, the inmates and the staff became so captivated you could hear a pin drop in that jail.

Q: Carlos, any special memories?

CARLOS MURILLO: During my solo performance class at DePaul, Tarell brought in the latest incarnation of a piece he was developing for his final—a remarkable autobiographical work drawing on his experience growing up in a world where he faced constant life-and-death peril for who he is as a human. In the final weeks of the course, the piece was starting to really fill out—he'd written a rich text, created an engrossing physical life, and built a makeshift set that, even with its rudimentary elements, contained a transporting power. He was clearly thinking of his theater as a totality—a three-dimensional, expressive integration of all the elements at his disposal to achieve that mythic transcendence he was aiming for.

That particular day I noticed that he was oddly disconnected from the words. It's hard to imagine it now, but Tarell seemed to be phoning his own text in, as if he had some fundamental doubt about the words that he had written. This was strange to me as the words themselves seemed written to explode outward from the body and voice that wrote them—visceral is the only way to describe it. While I work hard to maintain a sense of positivity, there are moments in classrooms where harder truths are necessary, especially when a student and their work in progress is on the edge of a breakthrough. Once Tarell was done, I carefully said something to the effect of "I'm wondering why in your performance you sounded like you were afraid of the words, that you didn't trust them or believe they were worthy of being sent out into the air. I've seen you act in plays and make other people's words, even ones that aren't nearly as good as the ones you've written, sound like they were coming from the deepest place in your body, and here you are making them sound like you're a little embarrassed that you wrote them." The room went silent, and I remember an illegible look come across Tarell's face and wondering, "Did I just lose him? Is he upset? Did I do the right thing?"

The next class, when he spoke those same words he'd written, they sounded like his body depended on them.

Specials

Tarell and the Royal Shakespeare Company: An Interview with Michael Boyd

Q: Tarell often speaks about how formative his time in residence at the Royal Shakespeare Company (RSC) was to his development as a writer and theater-maker. Were there particular things about his work and/or writerly voice that made him an especially auspicious choice to serve as the RSC's International Playwright in Residence?

MICHAEL BOYD: We asked Tarell to join us at the RSC because we loved his play *The Brothers Size*. He seemed perfect, primarily because he was clearly a brilliant, poetic playwright, with a voice that could speak beyond naturalism and express ideas and emotions of scale. Tarell's poetic "style" is no adornment, but the necessary virtuosic vehicle for the expression of his complex and sometimes painful relationship with a dysfunctional world. We knew he would be able to enter into a fruitful dialogue with our house playwright.

Tarell's experience and skills as an actor and dancer were also well suited to an institution that was trying to bring the different disciplines of theater into a closer working partnership. He was a writer who could talk and work with performers, and a true experimenter with theatrical form. Tarell would be forming an intimate relationship with an ensemble company of actors over a period of three years, working with them in a variety of ways, including writing a play specifically for them. He even stood in brilliantly as Rosalind for me one day in rehearsals when Katy Stephens was unwell.

Ironically, it was Tarell's work with the RSC in schools, and as a director, that was the standout success of our collaboration. His commissioned play, *American Trade*, written for our actors, was a dazzling love letter to the acting company.

Tarell's personal experience of theater as a redemptive and empowering force at his school in Miami made him a powerful advocate and driving force for our policy to bring our work with schools into the heart of our programming, and his adaptation and direction of *Hamlet* that toured schools in the U.K. and U.S. was excellent and seminal.

His life experience as a gay African American from a disadvantaged background helped us steel our resolve to give real opportunities to actors from diverse and excluded backgrounds. It was Tarell that successfully cast the U.K.'s first ever British Asian Hamlet, persuading our casting department that the young and, then, very inexperienced Dharmesh Patel had a Hamlet in him of which the RSC would be proud.

These qualities, together with his clear insightful mind and grace and charm, quickly made Tarell a very influential figure in RSC thinking and planning.

Q: The RSC, in collaboration with the Public Theater in New York and GableStage in Miami, produced a stripped-down, radical re-visioning of Shakespeare's *Antony and Cleopatra*, adapted and directed by Tarell. What new insights and meanings did Tarell's adaptation and production perhaps bring to Shakespeare's text?

MICHAEL BOYD: *Antony and Cleopatra*, with Kathryn Hunter as Cleopatra, had been programmed as part of our Long Ensemble repertoire, and I was interested in Tarell doing some work with me on the text of the play. He became very interested in parallels between ancient Egypt's relationship to Rome and Haiti's with Napoleonic France, and developed a version which I liked very much and thought he could direct with more authority than me. Eventually we pulled this off in a natural collaboration with the Public Theater, who had produced *The Brothers Size* in New York and whose program, like the RSC's, reflects a dialogue between Shakespeare's plays and contemporary work. However, I had left the RSC before this particular project went into rehearsal.

Q: Tarell also adapted and directed a "Young People's Shakespeare" production of *Hamlet* for the RSC. What are your reflections on this production?

MICHAEL BOYD: Tarell's *Hamlet* was a completely successful celebration of the young and diverse acting talent within the Long Ensemble, and displayed not only Tarell's beautifully clear storytelling but also his choreographic playfulness and his heartfelt commitment to the imaginative lives of school children.

Q: In the same way that some have argued that there are multiple Becketts (a British Beckett, a French Beckett, an American Beckett, and so on), there is also a developing sense that there are multiple McCraneys (particularly, an American McCraney and a British McCraney). Why do you think British audiences have responded so positively to his work—both his adaptations of Shakespeare as well as his new, more contemporary plays?

MICHAEL BOYD: I think Britain admires much the same qualities in Tarell's work as America does. Britain does still enjoy the remnants of meaningful public funding for the arts and has historically provided a benign space for American theater artists to be able to experiment with ideas that may only find full expression in their work later.

It has been valuable for authors from Arthur Miller to Will Eno to be celebrated by and touch base with the robust and reasonably experimental British theatrical tradition, and Tarell, too, has gained from early recognition and loyalty here.

The extraordinarily creative year of Tarell's life that produced *The Brothers Size* and the outline ideas for *Moonlight* may never be bettered, but if it is, his next golden time may owe some indirect and hidden debts to his work beyond what was familiar to him in the permissive environment of the U.K. and, specifically, the RSC. I hope so.

David Makes Man: An Interview with Jabari Ali, Music Supervisor

Q: You have served as a music supervisor on some of Hollywood's and TV's most notable films. How did you become involved with *David Makes Man* and what about the project made you say "Yes"?

JABARI ALI: I have been in this business for nearly two decades and have had the pleasure to serve in the capacity of music supervisor or consultant on great projects including: *The Equalizer 2*, *Shots Fired*, *Gun Hill*, *Training Day*, *Biker Boyz*, and many more. In that time, I've built some solid relationships with impactful people like Dee Harris-Lawrence. Dee asked that I join the team for *David Makes Man*, and I am so happy to be a part of something of this magnitude. The creativity and timeliness of this show's message is undeniable. Tarell is a fearless, trailblazing, refreshing beam of light in this world of film and television. I appreciate his bravery, transparency, and willingness to change lives. He's a genuine young leader with profound vision, and his storytelling talents are unmatched.

Q: For this process you asked Tarell to share with you a list of music that evoked feelings for *David Makes Man*. Was there anything that particularly struck you about Tarell's musical inspirations for the show? Any challenges involved?

JABARI ALI: Tarell is very intuitive and knowledgeable when it comes to the music integration for his projects. What I learned and loved most was his connection to the gospel. He grew up as a preacher's kid, so using gospel music in his stories is second nature to him. The music is such an important element in telling the story for this series, and his ability to feel the music for these scenes is impeccable. In terms of challenges, Tarell has a very busy schedule. The many important demands on his career don't allow him to be around as much as I would like.

Q: Phylicia Rashad has said that *David Makes Man* is unprecedented for television in various ways. Do you feel similarly? Is this show doing something for television that hasn't been done before?

JABARI ALI: *David Makes Man* is speaking the unapologetic language of our youth in the urban war zones of America. It is boldly and intentionally capturing the essence of the urban youth and telling their story. The show highlights the decisions and contemplations that these young people face every day. It is a show that will be remembered for years to come because it speaks life.

In Rehearsal with Tina Landau: About Tarell's Plays

TINA LANDAU: Tarell's plays function as music. They need to be played, sung, danced to. They need to be understood and felt for their tempi, their crescendos and diminuendos, their melodic motifs, their fermatas, and more. As a director, you need to conduct. You need to bond the orchestra, and conduct, and then let them play without a conductor.

Words I've repeated or written most often in rehearsal:

Quick Switches.
Precision.
Pace.
Play.

It often goes like this:

Make every quick switch found in the text. Make more. Instantly.
  Precisely.
Then do it fast. Then play it—or let it play you.

Moments

Embrace each moment of the play fully—moment by moment—even when they seem contradictory. Don't struggle to find or create a naturalistic logic. It will reveal itself in strange ways by following the map of the text, even if you don't understand "why." Do the beats, play the score as written and the "why" will reveal itself.

Pace

The key to the pace, remember, is to not let it make you lose the switches or the precision. You need to play the extremely committed beats, just faster. It requires, believe it or not, practice. You should take your scenes and practice—on your own and on a purely technical level: the speed *with* the switches (without allowing the fast to crank you into different acting choices or greater generality).

In the midst of the speed you can never lose intention, never go so fast that you are just saying words. You all are now finding the rhythm of the show. This is critical as the piece functions, so often, like a piece of music. It has a natural flow and rhythm in the speech that Tarell has written. The key now is to work on combining all three elements into one seamless whole:

> Rhythm (cadence, ebb, and flow).
> Tempo (speed).
> Intention (high stakes, strong motivation).

Ensemble

Tarell's work *requires* ensemble work. It is always *about* community, and always *requires* community. It's all about handoffs of the baton, or chords built from single notes—many forms of what it means to be an ensemble, a group, a family.

For directors: build the ensemble. Even if it seems that Shelah rules the roost. The actors are akin to players in a band. The music can't exist without them all. Even if/when some fall silent, when there is an extended solo, the solo has no definition without the context of the band's full force.

For actors: you are what Peter Brook calls "one story-teller with many heads." Show up. Focus. Give it your all. Give it up to your teammates. To your audience. Go that extra distance. It's not about pushing or going for results—it's about being present, alert, keeping the stakes high, listening to each other, and looking out for each other. Playing as one. The key is not only the individual athlete (actor) doing his or her part, but more so the teamwork, i.e., the ability of the team to work together, to follow and enter fully into the whole game, and yet for each to know their "role," what they must contribute and achieve as part of the whole.

Notes Specific to *Wig Out!*

Pacing and Pause

Take out the pause. The play needs to be played quick. The audience needs to be plunged into an experience, a vortex, as Eric is.

Act on the line—not before it. Make sure you know exactly what this means, and make sure you are doing it. Or, as Tarell once noted, "ACK [*sic*] on the lines."

Precision

The precision and the quickness of this play, especially once we get inside the house, is paramount because the audience, too, must feel whirlwinded. And it's not just in the language, it's in the body as well. Every action, whether mental or physical, needs to be clean, sharp, and definite. Nothing tentative, nothing grey or beige or milky. Go for sharp edges, spark, power, definition.

Opening Day Rehearsal Talk—*Brother/Sister Plays*

There is a tension—juxtaposition—in the piece between a naturalism/realness and a formalism/performative quality. In the acting, both need to be there. The actor never performs, but the character does. In the characters, it goes back and forth. Sometimes they are performing and sometimes not. Sometimes their performing is real/believable and sometimes it is intentionally not. In the production, it needs a balance—so that the evening in the theater is grounded in a kind of behavioral and psychological detail, a truth and simplicity to the acting, and also, the experience should soar as pure entertainment, spectacle, song and dance, and poetry.

In the acting, one needs to find a truth in the heightened language. Like acting Shakespeare, you don't play Tarell's work in a naturalistic, laid-back, mumbling fashion. Nor do you allow the formal quality of the poetry to make you artificial. You use the language to live in a new kind of truth and believability—you use the words, and you act on the line. For certain audiences, too, sometimes Tarell's work is like listening to Shakespeare. They might not understand all the word meanings, the slang, the cultural references, but they understand the sense, the sound, and the thought behind the text.

Tarell Alvin McCraney, in His Own Words

✦

*Interview with Sharrell D. Luckett, David Román,
and Isaiah Matthew Wooden*

EDITORS: At this point in your career, you've been asked to do countless interviews. One of the questions, it seems, that hasn't been asked, at least not directly, is: Who is Tarell Alvin McCraney?

MCCRANEY: "A strange beginning: 'borrow'd majesty!'" That's one of the first lines from *King John* [by William Shakespeare], and the first time I heard it—out loud—I knew I was in trouble . . . not like read it on the page but heard it from someone's mouth, from Eleanor to the court in defense of her son? I knew I was in trouble. Talk about a phrase that summed me up, that got me together, as the "kidz" and older church folks might say.

A strange beginning?

Indeed. My first memory is of me being beaten to a pulp by my mom and actual dad; they took turns because I had touched my cousin or brother's butt in the bathtub. I was four. Some of my other earliest memories are of the Challenger exploding; my little brother caressing the babysitter's breast, and her laughing and thinking of him as more manly than me; the man who I wished was my father being killed during a weekend while I was away, my mother explaining that he was dead and that I would never see him again; my mother pregnant with his child and being hospitalized for overdosing; the threat of being taken from my mother, the wish that I had never gone to call the police, the feeling that, if we were taken, then it would have been all my fault.

That was all by the age of six.

Borrow'd majesty . . .

I wish for the grace of my peers. When I meet with Kyle Abraham, I wish he could spin me into the brush strokes he paints with his choreography. When I walk with Jamar Roberts, I hope he will, for a moment, move next to me in such a way that someone will see grace in me in the way that I do in them, on them, with them.

My mother was graceful. Her mother was Grace. Then again, so was my father's mother. Grace. They taught me majesty: the King of Kings from Grace Ann, who taught me to know and fear God, and the King of Thought from Grace Rebecca, who taught me that knowledge was power. None of it feels like I wield it properly. I am neither a great worshiper, though I am reverent, or a great scholar, though I hold onto thoughts, ideas, and remembrances. I am lazy in that, if I must undo myself, disturb myself, in order to understand a thing, I retreat. I'd rather peace. Or maybe that's just the Venus in me . . .

I'd rather peace.

One time, on 43rd Street in New York City, in front of a rehearsal hall, I couldn't find my Uber. I was late to see my godson and was with a friend who I had offered a ride . . . if we could just find the right black car—in a sea of black cars—that day. I kept checking the phone, and checking my friend, and checking the cars until *finally* I found the correct one and popped in. My friend said, "Wow, I hope I never get like that!" I asked what he meant, and he went on to describe a scene of me ignoring the hell out of someone, a young person, who was trying to get my attention by calling my name. He said they seemed like a fan of my work.

In that instance, I was two things: relieved that I had missed out on having to live up to a stranger's expectations of me *and* really sad that the poor person might have thought I was ignoring them. Then the sadness won out. I started feeling so bad in the car, and calling myself all kinds of names. *Look at you acting like you are better than somebody.* But I wasn't. I honestly didn't hear them. But just like that I spiraled back to the first time I mistakenly or curiously went looking at something and got beat by two parents.

Even at thirty-seven, I was still four.

EDITORS: How would you describe your artistic development? Were there notable moments that inspired you to pursue theatermaking?

MCCRANEY: Thanks to Hurricane Andrew, I ended up in an arts magnet program at Mays Middle School. Thanks to my mom being in rehab, I met a man running a rehab-prevention theater program named Teo Castellanos, and that profoundly furthered my artistic development. Thanks to the retirement of an old stalwart, I got into New World School of the Arts High School in Miami. By that point, I was locked in . . . I've been all about theater and storytelling ever since.

My mom died when I was twenty-two, before I got to the Yale School of Drama. I wrote *The Brothers Size* and "In Moonlight Black Boys Look Blue" in the wake of her death. Lucky for me, both of those pieces have brought me back to Miami and Homestead.

EDITORS: What does your creative process look like? What practices and/or rituals do you engage in as you write?

MCCRANEY: Writing doesn't begin until I know the end. To find the end—as with any journey—you have to follow a path. Sometimes the path is before you. Sometimes the path is covered or hidden. Sometimes the path moves under you. But if you know where to stop or where to rest, then the path is all that matters.

EDITORS: Are there experiences that proved challenging that you would not change because they've indelibly shaped who you are?

MCCRANEY: I'm not sure that I would not change them. I think the powers that be are smart enough to give us limits on what we can change, and gives us the power of acceptance and wisdom to know that this is for our own good. Still, there is so much pain I would change.

EDITORS: What are some of the essential ingredients for a successful collaboration with you?

MCCRANEY: . . . Ask my successful collaborators.

EDITORS: What's unique about creating work for the theater (as opposed to film or television)?

MCCRANEY: . . . If you can see it—the story—then it's film. And if you can hear it, it's a play. The live interaction with the audience is *the* thing in theater.

EDITORS: How would you say the "distant present" differs from the present?

MCCRANEY: You are always telling a story. As you are telling it, it means it's already happened. It's distant. It's not quite present.

EDITORS: Do you feel the "burden of representation" as a black queer playwright?

MCCRANEY: Nothing is free. I write for the twelve blocks that make up Liberty City and, by doing so, feel I have to represent the truth of that place as best I can. I hope that truth resonates . . . and agitates more dialogue. But you have to always have an audience in mind when making dramatic stories.

EDITORS: How has teaching impacted your writing process?

MCCRANEY: Teaching is incredible because you get to remind people every day of the things that you wish someone would remind you of when you are working.

EDITORS: How has being a company member at Steppenwolf Theatre impacted your artistic development?

MCCRANEY: Steppenwolf was where I got my equity card. I became a card-carrying actor at Steppenwolf. I worked with Tina Landau on most of my early work, and Alana Arenas and I grew up together. Any place where I get to continue to work with them feels like home.

EDITORS: The world has come to know you as a writer, director, actor, and professor. What's something about you that we perhaps don't know?

MCCRANEY: I take Horton and ballet dance classes often at the Alvin Ailey American Dance Theater, where I once went for summer dance intensives.

EDITORS: What is the work that keeps you up at night?

MCCRANEY: I don't sleep, so all of it.

Introduction

1. The free "Artist Exchange" discussion was hosted by the Public Theater and the British Council in New York City on March 8, 2014, and livestreamed by HowlroundTV.

2. Jason Zinoman, "Two Brothers in a Gumbo of Bayou and West Africa," *New York Times*, January 20, 2007, https://www.nytimes.com/2007/01/20/theater/reviews/20size.html.

3. Patrick Healy, "Writer Digs Up Gods from the Bayou," *New York Times*, November 10, 2009, http://www.nytimes.com/2009/11/15/theater/15heal.html.

4. See "Backstage Pass: An Artist Roundtable on the Work of Tarell Alvin McCraney" in this volume.

5. Tarell Alvin McCraney, "Tarell Alvin McCraney on *The Brother/Sister Plays*," program for *The Brother/Sister Plays* at the McCarter Theatre Center, Princeton, New Jersey, April–June 2009.

6. Ibid.

7. Dan Rubin, "American Bayou: An Interview with Tarell Alvin McCraney," program for *Marcus; Or the Secret of Sweet* at the American Conservatory Theatre, San Francisco, California, October–November 2010.

8. See McCraney's acceptance speech for the HRC's 2017 Visionary Arts Award, which *Moonlight* received, https://www.youtube.com/watch?v=bGa65oBM8LI.

9. Harry J. Elam Jr. and Douglas A. Jones Jr., eds., "Introduction" in *The Methuen Drama Book of Post-Black Plays* (London: Bloomsbury Publishing, 2012), ix–xxxv (quoted on xi).

10. Isaiah Matthew Wooden, "*Head of Passes* by Tarell Alvin McCraney (review)," *Theatre Journal* 66, no. 2 (May 2014): 266–68 (quoted on 268).

11. Charles McNulty, "Rising Playwright Tarell Alvin McCraney Takes His Own, Wary Path to L.A.," *Los Angeles Times*, August 29, 2014, http://www.latimes.com/entertainment/arts/la-et-cm-ca-tarell-alvin-mccraney-20140828-column.html.

12. Ibid.

13. David Román, "The Distant Present of Tarell Alvin McCraney," *American Quarterly* 66, no. 1 (2014): 181–95 (quoted on 188).

14. McCraney, "Tarell Alvin McCraney on *The Brother/Sister Plays*."

15. Jill Dolan, *Utopia in Performance: Finding Hope at the Theater* (Ann Arbor: University of Michigan Press, 2005), 2.

16. McCraney, "Tarell Alvin McCraney on *The Brother/Sister Plays*."

17. Dolan, *Utopia in Performance*, 11.

18. McCraney, "Tarell Alvin McCraney on *The Brother/Sister Plays*."

19. Sandra L. Richards, "African Diaspora Drama," in *The Cambridge Companion to African American Theatre* (Cambridge: Cambridge University Press, 2013), 247; Jeffrey Q. McCune Jr., "A Good Black Manhood Is Hard to Find: Toward More Transgressive Reading Practices," *Spectrum: A Journal on Black Men* 1, no. 1 (2012): 121–40 (quoted on 132).

20. Tarell Alvin McCraney, *The Brother/Sister Plays* (New York: Theater Communications Group, 2010), 239.

21. See "Backstage Pass: An Artist Roundtable on the Work of Tarell Alvin McCraney" in this volume.

22. Susan Letzler Cole, *Playwrights in Rehearsal: The Seduction of Company* (New York: Routledge, 2001), 87.

23. This particular line is drawn from the version of the script performed in the premiere production at Steppenwolf Theatre Company.

24. See David Román, *Acts of Intervention: Performance, Gay Culture, and AIDS* (Bloomington: Indiana University Press, 1998).

25. Soyica Diggs Colbert, *The African American Theatrical Body: Performance, Reception, and the Stage* (Cambridge: Cambridge University Press, 2011).

Juxtaposing Creoles

Citations for the chapter's epigraphs are as follows: Isabel Berwick, "Interview with Tarell Alvin McCraney," *Financial Times*, November 1, 2013; Tarell Alvin McCraney, "The Distant Present," *'Cane Talks*, University of Miami, January 29, 2016.

1. McCraney's paternal grandparents are of Bahamian origins and his maternal roots are in the U.S. South. In earlier Wikipedia posts, the playwright is identified as "from the projects of Louisiana."

2. Tarell Alvin McCraney, *The Brother/Sister Plays* (New York: Theatre Communications Group, 2010); Tarell Alvin McCraney, *Head of Passes*, manuscript draft sent to me by McCraney. All subsequent references are to these versions of the scripts.

3. The playwright made this statement during his guest lecture in my "Housing in the Black Literary Imagination" course on April 12, 2017. His bayou plays include *Head of Passes* and *The Brother/Sister Plays*. McCraney also contributed to the collaborative play *The Breach*, which sought to capture the raw emotions in the immediate aftermath of Hurricane Katrina. *Choir Boy* and the screenplay "In Moonlight Black Boys Look Blue" are squarely set in Miami. The original "In Moonlight Black Boys Look Blue" manuscript draft was sent to me by McCraney; Tarell Alvin McCraney, *Choir Boy* (New York: Dramatist Play Service, 2014); Catherine Filloux, Tarell Alvin McCraney, and Joe Sutton's *The Breach* script performed at Seattle's Bagley Wright Theatre, January 10 to February 9, 2008. All subsequent references are to these versions of the scripts.

4. Juliet Hooker suggests that thinking juxtapositionally means placing thinkers and traditions that are viewed as disparate in proximity: "What can we see or understand differently by juxtaposing distinct and diverse . . . texts and contexts. However, juxtaposition does not assume prior similarities or differences between thinkers and traditions." Juliet Hooker, *Theorizing Race in the*

Americas: Douglass, Sarmiento, Du Bois, and Vasconcelos (New York: Oxford University Press, 2017).

5. Ruthmarie H. Mitsch, "Maryse Condé's Mangroves," *Research in African Literatures* 28, no. 4, Multiculturalism (Winter 1997): 54–70. Critics like Mitsch deploy the metaphor of the mangrove to capture "positive illustration[s] of multiculturalism." My reading of Miami, in contrast, attends to power hierarchies and racial and ethnic antagonisms.

6. Amy Kaplan and Donald E. Pease, *Cultures of United States Imperialism* (Durham, N.C.: Duke University Press, 1993); Allan Punzalan Isaac, *American Tropics: Articulating Filipino America* (Minneapolis: University of Minnesota Press, 2006).

7. Think, for example, about McCraney's rewriting of Shakespeare's *Antony and Cleopatra*, which he sets in Saint-Domingue. See Tarell Alvin McCraney's adaptation of *Antony and Cleopatra* performed at GableStage in January 2014.

8. *Moonlight*, directed by Barry Jenkins (2016; Santa Monica, Calif.: A24/Lionsgate, 2017). All subsequent references are to this version.

9. See John Stuart, "Liberty Square: Florida's First Public Housing Project," in *The New Deal in South Florida: Design, Policy, and Community Building, 1933–1940*, edited by John F. Stack and John A. Stuart (Gainesville: University Press of Florida, 2008); Nathan Connolly, *A World More Concrete: Real Estate and the Remaking of Jim Crow South Florida* (Chicago: University of Chicago Press, 2014); Chanelle Rose, *The Struggle for Black Freedom in Miami: Civil Rights and America's Tourist Paradise, 1896–1968* (Baton Rouge: Louisiana State University Press, 2015). Liberty Square housing projects were built to both "clean up" the substandard tropical housing many Blacks were subjected to as well as to "isolate Blacks from the white community." Segregated housing, nonetheless, led to the flourishing of the Black professional and entrepreneurial classes. In the 1960s, the construction of I-95, which cut through the Overtown neighborhood, was the death knell of such a visible, successful Black middle class in Miami.

10. Jessica Moulite, "Color of Climate: Is Climate Change Gentrifying Miami's Black Neighborhoods?" *The Root*, August 4, 2017. See also the short documentary film *Right to Wynwood*, which follows the displacement of the city's longstanding Puerto Rican community. *Right to Wynwood*, directed by Camila Alvarez and Natalie Edgar (Meraki Media, 2014).

11. Soyica Diggs Colbert, "Black Movements: Tarell Alvin McCraney's *In the Red and Brown Water*," *The African American Theatrical Body: Reception, Performance and the Stage* (Cambridge: Cambridge University Press, 2011). While Isaiah Matthew Wooden is not wrong to suggest that the playwright captures the idioms of "bayou cultures and hip-hop sensibilities," I want to make a claim that Miami matters to these sensibilities. See Isaiah Matthew Wooden, "*Head of Passes* by Tarell Alvin McCraney (review)," *Theatre Journal* 66, no. 2 (May 2014): 266–68.

12. *Crisis Magazine*, March 1942 (quoted on p. 83).

13. McCraney suggests that in *The Brother/Sister Plays* he is working out his relationship with his siblings and that he meets West African cosmology not in Africa or books but on the streets of Miami.

14. Jan Nijman, *Miami: Mistress of the Americas* (Philadelphia: University of Pennsylvania Press, 2011).

15. Three events with significant racial, ethnic, and linguistic overtones occurred in rapid succession in 1980 that have contributed to the present zeitgeist of Miami as a white Spanish bilingual and bicultural southern U.S. city: the Cuban Mariel boatlift from April 15 to October 31, 1980; the Miami race riots in the Black enclave of Liberty City on May 17, 1980; and amnesty for Haitian refugees who entered Miami via boat before October 10, 1980. The historian Chanelle Rose pushes back the dates of the city's turn to Latin America and Hispanicization to the 1940s and the tenure of Robert King High, who she calls the "Mayor of the Americas." See Rose, *The Struggle for Black Freedom in Miami*. Max J. Castro, "The Politics of Language in Miami," in *Miami Now!: Immigration, Ethnicity and Social Change*, edited by Guillermo J. Grenier and Alex Stepick III (Gainesville: University of Florida Press, 1992).

16. Alejandro Portes and Alex Stepick, *City on the Edge: The Transformation of Miami* (Los Angeles: University of California Press, 1993).

17. Louis Herns Marcelin, "Identity, Power, and Socioracial Hierarchies," in *Neither Enemies nor Friends: Latinos, Blacks and Afro-Latinos*, ed. Anani Dzidzienyo and Suzanne Oboler (New York: Palgrave Macmillan, 2000).

18. A Caribbean literary imagination has been particularly interested in tracing the connections within the Americas and especially with Louisiana. See, for example, Erna Brodber, *Louisiana* (London: New Beacon Books, 1994) and Roland Watson-Grant, *Sketcher* (Richmond, United Kingdom: Alma Books, 2015).

19. Guillermo J. Grenier and Alex Stepick III, *Miami Now!*; Elizabeth M. Aranda, Sallie Hughes, and Elena Sabogal, *Making a Life in Multiethnic Miami: Immigration and the Rise of a Global City* (Boulder, Colo.: Lynne Rienner Publishers, 2014).

20. Carole Boyce Davies, *Caribbean Spaces: Escapes from Twilight Zones* (Urbana: University of Illinois Press, 2013).

21. John Lowe, *Calypso Magnolia: The Crosscurrents of Caribbean and Southern Literature* (Chapel Hill: University of North Carolina Press, 2016).

22. Rose, *The Struggle for Black Freedom in Miami*. Rose makes an argument around tourism. I suggest that it also incorporates the agricultural industries and the elite power brokers from Latin America.

23. Jose Estaban Munoz, *Disidentifications: Queers of Color and the Performance of Politics* (Minneapolis: University of Minnesota Press, 1999).

24. McCraney, "The Distant Present."

25. My use of quiet draws on the work of Kevin Quashie who points us to quiet forms of protest focusing on interiority. See Kevin Quashie, *The Sovereignty of Quiet: Beyond Resistance in Black Culture* (New Brunswick, N.J.: Rutgers University Press, 2012).

26. In 1936, Miami Beach enacted Ordinance 457, which required more than five thousand seasonal workers at hotels, restaurants, and nightclubs, as well as domestic servants, to register with police and to be photographed and fingerprinted. Once registered, those workers—many of whom were Black—had to carry ID cards at all times in the city. Regarding the history of Virginia Key or Fisher Island, see Gregory Bush, *White Sand, Black Beach: Civil Rights, Public Space, and Miami's Virginia Key* (Gainesville: University Press of Florida, 2016).

27. Luther Campbell's urban weekend is the antagonist in the other direction, signaling the inability to incorporate Blackness within Miami—especially Miami Beach. See Luther Campbell, *The Book of Luke: My Fight for Truth, Justice and Liberty City* (New York: Amistad, 2015).

28. Darnell L. Moore, "Black+Gay+American: A Search for Sanctuaries," *Advocate*, July 15, 2013.

29. The Miaminess of McCraney's sensibilities invites the generational juxtaposition with Zora Neale Hurston, whose own North Florida roots and hemispheric crossings resulted in her epic, *Their Eyes Were Watching God*, written during her seven-week sojourn in Haiti. Keith Cartwright identifies the coastal south as the Black Gulf and describes Hurston as being grounded in "creole history, culture and landscapes of Florida." Where her stories were invested in elevating a rural folk, McCraney's Miami sensibility and different generational ethos evokes settings that are simultaneously urban, agriculturally rural, and suburban. And, where the Everglades and the porch sitters were key features of Hurston's classic texts, they, like the African-based orishas of Elegba and Oya, appear with an urban difference in McCraney's Black hemispheric southern epics. Unlike the propertied privacy of Janie's porch in *Their Eyes Were Watching God*, where one had to be invited, one lives with a sense of externality that occurs in the front of the housing structure. See Keith Cartwright, "'To Walk with the Storm': Oya as the Transformative 'I' of Zora Neale Hurston's Afro-Atlantic Callings," *American Literature* 78, no. 4 (2006): 741–67. See also Robin D. G. Kelley, *Freedom Dreams: The Black Radical Imagination* (New York: Beacon Press, 2003).

30. Vanessa Agard-Jones, "What the Sands Remember," *GLQ* 8, no. 2–3 (2012): 325–46.

31. Paul Gilroy, *The Black Atlantic: Modernity and Double Consciousness* (Cambridge, Mass: Harvard University Press, 1993); Peter Linebaugh and Marcus Rediker, *The Many-Headed Hydra: Sailors, Slaves, Commoners, and the Hidden History of the Revolutionary Atlantic* (Boston: Beacon Press 2000).

32. Quashie, *The Sovereignty of Quiet*; McCraney, *The Brother/Sister Plays*.

33. Donette Francis, *Fictions of Feminine Citizenship: Sexuality and the Nation in Contemporary Caribbean Women's Writings* (New York: Palgrave, 2012).

34. Jafari Sinclaire Allen, *There's a Disco Ball between Us: A Theory of Black/Queer Life* (Durham, N.C.: Duke University Press, forthcoming).

35. Randy Gener, "Dreaming in Yoruba Land: Tarell Alvin McCraney's Trio of Profanely Poetic Ritual Dramas Signals the Emergence of a Major New Voice," *American Theatre*, September 1, 2009.

36. Carolyn Dinshaw, *Getting Medieval: Sexualities and Communities, Pre and Postmodern* (Durham, N.C.: Duke University Press, 1999).

37. Germane Barnes, "[Housing] Destruction," *Journal of Architectural Education*, 72, no. 1 (February 2018): 20–21, doi:10.1080/10464883.2018.1410641; Audra, "On the Front Porch: Black Life in Full View," *New York Times*, December 4, 2018, https://www.nytimes.com/2018/12/04/us/porch-detroit-black-life.html.

38. Isaiah Matthew Wooden notes that the playwright addresses questions of ecology in his work, which is an element of his "dramaturgy that frequently goes unremarked." See Wooden's review of *Head of Passes*.

39. Boyce Davies, *Caribbean Spaces*, 95.

40. Ibid., 19.

41. Carlos Decena, *Tacit Subjects: Belonging and Same-Sex Desire among Dominican Immigrant Men* (Durham, N.C.: Duke University Press, 2011).

42. See Erica Moiah James, "Every Nigger Is a Star: Reimagining Blackness from Post-Civil Rights America to the Postindependence Caribbean," *Black Camera* 8, no. 1 (Fall 2016): 55–83.

43. Nathan Connolly made this statement in response to questions about what constitutes a distinctive Black Miami aesthestic at the "Creole Miami: Black Intellectual and Artistic Trajectories" convening at the University of Miami, April 20, 2018.

Theodicy and Hope

1. Tarell Alvin McCraney, *Head of Passes* (Center Theatre Group draft, August 20, 2017).

2. Tarell Alvin McCraney, *Wig Out!* (London: Faber and Faber, 2008), 5.

3. Robert S. Boynton, "Cornel West," *Rolling Stone*, November 15, 2007, 177.

4. Craig R. Prentiss, *Staging Faith: Religion and African American Theater from the Harlem Renaissance to World War II* (New York: New York University Press, 2014), 106.

5. Tarell Alvin McCraney, *Head of Passes* (Public Theater draft, March 23, 2016), 1. The 2017 Center Theatre Group draft does not feature this note, but the addition of Shelah's friend asking "What happened? Who gets punished like this? . . . What did you do, Shelah?" makes the later script even more Job-like (74). McCraney reports that, while developing the play, he and director Tina Landau "spent two weeks with a cast just reading the Book of Job out loud and then trying to decipher its makeup. When we walked away from it, my takeaway, again, was that it is a story about someone's personal faith, and how they use it as an aperture or a guide to try and understand the many, many, sometimes fraught, sometimes beautiful, often chaotic events of our lives." Julie McCormick, "Shining a Light on Tarell Alvin McCraney," *Berkeley Rep Magazine* 6 (2014–15): 21, https://www.berkeleyrep.org/season/1415/pdf/program-hp.pdf.

6. Ecclesiastes 8:15, *The New Oxford Annotated Bible: New Revised Standard Version with the Apocrypha*, ed. Michael D. Coogan (Oxford: Oxford University Press, 2010), hereafter NRSV.

7. Isaiah Matthew Wooden, "*Head of Passes* by Tarell Alvin McCraney (review)," *Theatre Journal* 66, no. 2 (May 2014): 267.

8. Voleine Amilcar, "Berkeley Rep Presents Tarell Alvin McCraney's *Head of Passes*," March 11, 2015, 1, https://www.berkeleyrep.org/press/pr/1415/Berkeley _Rep_Head_of_Passes.pdf.

9. 1 Kings 19:12 (NRSV).

10. This character is called "Angel" in the dramatis personae of each draft, but accounts suggest that its role on stage was ambiguous. Chris Jones, for example, reviewing the Steppenwolf production, calls this figure "McCraney's symbol of God, or the devil, or our psychotic delusions, or of that which passes all our understanding." The character did not return to the 2017 Center Theatre Group script. Chris Jones, "'Head of Passes': A family's trials, inspired by Job," *Chicago*

Tribune, April 15, 2013, http://www.chicagotribune.com/ct-ent-0415-head-passes-review-20130415-column.html.

11. Genesis 32:26 (NRSV).

12. David Román, "The Distant Present of Tarell Alvin McCraney," *American Quarterly* 66, no. 1 (2014): 186.

13. Ibid., 194.

14. Wooden, "*Head of Passes*," 267.

15. William A. Beardslee, *The Oxford Companion to the Bible* (Oxford: Oxford University Press, 1993), s.v. "Amen," 22–23; "Selah," 686.

16. McCraney, *Head of Passes* Public Theater draft, 4; Center Theatre Group draft, 57. "Pour. Oh, Pour!" is not in the later CTG draft, but Shelah recalls Lear there in new lines soliloquizing plans for her children: "What little I have, on this earth, I will divide it amongst them," 2.

17. Ecclesiastes 8:15 (Authorized King James Version).

18. Ecclesiastes 2:26 (NRSV).

19. On naming and Yoruba resonances in *The Brother/Sister Plays*, see Kevin J. Wetmore Jr., "Children of Yemayá and the American Eshu: West African Myth in African-American Theatre," in *Dramatic Revisions of Myths, Fairy Tales, and Legends: Essays on Recent Plays*, edited by Verna A. Foster (Jefferson, N.C.: McFarland & Company, 2012), 81–95.

20. Ecclesiastes 9:7 (NRSV).

21. Edward W. Said, *Humanism and Democratic Criticism* (New York: Columbia University Press, 2004), 11.

22. Robert Simonson, "Playbill.com's Brief Encounter with Tarell Alvin McCraney," *Playbill*, September 19, 2008, http://www.playbill.com/article/playbillcoms-brief-encounter-with-tarell-alvin-mccraney-com-176741.

23. Carol Wayne White, *Black Lives and Sacred Humanity: Toward an African American Religious Naturalism* (New York: Fordham University Press, 2016), 3.

24. Ecclesiastes 1:9 (NRSV).

25. White, *Black Lives*, 11–15.

26. Allen Dwight Callahan, *The Talking Book: African Americans and the Bible* (New Haven: Yale University Press, 2008), xiii. See also Vincent L. Wimbush, ed., *African Americans and the Bible: Sacred Texts and Social Textures* (New York: Continuum, 2000).

27. Eddie S. Glaude Jr., "Myth and African American Self-Identity," *Religion and the Creation of Race and Ethnicity*, ed. Craig R. Prentiss (New York: New York University Press, 2003), 32. Similarly to White, Glaude argues: "It is precisely in the African American struggle against the dehumanizing effects of racism that their religious imagination served as one of the key sources in the construction of an African American self," 28.

28. Wooden, "*Head of Passes*," 268.

29. Anthony B. Pinn, *Why Lord? Suffering and Evil in Black Theology* (New York: Continuum, 1995), 17.

30. Soyica Diggs Colbert, *The African American Theatrical Body: Reception, Performance, and the Stage* (Cambridge: Cambridge University Press, 2011), 262, 264.

The Distant Present of Tarell Alvin McCraney

1. Soyica Diggs Colbert, *The African American Theatrical Body: Performance, Reception, and the Stage* (Cambridge: Cambridge University Press, 2011), 268.

2. See Isaiah Matthew Wooden, "*Head of Passes* by Tarell Alvin McCraney (review)," *Theatre Journal* 66, no. 2 (May 2014): 266–68; Katherine Jean Nigh, "The Breach: *A Story about the Drowning of New Orleans* (review)," *Theatre Journal* 60, no. 3 (October 2008): 471–73.

3. This description appeared on the Steppenwolf website, https://www.steppen wolf.org/tickets--events/seasons/2018-19/ms-blakk/.

4. All quotations from *Head of Passes* are from the unpublished rehearsal draft dated March 1, 2013. My thanks to Steppenwolf Theatre for providing me with the text for this essay.

5. For a discussion of *Topdog/Underdog* by Suzan-Lori Parks, see my *Performance in America: Contemporary U.S. Culture and the Performing Arts* (Durham, N.C.: Duke University Press, 2005).

6. All quotes from *Choir Boy* are from the unpublished Manhattan Theatre Club 2013 press draft. My thanks to Manhattan Theatre Club for providing me with the text for this review.

7. Tarell Alvin McCraney, quoted in "*Choir Boy* Scribe Tarell Alvin McCraney on the Untold Story of African-American Gospel Singers," *Buzzfeed*, June 25, 2013, https://www.broadway.com/buzz/170337/choir-boy-scribe-tarell-alvin-mccraney -on-the-untold-story-of-african-american-gospel-singers/.

"My Grandmother Wore a Wig"

1. D. Soyini Madison and Judith Hamera, "Performance Studies at the Intersections," *The Sage Handbook of Performance Studies*, ed. D. Soyini Madison and Judith Hamera (Thousand Oaks, Calif.: Sage, 2006), xii.

2. E. Patrick Johnson, "'Quare' Studies, or (Almost) Everything I Know about Queer Studies I Learned from My Grandmother," *Text and Performance Quarterly* 21, no. 1 (2001): 1–25.

3. Michael Warner, *Fear of a Queer Planet: Queer Politics and Social Theory* (Minneapolis: University of Minnesota Press, 1993), xxvii.

4. Eve Kosofsky Sedgwick, *Touching Feeling: Affect, Pedagogy, Performativity* (Durham, N.C.: Duke University Press), 61.

5. Paulo Freire, *Pedagogy of the Oppressed* (London: Bloomsbury Publishing, 2001), 127.

6. Dustin Bradley Goltz and Jason Zingsheim, eds., *Queer Praxis: Questions for LGBTQ Worldmaking* (New York: Peter Lang, 2015), 1.

7. Norman K. Denzin, *Interpretive Ethnography: Ethnographic Practices in the 21st Century* (Thousand Oaks, Calif.: Sage, 1997), 34.

8. Drawn directly from the character descriptions in the published script. See Tarell Alvin McCraney, *Wig Out!* (London: Faber and Faber, 2008), 7. All subsequent references are to this version of the script.

9. While I delineate between Venus and The Fates in my rendering of the passage here, my focus is on Venus's primary narrative.

10. J. M. Barrie, *Peter Pan* (New York: Sterling, 2008), 22.

11. Stephen M. Whitehead, *Men and Masculinities* (Cambridge, Mass.: Polity Press, 2002), 210.

12. Ibid., 213.

13. Ibid.

14. The complex of this top/bottom relationality also plays out in more tensive ways between Venus and Deity.

15. Arthur Brittan, *Masculinity and Power* (Oxford: Basil Blackwell, 1989), 4.

16. Johnson, "'Quare' Studies."

17. Ibid., 2.

18. Ibid., 3–20.

19. See for example: Roderick A. Ferguson, *Aberrations in Black: Toward a Queer of Color Critique* (Minneapolis: University of Minnesota Press, 2004); E. Patrick Johnson, *No Tea, No Shade: New Writing in Black Queer Studies* (Durham, N.C.: Duke University Press, 2001); E. Patrick Johnson, *Sweet Tea: Black Gay Men of the South, An Oral History* (Chapel Hill: University of North Carolina Press, 2008); and E. Patrick Johnson and Mae G. Henderson, eds., *Black Queer Studies: A Critical Anthology* (Durham, N.C.: Duke University Press, 2005).

20. Johnson, "'Quare' Studies," 2. In this quote, Johnson references Mae G. Henderson, *Borders, Boundaries, and Frames: Cultural Criticism and Cultural Studies* (New York: Routledge, 1995), 147.

21. Ben Brantley, "Families Come in All Shapes and Hairstyles: *Wig Out!*," *New York Times*, September 30, 2008, http://www.nytimes.com/2008/10/01/theater /reviews/01wig.html. I am also reminded that in the scholarly text that chronicles his one-man show, "Strange Fruit," Johnson also talks about wearing his mother's wig. E. Patrick Johnson, "Strange Fruit: A Performance about Identity Politics," *TDR: The Drama Review* 47, no. 2 (Summer 2003): 88–116.

22. See Bryant Keith Alexander, "Queer/Quare Theory: Worldmaking and Methodologies," in *The Sage Handbook of Qualitative Research, 5th Edition*, ed. Norman K. Denzin and Yvonna Sessions Lincoln (Los Angeles, Calif.: Sage, 2017), 290.

23. For a glossary of terms, see https://www.hrc.org/resources/glossary-of-terms.

24. Chandan Reddy, "Home, Houses, Nonidentity: *Paris is Burning*," in *Burning Down the House: Recycling Domesticity*, ed. Rosemary Marangoly George (Boulder, Colo.: Westview Press, 1997), 356–57.

25. José Esteban Muñoz, *Disidentification: Queers of Color and the Performance of Politics* (Minneapolis: University of Minnesota Press, 1999).

26. Ferguson, *Aberrations in Black*, 4.

27. The quotes referenced throughout this paper are found in an older version of the script, in which the Cinderella Ball is not staged. In the more recent version of the script (including recent productions), the Cinderella Ball is staged.

The Breach

1. Scott McKinnon, Andrew Gorman-Murray, and Dale Dominey-Howes, "Disasters, Queer Narratives, and the News: How Are LGBTI Disaster Experiences Reported by the Mainstream and LGBTI Media?" *Journal of Homosexuality* 64, no. 1 (2017): 122–44 (quoted on 123).

2. Joe Sutton, "Eye of the Storm: 3 Playwrights Tap the Raw Emotions Left behind by Hurricane Katrina," *American Theatre*, 24, no. 7 (2007): 50.

3. Ibid.

4. Ibid.

5. Ibid., 51.

6. Catherine Filloux, Tarell Alvin McCraney, and Joe Sutton, *The Breach* in *Katrina On Stage: Five Plays*, ed. Suzanne M. Trauth and Lisa M. Brenner (Evanston, Ill.: Northwestern University Press, 2011), 77.

7. Sutton, "Eye of the Storm," 52.

8. Greg Szymanski, "Levees Blown Say Eyewitnesses: Media Ignores Them," *Rense.com*, January 9, 2006, http://www.rense.com/general69/blown.htm.

9. Benjamin R. Bates and Rukhsana Ahmed, "Disaster Pornography: Hurricanes, Voyeurism, and the Television Viewer," in *Through the Eyes of Katrina: Social Justice in the United States*, ed. Kristin A. Bates and Richelle S. Swan (Durham, N.C.: Carolina Academic Press, 2007), 187.

10. Ibid.

11. Anthony Hurst and Dreama G. Moon, "'Reasonable Racism': The 'New' White Supremacy and Hurricane Katrina," in *Through the Eye of Katrina: Social Justice in the United States*, ed. Kristin A. Bates and Richelle S. Swan (Durham, N.C.: Carolina Academic Press, 2007), 130.

12. Joe Scarborough, "Hurricane Katrina: Wrath of God?" NBC, October 5, 2005, http://www.nbcnews.com/id/9600878/ns/msnbc-morning_joe/t/hurricane-katrina-wrath-god/#.XHg2HdPwau5.

13. Charles Babington, "Some GOP Leaders Hit Jarring Notes in Addressing Katrina," *Washington Post*, September 10, 2005, http://www.washingtonpost.com/wp-dyn/content/article/2005/09/09/AR2005090901930.html?noredirect=on.

14. Gary Rivlin, "White New Orleans Has Recovered from Katrina. Black New Orleans Has Not," *Talk Poverty*, August 29, 2016, https://talkpoverty.org/2016/08/29/white-new-orleans-recovered-hurricane-katrina-black-new-orleans-not/.

15. Michael Eric Dyson, *Come Hell or High Water: Hurricane Katrina and the Color of Disaster* (New York: Basic Civitas Books, 2005), 19.

16. It is important to note that though the debate about race and Hurricane Katrina typically focuses (including in this chapter) on an African American /Caucasian binary, the Latino and Vietnamese populations of New Orleans, communities perhaps even more invisible in the city, were also disproportionately impacted in a negative way by the hurricane.

17. Cindi Katz, "Bad Elements: Katrina and the Scoured Landscape of Social Reproduction, Gender, Place, and Culture," *Gender, Place and Culture* 15, no. 1 (2008): 15–29 (quoted on 17).

18. Ibid., 16.

19. Dale Dominey-Howes, Andrew Gorman-Murray, and Scott McKinnon, "Queering Disasters: On the Need to Account for LGBTI Experiences in Natural Disaster Contexts," *Gender, Place and Culture* 21, no. 7 (2014): 905–18 (quoted on 907).

20. David Román, "The Distant Present of Tarell Alvin McCraney," *American Quarterly*, 66, no. 1, (2014): 181–95 (quoted on 188).

21. Russell Dynes and Havidán Rodríguez, "Finding and Framing Katrina: The Social Construction of Disaster," in *The Sociology of Katrina: Perspectives on a Modern Catastrophe*, ed. David Brunsma, David Overfelt, and J. Steven Picou (Lanham, Md.: Rowman and Littlefield, 2007), 33.

22. Catherine Filloux, Tarell Alvin McCraney, and Joe Sutton, *The Breach* (private copy, prepublication), 99. Subsequent references are to this version. Page numbers are included in the text parenthetically.

23. Brian Kaylor, "Fundamentalists View Hurricane Katrina as God's Punishment," *Ethics Daily*, September 9, 2005, htttps:// www.ethicsdaily.com /fundamentalists-view-hurricane-katrina-as-gods-punishment-cms-6269/.

24. Dominey-Howes, Gorman-Murray, and McKinnon, "Queering," 910.

25. Ibid., 912.

26. McKinnon, Gorman-Murray, and Dominey-Howes, "Disasters," 126.

27. Ibid., 125.

28. James T. Sears, "The Impact of Gender and Race on Growing Up Lesbian and Gay in the South," *National Women's Studies Association Journal* 1, no. 3 (Spring 1989): 422–57 (quoted on 448).

29. Ibid., 422–23.

30. Ibid., 423.

31. Gary Richards, "Queering Katrina: Gay Discourses of the Disaster in New Orleans," *Journal of American Studies* 44, no. 3, special issue, *Hurricane Katrina: Five Years After* (2010): 519–34 (quoted on 523).

32. Chris Rose, "Clueless in Seattle," *Times-Picayune*, January 16, 2008, http:// blog.nola.com/chrisrose/2008/01/chris_rose_clueless_in_seattle.html.

33. Ibid.

"Certainly No Clamor for a Kiss"

1. To Mary Helen, for the plug; Daniel, for handing me; and Al-Tariq, for being my friend.

2. Tre'vell Anderson, "Before the Buzz Began on 'Moonlight,' the Coming-of-Age Story Started with Playwright Tarell Alvin McCraney," *Los Angeles Times*, October 21, 2016, https://www.latimes.com/entertainment/movies/la-et-mn -moonlight-playwright-tarell-mccraney-20161017-snap-story.html. See also Kenneth Turan, "Barry Jenkins' Magical, Majestic 'Moonlight' is a Stunning Portrait of Young, Black Gay life," *Los Angeles Times*, October 20, 2016, http://www .latimes.com/entertainment/movies/la-et-mn-moonlight-review-20161017-snap -story.html.

3. Essex Hemphill, "American Wedding," *Ceremonies: Prose and Poetry* (New York: Plume, 1992), 170–71 (emphasis mine).

4. James H. Cone, *The Spirituals and the Blues* (New York: Orbis Books, 1991), 118.

5. Essex Hemphill, "Serious Moonlight," in *In the Life: A Black Gay Anthology*, ed. Joseph Beam (1986; repr., Washington, D.C: Redbone Press, 2008), 82.

6. Lauryn Hill and Bob Marley, "Turn Your Lights Down Low," *The Best Man—Music from the Motion Picture* Sony, 1999, compact disc.

7. Seye Isikalu, *monochrome.*, vimeo, accessed October 11, 2017, https://vimeo.com/204001499.

8. Hortense J. Spillers, "Mama's Baby, Papa's Maybe: An American Grammar Book," *Diacritics* 17, no. 2 (1987): 64–81 (quoted on 80).

9. Ibid.

10. "Embracing the bro hug," *CBS Sunday Morning*, February 12, 2017, https:// www.cbsnews.com/video/embracing-the-bro-hug/.

11. See Turan, "Barry Jenkins."

12. Toni Morrison, *Beloved* (1987; repr., New York: Plume, 1998), 15–16.

13. Turan, "Barry Jenkins."

14. Sharon P. Holland, "(Black) (Queer) Love," *Callaloo* 36, no. 3 (Summer 2013): 658–68 (quoted on 665).

15. Barry Jenkins and Tarrell Alvin McCraney, "Moonlight" screenplay, 16–18, accessed June 25, 2018, http://www.dailyscript.com/scripts/MOONLIGHT.pdf.

16. Dan Rubin, "American Bayou: An Interview with Playwright Tarell Alvin McCraney," in *Words on Plays—Insight into the Play, the Playwright, and the Production: Marcus; Or the Secret of Sweet*, ed. Elizabeth Brodersen (American Conservatory Theater, 2010), 9–10, https://www.act-sf.org/content/dam/act/education_department/words_on_plays/Marcus%20or%20the%20Secret%20of%20Sweet%20Words%20on%20Plays%20(2010).pdf (emphasis mine).

17. Anderson, "Before the Buzz Began on 'Moonlight.'"

18. Morrison, *Beloved*, 50.

19. Erykah Badu, "On & On," *Baduizm* (Universal, 1997).

20. Morrison, *Beloved*, 116–17. "IALAC" is an abbreviation for "I am Loveable and Capable." See Sidney B. Simon, *I Am Loveable and Capable: A Modern Allegory for the Classic Put-Down* (Niles, Ill.: Argus Communications, 1973), 27.

21. These are the words of Ali given during his acceptance speech for Best Supporting Actor at the 2017 Screen Actors Guild Awards. See "Mahershala Ali Acceptance Speech | 23rd SAG Awards," YouTube, January 29, 2017, https://youtu.be/e59q6jsWS6Q. I am interested in how these words intersect with the Beatitudes, namely "Blessed are ye, when *men* shall revile you, and persecute *you*, and shall say all manner of evil against you falsely." Matthew 5:11 (King James Authorized Version).

22. Morrison, *Beloved*, 88–89.

23. Ibid., 51 (emphasis mine).

24. Ibid., 51.

25. Tim Burton, *Batman* (Warner Bros. Pictures, 1989); and Hebrews 13:2 (King James Authorized Version).

26. This is Mark 1:9–11 (New Living Translation) reimagined. This biblical move is not lost on Jared Sexton, who extends this reading to suggest that Juan and Teresa, his partner played by Janelle Monáe, deserve "a perhaps more justified reading . . . in the tradition of the sixteenth-century Roman Catholic saints Juan de la Cruz (John of the Cross) and Teresa de Jesús (Teresa of Ávila), whose commitment to the Counter-Reformation in Habsburg Spain involved the promotion of a return to the austere monastic practices of the early Desert Fathers and Mothers." For more on the religious allusions in *Moonlight*, see Jared Sexton, *Black Masculinity and the Cinema of Policing* (New York: Palgrave Macmillan, 2017), 175–77.

27. Howard Thurman, *With Head and Heart: The Autobiography of Howard Thurman* (Orlando: Harcourt Brace, 1979), 24–25.

28. James Baldwin, *Tell Me How Long the Train's Been Gone* (1968; repr., New York: Vintage Books, 1998), 34–40. Hereafter, I will refer to the text as *TMHL*.

29. Robert Randolph Jr. opines, "Thus, his [Jenkins's] presentation of Chiron's quotidian life refuses the type of spectacle that we are used to seeing in American

cinema." Ironically enough, Randolph also intuits that "for [him], *Moonlight* resembles a great Toni Morrison novel," just as he documents a Baldwin-like aesthetic throughout the film. I, of course, agree! See Robert Randolph Jr., "Film Review: *Moonlight*, Barry Jenkins (2016)," *Queer Studies in Media and Popular Culture* 2, no. 3 (2017): 385–86.

30. Toni Morrison, "Home," in *The House that Race Built*, ed. Wahneema Lubiano (New York: Vintage Books, 1998), 7 (emphasis mine).

31. Louis Armstrong, "(What Did I Do to Be So) Black and Blue," *Satch Plays Fats: A Tribute to the Immortal Fats Waller* (Columbia, 2000).

32. Toni Morrison, "Life in His Language," in *James Baldwin: The Legacy*, ed. Quincy Troupe (New York: Simon & Schuster, 1989), 76. See also Morrison, "James Baldwin: His Voice Remembered; Life in His Language," *The New York Times*, December 20, 1987, https://archive.nytimes.com/www.nytimes.com/books/98/03/29/specials/baldwin-morrison.html?utm_campaign=pubexchange_article&utm_medium=referral&utm_source=huffingtonpost.com; and Baldwin, *TMHL*, 312–13.

33. Anderson, "Before the Buzz Began on 'Moonlight.'"

34. Jenkins and McCraney, "Moonlight" screenplay, 96–97.

35. Sexton, *Black Masculinity and the Cinema of Policing*, 183.

36. Jenkins and McCraney, "Moonlight" screenplay, 96.

37. Sexton, *Black Masculinity and the Cinema of Policing*, 180–81.

38. Fred Moten, "*Sonata quasi una fantasia*," in *Black and Blur* (Durham, N.C.: Duke University Press, 2017), 50–51.

39. DeBarge, "All This Love," *All This Love*, Gordy Records, 1982.

40. There is a moment in "American Wedding" when Hemphill writes, "They don't know / we are becoming powerful. / Every time we kiss / we confirm a new world coming." Elizabeth Freeman theorizes, "Finally, he decouples that rebellion [becoming powerful] from any nationalist project, moving from the nuptial ring to a kiss that is transubstantial with a world in the making, a wider social landscape not only saturated with but also animated by eroticism . . . in turn, the world seems to reach orgasm and emerge into being as the partners kiss." Here, one contrives a substantively different kind of clamor—compassionate and covert—aligned with the kiss. See Elizabeth Freeman, *The Wedding Complex: Forms of Belonging in Modern American Culture* (Durham, N.C.: Duke University Press, 2002), 217–20.

41. Alice Walker, "Womanist," *In Search of Our Mothers' Gardens: Womanist Prose* (1983; repr., Orlando: Harcourt Books, 2003), xii.

42. jayy dodd, *Mannish Tongues* (Platypus Press, 2017).

43. Anderson, "Before the Buzz Began on 'Moonlight'" (emphasis mine). Although this may seem to counteract the premise of the chapter, especially since McCraney himself calls the film "a well-done black, queer love story," the way he unpacks this sentiment regarding category is what I am tracking: "The thing that scares me is that people will try to use that [designation] to put it in this corner, because we can't consider it 'a great story.' We have to consider it '*this* kind of great story' . . . There is no part of me that wants to shirk this identity—it's just who I am, how I got here. At the same time, when you use [my identity] to relegate something I've done to a corner, it does [tick] me off." To me, based on

this interview with Anderson, it sounds like McCraney is saying: there should be no undue *clamor*, along lines of difference, for *Moonlight*. This move may also confirm Holland's parenthesized title . . .

44. Morrison, "Home," 7. Though the word for Baldwin is "homosexual," the point translates and still remains. See James Baldwin, *The Devil Finds Work* (1976; repr., New York: Vintage Books, 2011), 69. For more on Baldwin and touch, see Douglas Field, *All Those Strangers: The Art and Lives of James Baldwin* (New York: Oxford University Press, 2015), 96; and Ed Pavlić, *Who Can Afford to Improvise? James Baldwin and Black Music, the Lyric and the Listeners* (New York: Fordham University Press, 2016).

45. Octavia Butler, *Parable of the Sower* (New York: Grand Central Publishing, 2007), 3.

46. Sexton, *Black Masculinity and the Cinema of Policing*, 190.

47. Jenkins and McCraney, "Moonlight" screenplay, 97.

48. Erica Gonzales, "The Stars of 'Moonlight' Reacts to Their Calvin Klein Underwear Ads," harpersbazaar.com, March 7, 2017, https://www.harpersbazaar.com/celebrity/latest/news/a21201/moonlight-cast-calvin-klein-ads-reaction/.

Scenes of Vulnerability

1. Essex Hemphill, "Serious Moonlight," in *In the Life: A Black Gay Anthology*, ed. Joseph Beam (Boston: Alyson Publications, 1986), 120–21. The title of the poem also resonates with Barry Jenkins's film *Moonlight* (New York: A24 Films, 2016), which is based on McCraney's unpublished script, "In Moonlight Black Boys Look Blue." I talk about the central persona of the poem as the "speaker." In literary studies, so as not to conflate the poet with the persona in the poem, we refer to the central figure in a given poem as the "speaker."

2. Hemphill, "Serious Moonlight," 121.

3. Several critics have begun to pay attention to the aesthetic and social significance of these artists. See Dagmawi Woubshet, *The Calendar of Loss: Race, Sexuality and Mourning in the Early Era of AIDS* (Baltimore: Johns Hopkins University Press, 2015); Darius Bost, *Evidence of Being: The Black Gay Cultural Renaissance and the Politics of Violence* (Chicago: University of Chicago Press, 2018); Martin Duberman, *Hold Me Gently: Michael Callen, Essex Hemphill, and the Battlefield of AIDS* (New York: New Press, 2014); and Steven Fullwood and Charles Stephens, *Black Gay Genius: Answering Joseph Beam's Call* (New York: Vintage Entity, 2014).

4. Beam, *In the Life*.

5. I make the connection between McCraney's work and Beam's 1986 anthology, but through his emphasis on the gay search for history, which I discuss in this essay, one can also link McCraney's work specifically to Essex Hemphill's edited collection *Brother to Brother: New Writings by Black Gay Men* (1991; repr., Washington, D.C.: Redbone Press, 2007) and Rodney Evans's film *Brother to Brother* (New Almaden, Calif.: Wolfe Video, 2005).

6. *Marcus; Or the Secret of Sweet* is the final play in a dramatic trilogy about kinship and lineage published as *The Brother/Sister Plays*. Tarell Alvin McCraney, *Marcus; Or the Secret of Sweet* in *The Brother/Sister Plays* (New York: Theatre Communications Group, 2010), 241–361. The three dramas in the cycle are

In the Red and Brown Water, The Brothers Size, and *Marcus; Or the Secret of Sweet. Marcus* is set in the days before a great storm; the possibility of disaster provides the context for the exploration of Black queer life. The setting is the fictional small community in Louisiana of San Pere in late August. There are also references to a coming storm and floodwaters. Given the geographical and temporal setting as well as the references to a storm, one can discern that McCraney is alluding to the 2005 storm Hurricane Katrina and its aftermath, which devastated the U.S. gulf coast. This storm forms part of the backdrop for the play.

7. The basic plot of the play tracks the protagonist's attempt to learn about his absent father, Legba, in the context of other characters's mourning for another dead father/husband as well as a dead brother. However, this search for information about Legba is framed by Marcus's process of sexual self-discovery.

8. As the name "Marcus Eshu" signals, McCraney takes many of the names for his characters throughout the trilogy from West African Yoruban deities or orishas: Elegba, Eshu, Oshun, Ogun, etc. This technique reminds the reader that Black spirituality in the Americas represents a "synthesis of religions," or a combination of African indigenous practices and the modes of Christianity that enslavers encouraged. Temitope Adefarakan calls this feature of Black cultural expression "worldsense," alluding to how local Black cultures have woven together traditional ideas with those from the new world. Soyica Diggs Colbert argues that this naming technique allows the playwright to create a ritualistic theater and construct a cyclical reality, which suggests the possibility of temporal and spatial confusion in regard to the expression of Black identity. I will explore this idea at length. In addition, McCraney's allusions to Yoruban cosmology in his plays also suggest the queer potential that inheres in this worldview. See Adefarakan, *The Souls of Yoruba Folks* (New York: Peter Lang, 2015); Colbert, *The African American Theatrical Body* (New York: Cambridge University Press, 2011).

9. The term sweetness signals racialized and regional gender performance that is related but not always indicative. However, as I will show, in the context of the play, McCraney highlights the connection of sweetness to queer sexuality. In addition, there is an old connection between the word "sweet" in English and allurement and wantonness. According to the *Oxford English Dictionary,* "sweet" was used to describe song or discourse as pleasing or "alluring." Moreover, in Gordon Williams's *A Dictionary of Sexual Language and Imagery in Shakespearean and Stuart Literature* (London: Althone P, 1994), "sweet" indicates being "allusive of sexual pleasure" (1346). See *Oxford English Dictionary Online,* Oxford University Press, accessed February 1, 2019, http://www.oed.com.proxy-um.researchport.umd.edu/view/Entry/195665?rskey+g2Ee6d&result=2&isAdvanced=false; Gordon Williams, *A Dictionary of Sexual Language and Imagery in Shakespearean and Stuart Literature* (London: Althone Press, 1994).

10. McCraney, *Marcus,* 256.

11. Ibid. This moment reflects McCraney's unusual presentation of what we can think of as stage directions. Moments like this one that detail an actor's movement on stage are presented as if they are dialogue. They appear where spoken words would in the script instead of set off from them. Through this method, McCraney worries the lines between enacted experience and a character's thoughts.

12. Again, being characterized as sweet reflects an assessment of queer sexuality and nonnormative gender performance, but in this moment of the play, Shaunta is asking him about the nature of his sexual desire explicitly even as his answer has implications about how she has read and will read his gender performance.

13. See Eve Kosofsky Sedgwick's *The Epistemology of the Closet* (Berkeley: University of California Press, 1990).

14. See John D'Emilio, *Sexual Politics, Sexual Communities: The Making of a Homosexual Minority in the United States* (Chicago: University of Chicago Press, 1998); Christina Handhardt, *Safe Space: Gay Neighborhood History and the Politics of Violence* (Durham, N.C.: Duke University Press, 2013).

15. In her account, Shaunta suggests that this person is a woman who is envious of their relationship or motivated by religious ideology. See McCraney, *Marcus*, 257.

16. McCraney, *Marcus*, 257–58.

17. Sugarcane was first grown in Louisiana in 1751 when Jesuits brought it to the territory, and it was first successfully processed into sugar in 1794. See Alcée Fortier's *A History of Louisiana* (1904; repr., Baton Rouge, La.: Claitor's Book Store, 1966), 158. Again, the play is set in a mythical city in the Louisiana delta, which would have been the site of such production.

18. The link between sugar and the Black body is the primary element of Kara Walker's 2014 installation *A Subtlety, or the Marvelous Sugar Baby*. Walker created a sphinx-like figure made up of sugar that sat on the floor of the Domino sugar refining plant in the Williamsburg neighborhood of Brooklyn, New York City.

19. Michel Foucault, *History of Sexuality, Volume I* (1976; repr., New York: Vintage Press, 1990), 142–43.

20. It is significant that a heterosexual friend offers this narrative. McCraney chooses not to have the queer figure imagine this past; he only has access through an intermediary. The move to have Shaunta provide the narrative reflects queer figures' interrupted access to history. Phillip Brian Harper discusses the critical value of intuition and speculation in relation to the lived experience of sexual minorities. See Harper, "The Evidence of Felt Intuition: Minority Experience, Everyday Life, and Critical Speculative Knowledge," in *Black Queer Studies: A Critical Anthology*, ed. E. Patrick Johnson and Mae G. Henderson (Durham, N.C.: Duke University Press, 2005), 106–23.

21. Ashraf Rushdy, *Neo-Slave Narratives: Studies in the Social Logic of a Literary Form* (New York: Oxford University Press, 1999), 6.

22. Ibid., 7.

23. Fred Moten offers a discussion of fugitive movement and the theoretical possibilities of fugitivity in Black Studies in the essay "The Case of Blackness." See Fred Moten, "The Case of Blackness," *Criticism* 50, no. 2 (2008): 177–218.

24. Matt Richardson, *The Queer Limit of Black Memory: Black Lesbian Literature and Irresolution* (Columbus: Ohio State University Press, 2013), 12.

25. Ibid., 12–13.

26. See Aliyyah Abdur-Rahman, *Against the Closet: Black Political Longing and the Erotics of Race* (Durham, N.C.: Duke University Press, 2012).

27. McCraney, *Marcus*, 263–64.

28. McCraney, *Marcus*, 267.

29. Saidiya Hartman, "Venus in Two Acts," *Small Axe* 26, no. 2 (2008): 1–14.

30. Ibid., 14.

31. See Sharon Holland, *Raising the Dead: Readings of Death and (Black) Subjectivity* (Durham, N.C.: Duke University Press, 2000).

32. See David Román, "The Distant Present of Tarell Alvin McCraney," *American Quarterly* 66, no. 1 (2014): 181–95.

33. Sara Ahmed, *Queer Phenomenology: Orientations, Objects, Others* (Durham, N.C.: Duke University Press, 2006), 3.

34. McCraney, *Marcus*, 11.

35. Marcus's interaction with Shaunta is one clear example of the failure of the extension of the queer body into space, but his later encounters with Shua—discussed below—offer further examples.

36. My consideration of orientation and disorientation resonates with Sara Ahmed's work on queer phenomenology in *Queer Phenomenology*.

37. McCraney, *Marcus*, 299.

38. Ibid., 306.

39. Phillip Brian Harper, *Private Affairs: Critical Ventures in the Culture of Social Relations* (New York: New York University Press, 1999), 22.

40. McCraney, *Marcus*, 306.

41. Ibid., 330.

42. Ibid., 353–54.

43. This idea about temporal hybridity in the context of queer identity may find resonances with Carolyn Dinshaw's work on queer ways of being in time. See Carolyn Dinshaw, *How Soon Is Now? Medieval Texts, Amateur Readers, and the Queerness of Time* (Durham, N.C.: Duke University Press, 2012).

44. This discussion of a sensual relationship to the past in relation to the writing of history relates to Elizabeth Freeman's work on queerness and temporality. See Elizabeth Freeman, *Time Binds: Queer Temporalities, Queer Histories* (Durham, N.C.: Duke University Press, 2010).

45. McCraney, *Marcus*, 361.

46. Ibid.

Hip-Hop Nommo

1. Alvaro Toepke, Angel Serrano, and Vertamae Smart-Grosvenor, *The Language You Cry In: The Story of a Mende Song* (San Francisco: California Newsreel, 1998).

2. See John Lahr, "Been Here and Gone: How August Wilson Brought a Century of Black American Culture to the Stage," *New Yorker*, April 8, 2011, https://www.newyorker.com/magazine/2001/04/16/been-here-and-gone.

3. Paul Carter Harrison, *The Drama of Nommo* (New York: Grove Press, 1972) and *Kuntu Drama: Plays of the African Continuum* (New York: Grove Press, 1974).

4. Paul Carter Harrison, *Totem Voices: Plays from the Black World Repertory* (New York: Grove Press, 1989), xlii.

5. These forces are categorized as: Muntu—all human beings, spirits, certain trees, and God (only this category is endowed with intelligence); Kintu—things

and objects such as plants, animals, minerals, and unnamed babies; Hantu—time and place; Kuntu—the modality of image or, rather, the context from which an image is borne. See Harrison, *Kuntu Drama*, 22.

6. Ibid.

7. Harrison, *Totem Voices*, lxi.

8. Elegua is another manifestation of Elegba, also known as Esu (Eshu).

9. Harrison, *Kuntu Drama*, 259.

10. Sandra G. Shannon, "Audience and Africanisms in August Wilson's Dramaturgy: A Case Study," in *African American Performance and Theater History: A Critical Reader*, ed. Harry J. Elam and David Krasner (New York: Oxford University Press, 2001), 151–57.

11. Ibid., 154.

12. Sandra L. Richards, "Yoruba Gods on the American Stage: *Joe Turner's Come and Gone*," *African Drama and Performance*, ed. John Conteh-Morgan and Tejumola Olaniyan (Bloomington: Indiana University Press, 2004).

13. Ibid., 96.

14. Richards, "Yoruba Gods on the American Stage," 103–4.

15. Shannon, "Audience and Africanisms in August Wilson's Dramaturgy," 165.

16. McCraney describes the trilogy as a triptych; though the terms may seem to be similarly descriptive, a series of three related works designed to be appreciated together, a triptych can also have a religious connotation, for instance, a carved triptych that serves as an altar piece.

17. Harry J. Elam and Robert Alexander, eds., *The Fire This Time: African American Plays for the 21st Century* (New York: Theatre Communications Group, 2004), xxv.

18. Carole Woddis, "Interview with Tarell Alvin McCraney," October 31, 2007, http://www.youngvic.org/about-young-vic/news/interview-with-tarell-alvin -mccraney.

19. As the worship of Oya spread, she went from being the wife of Ogun to the wife of Shango. There is also a story that Oya worked the bellows for Ogun's forge. One day, Shango arrived to purchase a weapon, and he and Oya fell in love. When Ogun noticed that his bellows were not working, he came to realize that Oya had run off with Shango.

20. See Judith Gleason, *Oya; In Praise of an African Goddess* (San Francisco: Harper, 1987).

21. Though the word tragic may appear to be an overly strong term, I believe it is apt here when referring to traditional African cultures. As Michuku Kiiru notes, "There are proverbs that are insensitive to the humiliation that a childless woman undergoes: A barren woman should not scold a bad child (Minyanka, Burkina Faso). The woman whose sons have died is richer than a barren woman (Gîkûyû, Kenya). From Baganda we have this disparaging proverb: A useless person is like a woman, both lazy and barren." See Michuku Kiiru, "You Cannot Catch Old Birds with Chaff: The Woman's Multiple Images in Proverbs," *Wajibu: A Journal of Social and Religious Concern* 14, no. 1 (1999): http://web.peacelink .it/wajibu/6_issue/p3.html.

22. Christine Dolan, "Dreams of a Bright Moon: An Interview with the Playwright," *American Theatre* 25, no. 3 (March 2008): 54.

23. Tom Atkins, "20 Questions With . . . Tarell Alvin McCraney," *WhatsOn-Stage*, November 12, 2007, http://www.whatsonstage.com/index.php?pg=207& story=E8821194805596.

24. Dolan, "Dreams of a Bright Moon," 55.

25. Water is a vital element in religious rituals; it connects the physical with the metaphysical. In Santería, for example, Florida Water (a cologne) is a necessary element.

26. Tarell Alvin McCraney, *The Brother/Sister Plays* (New York: Theatre Communications Group, 2010), 22–23. All quotes from the triptych are taken from this volume.

27. Woddis, "Interview with Tarell Alvin McCraney."

28. Harry J. Elam Jr. and Douglas A. Jones Jr., eds., *The Methuen Drama Book of Post-Black Plays* (London: Methuen, 2012): xviii–xix.

29. Randy Gener, "Dreaming in Yoruba Land," *American Theatre* 26 (September 2009), 24–27, 81–82.

30. Elam and Jones, *Post-Black Plays*, xxi.

31. A personal observation: after viewing Lin-Manuel Miranda's brilliant work *Hamilton*, which has left an indelible impression as a new genre of Broadway show, I thought about the fact that Miranda drew on a story from the inception of the United States and told it in terms of its contemporary multicultural population and multiplicity of cultural idioms. I think McCraney, years before Miranda, did the same thing with taking a story from the beginning of the African presence in the Americas and telling it in those same terms.

32. Elam and Jones, *Post-Black Plays*, xvi.

Black Movements and Tarell Alvin McCraney's *In the Red and Brown Water*

1. Tarell Alvin McCraney, *The Brother/Sister Plays* (New York: Theatre Communications Group, 2010), 11. Further references are to this edition and will be cited parenthetically.

2. See the December 13, 2009, Public Theater production, directed by Tina Landau, of *In the Red and Brown Water*. It was recorded by the Theatre on Film and Tape Archive, in the Billy Rose Theatre Collection, New York Public Library for the Performing Arts, call no. NCOV 3570.

3. David Román, "The Distant Present of Tarell Alvin McCraney," *American Quarterly* 66, no. 1 (March 2014): 181–95 (quoted on 181).

4. Wole Soyinka, *Myth, Literature and the African World* (Cambridge: Cambridge University Press, 1976), 10.

5. See Ina J. Fandrich, "Yoruba Influences on Haitian Vodou and New Orleans Voodoo," *Journal of Black Studies*, 37 (May 2007): 775–91 (quoted on 784).

6. Soyica Diggs Colbert, *The African American Theatrical Body: Reception, Performance and the Stage* (Cambridge: Cambridge University Press, 2011).

7. Soyica Diggs Colbert, *Black Movements: Performance and Cultural Politics* (New Brunswick: Rutgers University Press, 2017).

8. Benedict M. Ibitokun, *African Drama and the Yoruba World-View* (Ibadan, Nigeria: Ibadan University Press, 1995), 21.

9. Joseph Roach, *Cities of the Dead: Circum-Atlantic Performance* (New York: Columbia University Press, 1996), 36.

10. Peggy Phelan, *Unmarked: The Politics of Performance* (New York: Routledge, 1993), 146.

11. Ibid.

12. Fred Moten, *In the Break: The Aesthetics of the Black Radical Tradition* (Minneapolis: University of Minnesota, 2003), 6.

13. Cedric Robinson, *Black Marxism: The Making of the Black Radical Tradition*, with a foreword by Robin D. G. Kelley (Chapel Hill: University of North Carolina Press, 1983), 200.

14. L. H. Stallings, *Funk the Erotic: Transaesthetics and Black Sexual Cultures* (Urbana: University of Illinois Press, 2015), 40.

15. Toni Morrison, *The Bluest Eye* (New York: Vintage, 2007); Soyinka, *Myth, Literature, and the African World*, 2.

16. E. Patrick Johnson, *Appropriating Blackness: Performance and the Politics of Authenticity* (Durham, N.C.: Duke University Press, 2003), 77.

17. Soyinka, *Myth, Literature and the African World*, 4.

18. Paul Carter Harrison, "Praise/Word," in *Black Theatre: Ritual Performance in the African Diaspora*, ed. Paul Carter Harrison, Victor Leo Walker II, and Gus Edwards (Philadelphia: Temple University Press, 2002), 4.

19. Soyinka, *Myth, Literature and the African World*, 26.

20. McCraney quoted in Randy Gener, "Dreaming in Yoruba Land," *American Theatre* 26 (September 2009), 24–27, 81–82.

21. Ibid.

22. Ibid.

23. Andrea Allen, "Tarell McCraney is Talking to You: How *The Brothers Size* Calls On the Audience to Share the Story," Seattle Repertory Theatre, accessed February 2, 2018, http://www.seattlerep.org/Plays/1011/BZ/DeeperLook/McCraney.

24. Ibid.

25. Harry J. Elam Jr., *The Past as Present in the Drama of August Wilson* (Ann Arbor: University of Michigan Press, 2006), 171.

26. Soyinka, *Myth, Literature and the African World*, 142–49.

27. Ibid., 142–43.

28. Elam, *The Past as Present*, 171.

29. Henry Louis Gates Jr., *The Signifying Monkey: A Theory of African-American Literary Criticism* (Oxford: Oxford University Press, 1989), 5.

30. Ibid., 6.

31. Soyinka, *Myth, Literature and the African World*, 143.

The Brother/Sister Plays and the Black Real

1. In Western theater, "real" or "realism" has a particular history that my coinage of the Black Real is speaking to. I want to engage what "real" means for many Black people. In Western theater, realism developed, in part, out of an opposition to the formulaic realities of melodrama, with its obvious truths, one-dimensional characters, and predictable narrative devices. Realism worked to reveal the complexity of human life by foregrounding ambiguous ethical choices and examining social issues of the day. This shift to realism did not address ethical or social issues surrounding race, the construct that is central to understanding the reality of Black

lives. Neither did this shift derive from African diasporic cosmologies. Even as Western theatrical realism was being solidified as a genre through the landmark production of Henrik Ibsen's *A Doll's House*, set in 1879 Norway, the world was enacting racially inspired acts of war and other forms of violence. In the Anglo-Zulu War of the same year, after the Zulu won a major battle against the British, British forces eventually won the war that ultimately laid the foundation for the vicious and protracted enactment of Apartheid in 1948. The Black Real borrows from realism the sense of urgency in addressing social issues and an insistence on a nonromanticized understanding of life, *and* does so from a decidedly Black lens. This lens significantly reimagines what "real" is. For many Black people in the United States, "real" includes the social abjection and attendant terrors that are required for a rife white supremacy *alongside* a persistent, vibrant aliveness.

2. "For, by, about, and/or near Black people" is taken from the Krigwa Players' manifesto of the 1920s. Founded by W. E. B. Du Bois, the Crisis Guild for Writers and Artists (CRIGWA) produced a range of theatrical works that were the result of literary contests sponsored by the NAACP's *Crisis Magazine*. For more information on the Krigwa Players, see Ethel Pitts Walker, "Krigwa: A Theatre by, for, and about Black People," *Theatre Journal* 40, no. 3 (October 1988): 347–56.

3. In the distillation of an interview Dan Rubin conducted with McCraney as part of the extensive production materials provided by the American Conservatory Theatre for their 2010 production of *Marcus; Or the Secret of Sweet*, Rubin notes that McCraney refers to *The Brother/Sister Plays* as a triptych rather than the more expected trilogy. Triptych is more commonly associated with visual art, and using it in describing this theatrical piece foregrounds San Pere as a visual epic.

4. Tarell Alvin McCraney, *The Brother/Sister Plays* (New York: Theatre Communications Group, 2010). Subsequent references are cited in the text parenthetically.

5. Andrea Allen, "Tarell McCraney Is Talking to You: How *The Brothers Size* Calls On the Audience to Share the Story," Seattle Repertory Theatre, http://www.seattlerep.org/Plays/1011/BZ/DeeperLook/McCraney.

6. McCraney's staged storytelling is distinct from both Robert Breen's emphasis on character psychology in his development of Chamber Theatre—the embodiment of narration and retention of the third person within that narration—and Bertolt Brecht's dialectical strategies that sought to create distance between the character and the actor for the purpose of foregrounding the ideas and action rather than the emotions and identification in the work. McCraney's approach feels more communally driven and attentive to orality than that of Breen or Brecht. The Black Brazilian theater company Cia dos Comuns has also employed a narrative style that explores ways of marking the Black performers as corporeal beings separate from theatrical characters through direct address to the audience as an unmasked self. In *Bakulo, Os Bem Lembrados (Bakulo, the Well Remembered)*, the performers spoke as themselves directly to the audience/witnesses, read political treatises, and performed as fictional characters speaking to each other without a direct awareness of the audience/witnesses. Cia dos Comuns's aims with this dramaturgical strategy seem to be a specific confrontation with the complexities of perceiving Black bodies on stage outside of well-worn stereotypes that haunt theater. This aim is different than McCraney's usage, though it is important

that both McCraney and Cia dos Comuns are invested in moments when the performers' direct address to the audience/witnesses opens up a way of doing theater that lets Black performers go beyond the expected, obtaining greater agency (McCraney) and challenging stifling predictability (Cia dos Comuns). I am indebted to discussions with artist/scholar Gustavo Melo Cerqueira for my comparisons of the varied approaches and implications of what I am calling storytelling by Black artists in theatrical productions. For a detailed examination of Cerqueira's analysis of Cia dos Comuns, see Gustavo Melo Cerqueira, *The Black Body in Teatro Negro of Cia Dos Comuns* (forthcoming). Also, see Robert Breen, *Chamber Theatre* (Englewood Cliffs, N.J.: Prentice-Hall, 1978), and Bertolt Brecht, "Short Description of a New Technique of Acting Which Produces an Alienation Effect," *The Twentieth Century Performance Reader*, ed. Teresa Brayshaw and Noel Witts (London: Routledge, 2014), 101–12.

7. I set the text on the page in the way it appears in the script so that the emphasis on the shift in realities that is implied between each "What I say," is made visible. I believe McCraney provides such cues in the pagination not only to signal the shift in address to the performer, but to underscore the psychic shift from one time and space to another.

8. McCraney sets *In the Red and Brown Water* and *The Brothers Size* in "the distant present," while *Marcus* is set in the almost similarly unspecified "late August."

9. Allen, "Tarell McCraney Is Talking to You."

10. From a conversation between performance studies scholar Aymar Jean Christian and Tarell Alvin McCraney. Black Arts Initiative Conference, "Black Arts International: Temporalities and Territories," Northwestern University, October 13, 2017.

11. Yoruba-based spiritual traditions have been significantly shaped by their diasporic crisscrossings. In Lukumi *pataki* from Cuba, it is Oba who cuts off her ear for Sango, not Oya, as presented in *In the Red and Brown Water*. By subtitling the play *A Fast and Loose Play on Spanish* Yerma *and African Oya/Oba*, McCraney is clearly aware of the ways that the diaspora has reformulated these Divinities. The regional distinctions reflect the ways the Divine forces morphed to suit the people and environments where they were experienced and the intriguing slipperiness of oral traditions where each storyteller edits and embellishes as Spirit moves them.

12. In *Black and Blur*, Moten details the "rituals of renomination" that occur "serially and variously" in the formations of Blackness. It is the practice of self-naming/self-narrating that creates the space for Black multiplicity. Fred Moten, *Black and Blur* (Durham, N.C., Duke University Press, 2017), vii.

13. As Christina Sharpe explores the position of art "in the wake" of enslavement, she speaks of the "quotidian disasters" that characterize Black life. The oxymoronic nature of that phrase is itself an understanding of Black realities— social annihilation *and* the many everyday moments of asserting Black aliveness, of creating/embodying art beyond social and political definitions even as it exists, in part, within them. Christina Sharpe, *In the Wake: On Blackness and Being* (Durham, N.C.: Duke University Press, 2016), 11–14.

14. While "the break" in jazz typically opens a space for musicians to take an improvised solo, here I am expanding the use of the term to include moments of innovation and creativity that resonate with improvisation.

15. Ben Brantley, "Lives in the Bayou Tap All the Realism of Dreams," *New York Times*, November 17, 2009, https://www.nytimes.com/2009/11/18/theater/reviews/18brother.html.

16. In *M Archive: After the End of the World*, Alexis Pauline Gumbs explores the staying power of spirit, or "you beyond you," that situates the presumed past and future into the multiverse of now. In an apocalyptic landscape, her scientists know artifacts not only for their material presence but for the residue of past vibrations they carry, the very spirit of what they are. Similarly, Blackness does not stop with the end of a story or even the "spilling" of life; Blackness is, instead, "sticky" because of its rootedness in spiritual verity which can "stay." Alexis Pauline Gumbs, *M Archive: After the End of the World* (Durham, N.C.: Duke University Press, 2018).

17. In lengthy conversations with performance studies scholar Dotun Ayobade, I have come to think of *aiye*—often understood as the earth plane—as the idea of the "real" that includes unseen beings and forces that move between *orun* (the realm of Divinities and ancestors) and *aiye*. While Ayobade has helped me to explore the depth of Yoruba language and cosmology, any insufficiencies in my thinking are solely my own.

18. In a public presentation on Yoruba conceptualizations of gender and sexuality at the University of Texas, Yoruba studies scholar Abimbola Adunni Adelakun discussed the complexities of *daudu*. Her talk, "'A Man Acting Like a Woman': Double Entendre, Language, and Ideology," has yet to be published. I thank Adelakun for introducing me to this concept and for sharing her insights on these themes.

19. In my discussions of theatrical jazz, I have explored "the break" as indeterminacy as it relates to spiritual and artistic realities. Here, I expand indeterminacy to include a more explicit discussion of sexuality and gender expression.

20. Richard Iton, *In Search of the Black Fantastic* (New York: Oxford University Press, 2008), 29.

21. It is difficult to disentangle diaspora from indeterminacy; the concepts work in tandem. The unfixed location is the very homeplace for diaspora dwellers, haunted subtly or audaciously by an originary homeland that has transformed through the vagaries of memory or, in the case of second- and third-generations, was fabricated from an amalgamation of others' stories. In thinking of the African diaspora as nonphysical space, I am stimulated by Kellie Jones's discussion of the migrations of Black visual artists in Los Angeles. She describes how Black social abjection creates a host of migrants in search of homeplace, with the acknowledgment that Black people are "patently ungeographic." Perhaps this is a fertile rather than vexing site, surely a space of the imagination which is unfettered by place. Kellie Jones, *South of Pico: African American Artists in Los Angeles in the 1960s and 1970s* (Durham, N.C.: Duke University Press, 2017).

22. I have worked with Yoruba-based communities in Brazil, Trinidad, Nigeria, and Cuba, as well as Austin, Miami, and New York City. These experiences form the basis for much of my understanding of and experience with the Yoruba cosmology I discuss in this essay. N. Fadeke Castor offers a similar investigation in *Spiritual Citizenship: Transnational Pathways from Black Power to Ifa in Trinidad* as she explores the mutually influencing spiritual practices around the African diaspora.

23. Isaac Butler, "That August Wilson Feeling," *American Theatre*, January 18, 2014, https://www.americantheatre.org/2014/01/18/almost-10-years-after-his-death-august-wilsons-work-is-still-resonating-with-audiences/.

24. Terry Teachout, "'The Piano Lesson' Review: The Year of August Wilson," *Wall Street Journal*, January 24, 2017, https://www.wsj.com/articles/the-piano-lesson-review-the-year-of-august-wilson-1485287676.

25. Zora Neale Hurston, "Characteristics of Negro Expression," in *Negro: An Anthology*, ed. Nancy Cunard (New York: F. Ungar Publishing Company, 1934), 50–51.

One *Size* Does Not Fit All

1. Tarell Alvin McCraney, *The Brother/Sister Plays* (New York: Theatre Communications Group, 2010), 137. All subsequent references are to this version and are cited parenthetically.

2. Isaiah Matthew Wooden, "How to Do Things with Stage Directions: Lessons from Contemporary African American Drama," *Theatre Topics* 28, no. 3 (2018): 217–26.

3. James Baldwin, *The Fire Next Time* (New York: Vintage Books, 1993), 3–4.

4. See Keith Clark, *Black Manhood in James Baldwin, Ernest Gaines, and August Wilson* (Urbana: University of Illinois Press, 2002), 101.

5. Jeffrey Q. McCune Jr., "A Good Black Manhood Is Hard to Find: Toward More Transgressive Reading Practices," *Spectrum: A Journal on Black Men* 1, no. 1 (2012): 121–40.

6. Anaya McMurray, "Hotep and Hip Hop: Can Black Muslim Women Be Down with Hip Hop?" *Meridians* 8, no. 1 (2008): 74–92.

7. Eve Kosofsky Sedgwick, *Between Men: English Literature and Male Homosocial Desire* (New York: Columbia University Press, 1985), 25–26.

8. Marlon Riggs, *Tongues Untied* (1989; Frameline, 2008), DVD.

9. Rashad Shabazz, "Kitchenettes, the Robert Taylor Homes, and the Racial Spatial Order of Chicago: The Carceral Society in an American City," in *Justice et Injustice Spatiales*, ed. Bernard Bret, Phillippe Gervay-Lambony, Claire Hancock, and Frederic Landy (Paris: Presses Universitaires de Paris Oeste, 2010).

10. Baldwin, *The Fire Next Time*, 2.

11. Simone Drake, *When We Imagine Grace: Black Men and Subject Making* (Chicago: University of Chicago Press, 2016).

12. Calvin Warren, *Ontological Terror: Blackness, Nihilism, and Emancipation* (Durham, N.C.: Duke University Press, 2018).

13. Ibid., 6.

14. Rinaldo Walcott, "Freedom Now Suite: Black Feminist Turns of Voice," *Small Axe: A Caribbean Journal of Criticism* 22, no. 3 (2018): 151–59 (quoted on 156).

15. Ibid.

Backstage Pass

1. This quote is found later in this chapter in the section titled "In Rehearsal with Tina Landau."

2. Historically, the academic field of theater has often separated the Ph.D.'s from the M.F.A.'s, i.e., the researchers from the practitioners, though both groups often

write about and practice theater. The vestiges of this separation can now be seen at theater conferences in and outside of the academy. For instance, academic conferences, such as the Association for Theatre in Higher Education and the American Society for Theatre Research, are mostly attended by theater researchers and practitioners (Ph.D.'s) who work in the academy, whereas public theater conferences, such as Theatre Communications Group's national conference, are mostly attended by theater practitioners and researchers (M.F.A.'s) outside of the academy. Therefore, a visible gap has been created between the academy and the public sphere in theater.

3. Patricia Leavy, *Method Meets Art: Arts-Based Research Practice* (New York: Guilford Press, 2015), 41–42.

4. Long before academic articulations of the importance of narratives existed in the United States, West African cultures shared and created knowledge through storytelling, often via griots and *djelis* within their communities. For further readings about this, see: Paul Carter Harrison, *Drama of Nommo: Black Theatre in the African Continuum* (Ultramarine: New York, 1972); Nilgun Andolu-Okur, *Contemporary African American Theater: Afrocentricity in the Works of Larry Neal, Amiri Baraka, and Charles Fuller* (New York: Garland Publishing, 1997); and Sharrell D. Luckett with Tia M. Shaffer, eds., *Black Acting Methods: Critical Approaches* (New York: Routledge, 2017). For discipline-specific readings about the values of narrative inquiry, see: Patricia Hill Collins, *Black Feminist Thought* (New York: Routledge, 2008); James A. Holstein and Jaber F. Gubrium, *The Active Interview* (Thousand Oaks, Calif.: Sage, 1995); Ivor Goodson et al., eds., *The Routledge International Handbook on Narrative and Life History* (New York: Routledge, 2018); Tony E. Adams, Stacy Holman Jones, and Carolyn Ellis, *Autoethnography* (Oxford: Oxford University Press, 2014); and Jonny Saldana, *Ethnotheatre: Research from Page to Stage* (New York: Routledge, 2016), 45–46.

5. The majority of work that we do is only marginalized when approached from an imperialistic White-European, hetero framework/gaze.

6. Sarojini Nadar, "Stories Are Data with Soul: Lessons from Black Feminist Epistemology," *Agenda: Empowering Women for Gender Equity* 28, no.1 (2014): 26.

7. Tarell later skyped with a group of my students at Muhlenberg College for their production of *Wig Out!* He also visited Isaiah M. Wooden's students at Georgetown University for a two-day residency in September 2014, where, in addition to actively participating in rehearsals for the university's production of *In the Red and Brown Water*, he engaged in a public conversation with Wooden about his career and artistic process.

8. James Baldwin, "Sweet Lorraine," in *To Be Young, Gifted and Black: Lorraine Hansberry in Her Own Words*, adapted by Robert Nemiroff (Englewood Cliffs, N.J.: Prentice Hall Publishing, 1969), x–xi.

9. This isolation of black playwrights is often evident in America when black plays are produced, yet black directors or designers, among others, are rarely hired to work on the production, evidencing a profound undervaluing and rejection of the importance of blackness and black culture in the artistic process. Unfortunately, this practice is also visible when works from other, nonwhite playwrights are produced.

10. Tarell is not alone. Many black artists have often strategized ways to stay connected with their communities after becoming famous in the theater world,

whether it be starting an educational nonprofit program, a theater program for the community, meeting with the community, or advocating for their peers.

11. Special thanks to Isaiah M. Wooden for developing the questions for "Tarell and the Royal Shakespeare Company: An Interview with Michael Boyd."

12. Anne Bogart and Jackson Gay, "The Art of Collaboration: On Dramaturgy and Directing," in *The Routledge Companion to Dramaturgy*, ed. Magda Romanska (New York: Routledge, 2016), 216.

13. These interviews were collected via email throughout the spring of 2018. Email correspondence was the most effective strategy given everyone's career obligations and schedules.

14. "Workin' without a net" simply means to improvise, take chances, see where a moment leads, and deeply explore aspects of the piece in pursuit of truth.

15. Saint Augustine was a fourth-century Roman African philosopher, a Berber born in Numidia (modern day Algeria). He is most famous for his treatises and his writings, which greatly influenced Western Christianity and philosophy. Saint Augustine eventually turned from his lifelong pursuit of self-satisfaction, embraced celibacy, and dedicated himself to meditation and prayer. This information was provided by Cheryl Lynn Bruce.

CONTRIBUTORS

Editors

SHARRELL D. LUCKETT, PH.D., is director of the Helen Weinberger Center for Drama and Playwriting and associate professor of drama and performance studies in the Department of English and Comparative Literature at the University of Cincinnati. She is also affiliate faculty in the departments of Africana Studies and Women's, Gender, and Sexuality Studies, and faculty collaborator with the College-Conservatory of Music (CCM). Luckett is the editor of *African American Arts: Activism, Aesthetics, and Futurity*; author of *YoungGiftedand-Fat: An Autoethnography of Size, Sexuality, and Privilege*; and lead editor of *Black Acting Methods: Critical Approaches*, an award-winning book that highlights diverse acting and directing methods rooted in Black American culture. She is also the founding director of the Black Acting Methods Studio, a mobile and online training program in performance theory and practice. A sought-after scholar and artist, Luckett has had residencies at renowned institutions, such as the Lincoln Center, Harvard University, and 92Y. Her upcoming research projects engage with transweight celebrity performance and the work of Freddie Hendricks of the Freddie Hendricks Youth Ensemble of Atlanta.

DAVID ROMÁN is professor of English and American studies at the University of Southern California. He is the author of two books, *Acts of Intervention: Performance, Gay Culture, & AIDS* and *Performance in America: Contemporary U.S. Culture and the Performing Arts*, and several edited volumes, including *O Solo Homo: The New Queer Performance*, which he coedited with Holly Hughes. He is a former editor of *Theatre Journal* and a founding editorial member of *GLQ*. He served as the scholar-in-residence at the Mark Taper Forum in Los Angeles under the leadership of founding artistic director Gordon Davidson, and was the chair of the board of directors at Highways Performance Space in Los Angeles under the leadership of founding artistic director Tim Miller. He has won multiple awards for his scholarship, teaching, and service.

ISAIAH MATTHEW WOODEN is a director-dramaturg, critic, and assistant professor of theater arts at Brandeis University. A scholar of twentieth- and twenty-first-century African American art, drama, and performance, he has published work in *Black Camera, The Black Scholar, Callaloo, Journal of American Drama and Theatre, Journal of Dramatic Theory and Criticism*,

Modern Drama, *PAJ: A Journal of Performance and Art*, *Theater*, *Theatre Journal*, and *Theatre Topics*, among other scholarly and popular venues. Wooden is currently at work on a book that explores the interplay of race and time in post–Civil Rights Black expressive culture. He has directed new and canonical works in both the United States and abroad, including plays by Eisa Davis, Nilaja Sun, Sarah Ruhl, Mary Zimmerman, Robert O'Hara, Charles L. Mee, and Tarell Alvin McCraney. A past performance review editor of *Theatre Journal* (2017–2019) and a contributing editor to *PAJ*, Wooden previously taught at Georgetown University and American University.

Chapter Authors

BRYANT KEITH ALEXANDER is professor of communication, cultural, and perfor-mance studies. He currently serves as dean of the College of Communication and Fine Arts at Loyola Marymount University. He is an active scholar, lec-turer, and performer, with publications in leading journals along with major contributions to such volumes as the *Handbook of Critical and Indigenous Methodologies*, *Handbook of Performance Studies*, *Handbook of Qualita-tive Research*, *Handbook of Communication and Instruction*, *Handbook of Critical Intercultural Communication*, and *Handbook of Autoethnogra-phy*. Alexander is the coeditor of *Performance Theories in Education: Power, Pedagogy and the Politics of Identity* and the author of *Performing Black Masculinity: Race, Culture, and Queer Identity* and *The Performative Sus-tainability of Race: Reflections on Black Culture and the Politics of Identity*.

GERSHUN AVILEZ is associate professor of English at the University of Maryland, College Park. He is a cultural studies scholar who specializes in contemporary African American literary and visual culture, with a particu-lar focus on gender and sexuality. Avilez is the author of *Radical Aesthetics and Modern Black Nationalism*, which won the 2017 William Sanders Scar-borough Prize from the Modern Language Association (MLA). The prize is given to an outstanding scholarly study of African American literature or culture. His publications appear in the journals *African American Review* and *Callaloo* and the edited collections *The Cambridge History of Gay and Lesbian Literature* and *The Psychic Hold of Slavery*, among others. Avilez has completed a new book manuscript on Black diasporic queer artists and experiences of vulnerability. An experienced teacher, he received the Poorvu Family Award for Interdisciplinary Teaching in 2011 from Yale University. Avilez has held professorships at Yale University and the University of North Carolina, Chapel Hill.

SOYICA DIGGS COLBERT is professor of African American studies and theater and performance studies at Georgetown University. She is the author of *The African American Theatrical Body: Reception, Performance and the Stage* and *Black*

Movements: Performance and Cultural Politics. Colbert edited the Black Performance special issue of *African American Review*, and coedited *The Psychic Hold of Slavery.* She is currently working on two book projects: a monograph, *Staging Identity: Lorraine Hansberry, an Intellectual Biography,* and an edited collection, *Time Signatures: Race and Performance after Repetition.*

I. AUGUSTUS DURHAM is the 2018–2020 President's Postdoctoral Fellow in the Department of English at the University of Maryland, College Park. He completed his master's and doctorate degrees in English at Duke University. His current book project takes up black studies, primarily through the twentieth and twenty-first centuries, in order to interrogate melancholy and how the affect catalyzes performances of excellence, otherwise known as genius. Durham has published work in *CAA Reviews, Black Camera: An International Film Journal, Palimpsest: A Journal on Women, Gender, and the Black International,* and *Journal of Religion and Health.*

DONETTE FRANCIS directs the American Studies Program at the University of Miami, where she is associate professor of English and a founding member of the Hemispheric Caribbean Studies Collective. She is cofounder of the Jamaican Cultural Political Modern Project, a collective that rethinks Jamaica's historiography, and has edited proceedings from the symposia, such as *The Jamaican 1960s* and *The Jamaican 1970s* in *Small Axe: A Caribbean Journal of Criticism.* Dr. Francis is the author of *Fictions of Feminine Citizenship: Sexuality and the Nation in Contemporary Caribbean Literature.* She is currently working on two book projects: *Illegibilities: Caribbean Cosmopolitanisms and the Problem of Form,* an intellectual history of the Anglophone Caribbean's transnational literary culture from 1940 to 1970; and *Creole Miami: Black Arts in the Magic City,* a sociocultural history of black arts practice in Miami from the 1980s to the present.

FREDA SCOTT GILES earned her Ph.D. at the City University of New York. A specialist in African American theater, directing, and acting, she is the author of several articles focusing on drama and theater of the Harlem Renaissance and contemporary African American theater practitioners. Before her joint appointment in theatre and film studies and African American studies at the University of Georgia (UGA), Dr. Giles taught at the State University of New York at Albany and City College of the City University of New York. She recently retired from UGA as a General Sandy Beaver Teaching Professor. She served as associate director for the Institute for African American Studies and was an affiliate faculty member in the African Studies Institute and the Institute for Women's Studies. Dr. Giles is a founding editor of *Continuum,* an online, open-access journal of African diaspora theater, drama, and performance published by the Black Theatre Network.

OMI OSUN JONI L. JONES is an artist, scholar, and professor emerita in the African and African Diaspora Studies Department at the University of Texas at Austin. Jones's scholarship focuses on ethnography, theatrical jazz, Yoruba-based aesthetics, Black Feminisms, and activist theater. Her original performances include "Sista Docta," a critique of the academy, and "Searching for Osun," a performance ethnography around Yoruba identity. She has served as an Artist-in-Residence with Thousand Currents, a member of the Urban Futures Think Tank at the Yerba Buena Center for the Arts, and as an art-for-social-change facilitator with Educafro in Sao Paulo, Brazil. Jones is coeditor of *Experiments in a Jazz Aesthetic: Art, Activism, Academia, and the Austin Project* and author of *Theatrical Jazz: Performance, Àṣẹ, and the Power of the Present Moment.*

PATRICK MALEY is associate professor of English at Centenary University in Hackettstown, New Jersey, where he teaches a wide variety of courses on topics including drama, theory, Shakespeare, the Bible, classics, and religion. He is the author of *After August: Blues, August Wilson, and American Drama,* which argues that Wilson's blues dramaturgy allows for a productive rethinking of the American dramatic tradition. Other work appears in *Modern Drama, Theatre Journal, Comparative Drama, Eugene O'Neill Review, New Hibernia Review, Irish Studies Review,* and *Field Day Review.* Maley currently serves as performance review editor at both *Theatre Journal* and *August Wilson Journal,* and is an active theater critic in New York and New Jersey, contributing regularly to *The Star-Ledger,* New Jersey's largest newspaper.

JEFFREY Q. MCCUNE JR. is associate professor of African and African American studies and women, gender, and sexuality studies at Washington University in St. Louis. He is the author of the award-winning book *Sexual Discretion: Black Masculinity and the Politics of Passing.* His work has been featured in *Journal of Homosexuality, QED: A Journal of GLBTQ Worldmaking, American Quarterly, Spectrum,* and *Text & Performance Quarterly.* He is presently completing two book manuscripts: *On Kanye,* a critical engagement with the impossibility of black genius, iconography, and monster aesthetics; and *Disobedient Readings: An Experiment in Seeing Black,* a monograph which utilizes black gay men's vernacular use of "reading"—an interpretation and critique of performance which is centered in one's love and/or proximity to a black object—as a new way to theorize and analyze blackness. He has been featured on *Left of Black, Sirius XM's Joe Madison Show, HuffPost Live, Pitchfork,* and as a guest expert on *Bill Nye Saves the World.*

KATHERINE NIGH, PH.D., is an artist, activist, and scholar whose work primarily deals with art and social justice. She received her doctorate from Arizona State University in the Theatre and Performance of the Americas program. She is an instructor of Theater Arts at Pasadena City College and has previously been a professor at Whittier College, Florida State University, and Temple University. She has worked as a director, playwright, dramaturg, stage manager, and performer all over this complicated but beautiful nation, as well as internationally. Nigh is the producer and host of "My Year Without A Man," a podcast focused on womxn in the fields of theater and performance that can be found at www.soundcloud.com/myyearwithoutaman. Her website is http://katherinenigh.wixsite.com/dr-katherine-nigh.

Backstage Pass Contributors

TEA ALAGIĆ is an internationally acclaimed Bosnian American multilingual director. Based in New York City, her credits include Off-Broadway, regional, and international productions of both traditional theater and devised work. She holds a B.F.A. in acting from Charles University in Prague, Czech Republic, and an M.F.A. in directing from the Yale School of Drama, where she received the Julian Milton Kaufman Prize in Directing. Alagić directed the world premiere of Tarell Alvin McCraney's *The Brothers Size* at The Public Theater in New York City, and subsequent productions at the Studio Theatre in Washington D.C., Actors Theatre of Louisville, The Old Globe in San Diego, and The Abbey Theatre in Dublin. Alagić is presently the head of the M.F.A. and B.F.A. Directing Department at The New School for Drama in New York City. Other select credits include the North American premiere of Nobel laureate Elfriede Jelinek's *Jackie*, starring Tina Benko at New York City Center (multiple Lortel Award nominations); Charise Smith's *Washeteria* at Soho Rep; Shakespeare's *Romeo and Juliet*, starring Elizabeth Olsen and Julian Cihi at CSC Rep; the Broadway-bound revival of *Passing Strange* by Stew and Heidi Rodewald at The Wilma Theater; Frances Ya-Chu Cowhig's *Lidless* at Page 73; and productions of a wide repertory of plays and musicals.

JABARI ALI is a music supervisor and curator with Paragon Film Music, LLC, in addition to working as a consultant and business-personal manager. He has served as music supervisor or consultant on several notable projects, including, *David Makes Man* (OWN), *The Equalizer 2* (Sony Pictures), *Shots Fired* (FOX), *Training Day* (Warner Bros.), and *ESPN's 30 for 30: Tupac Shakur*. Ali, who is a Guild of Music Supervisors Award nominee, is a graduate of California State University, Northridge (Bachelor of Arts degree in Pan-African studies), and the esteemed Crenshaw High School in Los Angeles. Ali also attended the University of California, Los Angeles, where he completed several extension courses in publishing and film and television music licensing. With a great desire to use his skills to enhance, encourage, and empower those around him, he has worked in the fields of education, coaching, mentoring, and promotions, as well as marketing, publishing, and producer-songwriter management. While leveraging a propensity for "deal making" and an immense knowledge of the entertainment industry, record company distribution, and film and television music, Ali cofounded one of the industry's premier management firms, Paragon Management Corporation, and an urban soundtrack record label, Paragon Soundtracks.

ALANA ARENAS joined the Steppenwolf Theatre Company ensemble in 2007 and created the role of Pecola Breedlove for the Steppenwolf for Young Adults' production of *The Bluest Eye*, which also played at the New Victory Theater Off-Broadway. She recently appeared in productions including *The Fundamentals*; *Marie Antoinette*; *Tribes*; *Belleville*; *Head of Passes*; *Good People*; *Three Sisters*; *The March*; *Man in Love*; *Middletown*; *The Hot L Baltimore*; *The Etiquette of Vigilance*; *The Brother/Sister Plays* (Steppenwolf Theatre Company); *Disgraced* (American Theater Company); and *The Arabian Nights* (Lookingglass Theatre Company, Berkeley Repertory Theatre and Kansas City Repertory Theatre). Other theater credits include *The Tempest*; *The Crucible*; *Spare Change*; *The Sparrow Project* (Steppenwolf Theatre Company); *Black Diamond* (Lookingglass Theatre Company); *Eyes* (eta Creative Arts); *SOST* (MPAACT); *WVON* (Black Ensemble Theater); and *Hecuba* (Chicago Shakespeare Theater). Television and film credits include *David Makes Man*, *Crisis*, *Boss*, *The Beast*, *Kabuku Rides*, and *Lioness of Lisabi*. Arenas is originally from Miami, Florida, where she began her training at the New World School of the Arts. She holds a B.F.A. from The Theatre School at DePaul University.

MICHAEL BOYD's career has taken him from training in Moscow to artistic directorships at the Tron Theatre Glasgow (1985–1996) and the Royal Shakespeare Company (2002–2012), where he commissioned and developed *Matilda the Musical*, produced the Complete Works and World Shakespeare Festivals, rebuilt the Royal Shakespeare Theatre, and directed Shakespeare's eight-play history cycle (described by the Guardian as "one of the great moments of modern theatre"). Recent work includes *Orfeo* with the Royal Opera House, London, and *Tamburlaine* at Theater for a New Audience in Brooklyn and the Royal Shakespeare Company. Boyd was Visiting Professor of Contemporary Theatre at the University of Oxford, and was knighted in 2012 for services to drama.

CHERYL LYNN BRUCE has performed on numerous regional stages as well as in Europe and Mexico. She originated the role of Elizabeth Sandry in Steppenwolf Theatre's Tony Award–winning *The Grapes of Wrath* (Cort Theatre, National Theatre in London, La Jolla Playhouse). Other credits include *Familiar* (Woolly Mammoth); *Hillary and Clinton*; *The Snow Queen*; *Eurydice*; *Hortensia and the Museum of Dreams*; *Voice of Good Hope* (Victory Gardens); *The Convert* (McCarter Theatre, Goodman Theatre, Kirk Douglas Theatre); *Death and the King's Horseman*; *Nomathemba* (Kennedy Center); *Cry, The Beloved Country*; *Trojan Women* (Goodman Theatre); *Joe Turner's Come and Gone*; *Harriet Jacobs* (Kansas City Rep); *Intimate Apparel*; *Everyman* (Steppenwolf Theatre); *The Old Settler* (Writers' Theatre); *From the Mississippi Delta* (Northlight Theatre, Hartford Stage, Arena Stage, Old Globe, Circle-in-the-Square); and *RACE* (Lookingglass). Film credits include *Daughters of the Dust*; *The Fugitive*; and *Stranger Than Fiction*. Television credits include *Prison Break*; *There Are No Children Here*; *Separate but Equal*; and *To Sir with Love, Part 2*. Bruce directed *Jitney* for Congo Square and Sandra Delgado's *La Havana Madrid* (Steppenwolf Theatre, Goodman Theatre, the Miracle Center, Navy Pier Lake Stage). She studied Bunraku puppetry in Iida, Japan, for her 2008 staging of *Rythm Mastr*, the urban comic by her husband, artist Kerry James Marshall, presented at the Wexner Center for the Arts. *Some Ra*, her poetical musings on Afro-Futurist musician-philosopher Sun-Ra, is included in *Traveling the Spaceways: Sun-Ra, the Astro Black and Other Solar Myths*. Honors include the following: Helen Hayes Award (1991); Joseph Jefferson Award (1992); 3Arts Award (2010); Rauschenberg residency (2015); Yale University Art Gallery residency (2011); Jane Addams Hull House Association Woman of Valor Award (2010); and Inaugural Fellow of the Ellen Stone Belic Institute for the Study of Women and Gender in the Arts and Media from Columbia College (2006).

TEO CASTELLANOS is an actor, writer, and director who works in theater, film, and television. His award-winning solo show *NE 2nd Avenue* toured extensively for a decade and won the Fringe First Award at the Edinburgh Fringe Festival in Scotland in 2003. His most recent solo show, *Third Trinity*, was directed by Tarell Alvin McCraney. He founded the dance and theater company *Teo Castellanos D-Projects* in 2003. For the past twenty-five years, Teo has toured solo and company works throughout the United States, Europe, South America, China, and the Caribbean. Select acting theater credits include playing Elegba in *The Brothers Size* (Miami), and Santos in The Hittite Empire's *Skeletons of Fish* (London). Film credits include playing opposite Matt Dillon in "Sunlight Jr." and opposite John Leguizamo in "Empire," as well as in "A Change of Heart" with Jim Belushi. Teo is the recipient of several awards and grants, including the following: NEA; NEFA; MAP; NPN; Knight Arts Challenge; Knight Foundation People's Choice Award; and Miami-Dade County Cultural Affairs. He also won the State of Florida Individual Artist Fellowship in 2005 and 2013. In 2015, Castellanos was a Sundance Institute Screen Writers Intensive Fellow. Castellanos is a member of SAG/AFTRA, and the Society of Stage Directors and Choreographers. He holds a B.F.A. in theater from Florida Atlantic University.

TRIP CULLMAN is an accomplished director. His credits on Broadway include Tarell Alvin McCraney's *Choir Boy* (MTC at the Friedman); Kenneth Lonergan's *Lobby Hero* (Second Stage at the Hayes); John Guare's *Six Degrees of Separation* (Barrymore); and Joshua Harmon's *Significant Other* (Booth). Select Off-Broadway credits include Leslye Headland's *The Layover*; Jon Robin Baitz's *The Substance of Fire*; Paul Weitz's *Lonely I'm Not*; Headland's *Bachelorette*; Terrence McNally's *Some Men*; Adam Bock's *Swimming In The*

Shallows (Second Stage); Anna Jordan's *Yen*; Simon Stephens' *Punk Rock* (Obie Award); Halley Feiffer's *A Funny Thing Happened On The Way To The Gynecologic Oncology Unit At Memorial Sloan Kettering Cancer Center Of New York City* (MCC); Headland's *Assistance*; Bock's *A Small Fire* (Drama Desk nomination); Bock's *The Drunken City* (Playwrights Horizons); Tarell Alvin McCraney's *Choir Boy* (MTC); Julia Jordan and Juliana Nash's *Murder Ballad* (MTC and Union Square Theatre); Feiffer's *I'm Gonna Pray For You So Hard* (Atlantic); Weitz's *Roulette* (EST); Adam Rapp's *The Hallway Trilogy: Nursing* (Rattlestick); Bert V. Royal's *Dog Sees God* (Century Center); Jonathan Tolins's *The Last Sunday In June* (Rattlestick and Century Center); Gina Gionfriddo's *US Drag* (stageFARM); and several productions with The Play Company. Credits in London include Bock's *The Colby Sisters of Pittsburgh, PA* (Tricycle). Select regional credits include McCraney's *Choir Boy* (Ovation nomination); Bess Wohl's *Barcelona* (Ovation nomination); Feiffer's *A Funny Thing Happened* (Geffen Playhouse); McCraney's *Choir Boy* (Alliance); Guare's *Six Degrees of Separation* (Old Globe); Richard Greenberg's *The Injured Party* (South Coast Rep); McNally's *Unusual Acts of Devotion* (La Jolla Playhouse); Christopher Durang's *Betty's Summer Vacation* (Bay Street); Wohl's *Touched*; Michael Friedman and Daniel Goldstein's *Unknown Soldier*; Tennessee Williams's *The Rose Tattoo*; and Feiffer's *Moscow, Moscow, Moscow, Moscow, Moscow, Moscow* (Williamstown Theater Festival).

OSKAR EUSTIS has served as the artistic director of The Public Theater since 2005. In the last three years, he has produced two Tony Award–winning Best Musicals (*Fun Home* and *Hamilton*), and back-to-back winners of the Pulitzer Prize for Drama (*Hamilton* and *Sweat*). He came to The Public Theater from Trinity Repertory Company in Providence, Rhode Island, where he served as artistic director from 1994 to 2005. Eustis served as associate artistic director at Los Angeles's Mark Taper Forum from 1989 to 1994, and prior to that he was with the Eureka Theatre Company in San Francisco, serving as resident director and dramaturg from 1981 to 1986 and artistic director from 1986 to 1989. Eustis is currently professor of dramatic writing and arts and public policy at New York University, and has held professorships at UCLA, Middlebury College, and Brown University, where he founded and chaired the Trinity Rep/Brown University Consortium for professional theater training. At The Public Theater, Eustis directed the New York premieres of Rinne Groff's *Compulsion* and *The Ruby Sunrise*; Larry Wright's *The Human Scale*; and, most recently, *Julius Caesar* at Shakespeare in the Park. He has funded numerous groundbreaking programs at The Public, from Public Works and Public Forum to the EWG. At Trinity Rep, he directed the world premiere of Paula Vogel's *The Long Christmas Ride Home* and Tony Kushner's *Homebody/Kabul*, both recipients of the Elliot Norton Award for Outstanding Production. While at the Eureka Theatre, he commissioned Tony Kushner's *Angels in America*, and directed its world premiere at the Mark Taper Forum. Eustis has also directed the world premieres of plays by Philip Kan Gotanda, David Henry Hwang, Emily Mann, Suzan-Lori Parks, Ellen McLaughlin, and Eduardo Machado, among many others. In 2017, Eustis was inducted into the Theater Hall of Fame.

SHIRLEY JO FINNEY is an award-winning international theater and film director and actress. She has directed at some of the most respected regional theater houses across the country, including The McCarter Theatre; The Pasadena Playhouse; The Goodman Theatre; the Alabama Shakespeare Festival; the Cleveland Playhouse; The Fountain Theatre; L.A. Theatre Works; Crossroads Theatre Company; Actors Theatre of Louisville Humana Festival; the Sundance Theatre Workshop; The Mark Taper Forum; Kennedy Center for the Performing Arts; and the State Theatre in Pretoria, South Africa. Finney's awards include the L.A. Stage Alliance Ovation Award; The Los Angeles Drama Critics Award; L.A. Weekly Award; The NAACP and the Santa Barbara Independent awards; the UCLA School of Theater, Film and Television Distinguished Alumni Award; The Black Alumni Associations' Dr. Beverly Robinson Award for Excellence in the Arts; and The African American Film Marketplace Award of Achievement for Outstanding Performance and Achievement in Entertainment. Most recently Finney directed and developed the critically acclaimed world premiere of *Citizen: An American Lyric* by the award-winning PEN poet Claudia Rankine. She also helmed the acclaimed opera *Winnie*, based on the life of political icon Winnie Mandela. Finney is an alumna of the American Film Institute's Director Workshop for Women and holds an M.F.A. degree from UCLA. She has been an artist in residence at several colleges and universities, including Columbia College in Chicago, UCSB, USC, and UCLA. Finney is also a member of the Society of Stage Directors and Choreographers, the Directors Guild, and the Screen Actors Guild.

TINA LANDAU is a writer and director whose work in New York City includes *SpongeBob SquarePants: The Broadway Musical* (Drama Desk and Outer Critics Circle winner for Best Direction and Best Musical and recipient of Tony Award nominations); Tracy Lett's *Superior Donuts* and the revival of *Bells Are Ringing* on Broadway; Off-Broadway productions of Bill Irwin and David Shiner's *Old Hats*, Chuck Mee's *Big Love*, and *Iphigenia 2.0* (all Signature Theatre); and Paula Vogel's *A Civil War Christmas* (New York Theatre Workshop), and the musicals *Floyd Collins* (Playwrights Horizons) and *Dream True* (Vineyard Theatre), both of which she also cowrote. Landau's numerous collaborations with Tarell Alvin McCraney include *Head of Passes* (Mark Taper Forum, Berkeley Rep, the Public Theater, and Steppenwolf); *The Brother/Sister Plays* (Steppenwolf); *Wig Out!* (Vineyard); *In the Red and Brown Water* (Alliance, McCarter, Public Theater); *Theatrical Essays* (Steppenwolf); and *Ms. Blakk for President*, which they cowrote and Tarell starred in at Steppenwolf in the spring of 2019. Landau is an ensemble member at Steppenwolf, where her more than twenty productions also include *The Doppelgänger*; *The Wheel*; *The Tempest*; *Time of Your Life* (also Seattle Rep, ACT); *The Cherry Orchard*; *The Diary of Anne Frank*; *Berlin Circle*; *Time to Burn*; and her own play *Space* (also Mark Taper Forum, the Public). Landau has taught regularly at such schools as Yale, Columbia, Harvard, and Northwestern, has received numerous awards and grants for her work, and is the coauthor, with Anne Bogart, of *The Viewpoints Book*.

CARLOS MURILLO is a Chicago-based, internationally produced, award-winning playwright of Colombian and Puerto Rican descent. Select awards include Doris Duke Impact Award (2015); Mellon Foundation Playwright Residency at Adventure Stage in Chicago (2016); Met Life Nuestros Voces Award from Repertorio Español; the Frederick Loewe Award from New Dramatists; the Ofner Prize from the Goodman Theatre; the Otis Guernsey Award from the William Inge Theatre Festival; Distinguished Play Award from the American Alliance for Theatre and Education; a Jerome Fellowship at The Playwrights' Center; and two National Latino Playwriting Awards from Arizona Theatre Company. His most notable play is *Dark Play or Stories for Boys*, which has been produced internationally. *The Javier Plays*, a trilogy of works published in spring of 2016 by 53rd State Press, was called by *American Theatre Magazine* "an absolutely extraordinary achievement from a writer at the height of his powers." Murillo has served on numerous selection panels, including the National Endowment for the Arts and the Creative Capital MAP Fund. Murillo served as the associate literary manager at The Public Theater in New York from 1993 to 1995, and now serves on the board of directors of the MacDowell Colony. Murillo heads the B.F.A. Playwriting Program at The Theatre School at DePaul University, and is a proud alumnus of New Dramatists. He lives on the south side of Chicago with his wife, the director Lisa Portes, and their children, Eva and Carlitos.

ROBERT O'HARA is an acclaimed director and playwright. Awards include NAACP Best Director Award; NAACP Best Playwright Award; Helen Hayes Award for Outstanding New Play; two Obie Awards; and the Oppenheimer Award. He directed the world premieres of Nikkole Salter and Danai Gurira's *In the Continuum*, Tarell Alvin McCraney's *The Brothers Size*, Colman Domingo's *Wild with Happy*, and Kirsten Childs's *Bella: An American Tall Tale*, as well as his own plays, *Mankind*, *Bootycandy*, and *Insurrection: Holding History*. O'Hara's recent plays, *Zombie: The American* and *Barbecue*, had world premieres at Woolly Mammoth Theater and the New York Shakespeare Festival, respectively. His recent directing projects include Kirsten Childs's *Bubbly Black Girl* at City Center/Encores Off Center; UNIVERSES Theater's *UniSon*, inspired by the poetry of August Wilson, at the Oregon Shakespeare Festival; and Shakespeare's *Macbeth* at the Denver Center for the Performing Arts. He directed the world premiere of Jeremy O. Harris's *Slave Play*, which originated at New York Theatre Workshop in 2018 before transferring to Broadway in 2019. O'Hara holds an M.F.A. in directing from Columbia University.

INDEX